# INSIDER BUY

POT
VPHM
DXPE
ALDA
TRLG
TZOO
WPRT
FORD
AAPL
BOOM

# SUPERSTOCKS

JESSE C. STINE

# INSIDER BUY

# SUPERSTOCKS

## JESSE C. STINE

*Insider Buy Superstocks*

Book Interior Design by Vyrdolak, By Light Unseen Media

Cover design by Lenka K Design Studio

### Disclaimer:

This publication is designed to provide accurate and authoritative information in regard to the subject matter covered. It is sold with the understanding that the publisher is not engaged in rendering legal, accounting, or other professional services. If you require legal advice or other expert assistance, you should seek the services of a competent professional.

Under no circumstances does the information in this book represent a recommendation to buy or sell stocks or funds. It should not be assumed that the methods presented in this book will be profitable or that they will not result in losses. Past results are not necessarily indicative of future results. Examples in this book are for educational purposes only.

All charts herein are presented through courtesy of Stockcharts.com and Worden.com. Some charts (or data) produced by TC2000® which is a registered trademark of Worden Brothers, Inc., Five Oaks Office Park, 4905 Pine Cone Drive, Durham, NC 27707. Ph. (800) 776-4940 or (919) 408-0542. www.Worden.com.

# TOP TWENTY-FIVE BOOK HIGHLIGHTS
## *Many of Which May Shock You!*

1. My story: the steps I took to make several small fortunes.

2. How to spot elusive "Superstocks," the stock market's biggest winners.

3. Free online sources I use to help me discover future "Superstocks."

4. Why you can't follow Peter Lynch; how it pays NOT to buy what you know best or what makes you "feel good."

5. Learn about the most potent "drug" ever developed that will absolutely *destroy* your investment returns.

6. The "Canary in a Coalmine" indicator I use that precedes market crashes within 6 days.

7. How high-level investment returns require you to go against everything you've ever been taught.

8. Discover that the market is more manipulated than you could ever imagine.

9. Why some stocks must be sold at $25.

10. Why you can never invest in an ETF or mutual fund ever again.

11. Learn how the "Magic Line" triggers gigantic stock thrusts.

12. How to dramatically increase your trading focus, creativity, and energy.

13. Why you should dump a majority of the methods you currently employ to research stocks.

14. Why you must become George Clooney, Jack Nicholson, or Colin Ferrell.

15. Learn how to find *Investor's Business Daily* 100 ("IBD 100") stocks in the single digits—months before anyone else.

16. What to look for in the rare blockbuster "Superstock" earnings press release.

17. Why you must do everything in your power to never watch *CNBC* ever again... not even for a second.

18. Why only suckers "back out cash."

19. Why you must learn to sell like Mark Cuban.

20. How to determine your Superstock's lowest risk, highest reward entry price.

21. The charts, fundamentals, and stories behind my biggest winners.

22. Why all insider-buying is not created equal.

23. Inevitable account drawdowns and how to cope with them.

24. How to spot manipulated bogus BS media groupthink and how to profit from it.

25. Honest lessons from my many failures.

## ABOUT THE AUTHOR

From Oct 2003 to January 2006, the value of Jesse Stine's self-managed individual stock portfolio appreciated 14,972% from $45,721 to $6,845,342. During this time frame, the S&P 500 returned 25%. A complete biography and financial documentation can be found at www.jessestine.com.

For questions, comments, or to swap stories, feel free to contact Jesse at jesse@jessestine.com. To follow Jesse on Twitter, go to @InsiderbuySS.

To be included in his "friends and family" market inflection points email (complimentary of course), contact jesse@jessestine.com or visit www.jessestine.com. Your email address is 100% confidential. It is not shared or sold. Past alerts can be read at his website.

## ACKNOWLEDGMENTS

Nicole, Mom, Dad, Bill, Lenka, Donna, Ted, Tony, Inanna, Jen, and 2008. Each of you played an essential role in the "birth" of this book. A couple of you provided the inspiration. A couple of you played a hands-on role during the development process. And you all provided immense support along the way. I will forever be grateful for your contributions. Thank you.

## A SPECIAL THANK YOU TO MY COLLEAGUES ON TWITTER

A very special thank you to the "Twitterverse". After being a total stranger to Twitter since its inception, I decided to create an account in late November of 2012. I had no idea how it would happen, but I thought Twitter might be a good way to promote this book. After sending "Superstocks" out to a dozen or so followers, I was shocked by their positive response. As word spread, other people starting sending me direct messages asking if they too could receive an advance reviewer's copy. I initially sent it out to anybody who was willing to read it. I received priceless comments from the people who knew the subject best—fellow traders and investors.

During this process, I was able to connect with like-minded people from every corner of the world. The feedback, edits, suggestions, and support were invaluable. The final version of this book is a direct result of this global collaboration. Again,

I want to thank everybody I met during this initial stage. Your efforts were truly instrumental in getting this book released.

## *A NOTE FROM THE EDITOR*

When Jesse Stine asked me to edit his book, I jumped at the chance. I know of no other book that so nicely reflects my own trading philosophy—a philosophy that has seen my trading portfolio fall by as much as 50% (or even more) en route to achieving an embarrassingly-high 3000% return within as little as six months. In a nutshell, I know that it is perfectly possible to make a lot of money (relatively) from very little, but that you may need to prepare yourself for significant drawdowns along the way.

I read the initial manuscript for this book from three perspectives:

- As a fellow trading author and editor of several books in this genre.

- As a fellow financial trader with my own successes and failures to draw on.

- As a member of the target audience, i.e. as someone who would likely have bought the book if he hadn't been involved with the editing of it.

The approach is not without its risks, but all speculation is risky, and as I once wrote as the tag-line for one of my own books:

**WARNING!** This strategy could seriously damage your wealth... or make you rich!

I commend this book to readers, and I hope you enjoy it as much as I have.

*Tony Loton at trading.lotontech.com*

# CONTENTS

Preface                                                                                          8

Introduction                                                                                    12

Chapter 1: My Story                                                                      20

Chapter 2: Today is the Day to Divorce Yourself from Mediocrity         36

Chapter 3: The Most Potent Drug the World Has Ever Seen                 44

Chapter 4: Wall Street's Worst Kept Secret                                          55

Chapter 5: Becoming a Better Trader                                               59

Chapter 6: Systems and Simplicity                                                   71

Chapter 7: The Elusive Superstock                                                   78

Chapter 8: Stacking the Odds in Your Favor                                    105

Chapter 9: Low Risk Entry Super Laws                                          111

Chapter 10: The Super Laws of Selling--Mastering the Art of
Selling High Risk                                                                             128

Chapter 11: The "Lazy Man's Guide" to Superstocks                        152

Chapter 12: Eleven Charts that Changed My Life and May
Change Yours                                                                                    154

Chapter 13: Superstock Resources                                                    185

Chapter 14: Major Lessons from My Failures, Warts and All            188

Chapter 15: Top Sixteen Things You Must Do Differently to
Achieve Massive Success                                                                  195

Chapter 16: The Road Less Traveled                                                202

Appendix A- How to Spot Global Inflection Points                          204

Appendix B- My Annual Global Market Forecasts 2010-2013            238

Appendix C- "Some Things Never Change"                                      246

# PREFACE

This book is an account of how I broke the traditional rules of investing to achieve the unthinkable—what is believed to be a world record-setting personal portfolio return in the post-Dot-com bubble era. My style of trading "Superstocks" is for the rare breed; those who not only embrace calculated risk but also have the ability to stomach the consequences of occasional failure. This case study is meant for those who dream big and have a passion for the markets. It is not for the timid or faint of heart.

Constructed in pieces in several countries throughout the world, what is to follow truly is my life's work. I tried to refine and include every ounce of actionable knowledge I've picked up over the years. It is the result of studying everything I could find about the characteristics of the market's biggest winners throughout history.

The book is the culmination of some $2.5 Billion in personal stock sales and 30,000 hours of hand-to-hand combat in the market trenches. I want you to learn as much as you possibly can from my achievements. I want you to learn even more from my failures.

This is not a book devoted to portfolio management, diversification, bonds, currency, or abstract theory. All of the personal experiences described within these pages are true and almost every example was taken from my personal trading history.

My method is simple. There is nothing "Earth-shattering" about it; strike when you find a stock with the absolute best fundamentals in alignment with the very best technicals while trading at a distressed price. Like the claims of so many others before it, this book is certainly not a "Foolproof Lazy Man's Guide to Riches." If there were any "foolproof" methods, I assure you that everybody would be making millions in the stock market. Although my method is simple in its premise, a new investor must first master the fundamental investing laws presented in this book before the method can become "second nature."

For this reason, it is my hope that you will treat this book more as a "textbook" to refer to from time to time rather than as your typical "weekend read." Since the market is a rigged game, you must first understand and master the fundamental rules of the game before you can excel at a high level on the playing field.

There certainly are no guarantees in life, but with the proper tools, focus, and vision, it is indeed possible to make millions as an individual investor.

## ASSUMPTIONS AND THINGS TO NOTE:

- I use the terms "investor" and "trader" interchangeably throughout the book. Although I am a longer-term investor at heart, my hybrid approach requires that I "invest" at low-risk weekly buy points and to "trade" out of positions when the risk/ reward is no longer in my favor (My longest hold during my 28 month portfolio advance was 8 months).

- I assume that the reader has some experience in trading and investing. I assume that you know the basics of technical analysis (volume, breakouts, moving averages etc.) and that you will refer to the "Resources" section of this book if you would like to learn more about technical analysis.

- Warning—the first half of the book can best be described as an "easy narrative". The second half presents "The Super Laws of Superstocks" and reads more like a textbook. This section can be more difficult to absorb. Prepare yourself

- In the spirit of simplicity, for the "Cliffs Notes" on the Super Laws of Superstocks, please refer to chapter 11 which is titled "The Lazy Man's Guide to Superstocks." This may help you see the bigger picture before getting bogged down in the details.

- A vast majority of stocks fall during bear markets. Superstocks are no exception.

- Yes, I know "Super Stocks" should be two words. Like Superman, "Superstocks" are Superhuman, Supernatural, and Supercharged and thus deserve their own word.

- Most of the charts are courtesy of Stockcharts.com. In a few instances, the stock prices seen in the charts are different from other chart vendors and different from the actual prices I transacted during the period in question. The important thing to note is that any potential price discrepancies do not affect the chart pattern or technical conditions.

- Most importantly, I assume that you are highly motivated and have an incredible belief in what's possible.

# INTRODUCTION

*"It is literally true that millions come easier to a trader after he knows how to trade than hundreds did in the days of his ignorance."*

Investment legend Jesse Livermore

Hello. My name is Jesse Stine, and I want to express my gratitude to you for purchasing this book out of the thousands of others available. Although I may not know you personally, it means a great deal to me to connect with readers like you who take an interest in what I have to say.

Unlike a majority of the people I encounter, I hope you share my passion for financial markets and have an equally intense desire to do whatever it takes to achieve your financial dreams. In these pages, I return to the market after a three and a half year "trading retirement" and open up my playbook for the very first time. After reading this book you'll know that "investing as usual" is dead.

Before we begin, I must confess that although I wake up every morning with a burning passion for the financial markets, I am definitely not a professional writer. My goal is to share my money-making secrets. The goal is not to win the Pulitzer Prize. I will do my best to provide you with a straightforward, accurate, and honest account of my experiences.

My goal for this book is for it to be 100% raw and uncut—a genuine, accurate, and brutally honest depiction of my victories as well as my extraordinary defeats. My hope is that this book will be seen as an outlier in the sea of investing books, many seemingly written by the same two or three ghostwriters.

## WHY ME?

You might be asking yourself what sets this guy apart from everyone else in this field? I am a specialist who focuses on one single "bread and butter" approach, and my results indicate that I do it better than the biggest names in the business. Like a surgeon performing the same surgery for years on end, I find that it becomes easier and easier over time to identify the market's biggest future winners. Unlike the "agenda-rich" snake-oil salesmen you see on financial television and in financial mass-media, I will give you the honest-to-goodness straight scoop on how to beat the market by investing differently from just about everybody else.

Because investing is my one true passion, and my one core area of excellence, I channel every single ounce of energy I have into it. I am a liquidity prognosticator seeking outlier situations where price and fund flows are likely to increase over time. I search every corner of the market universe to exploit extreme information imbalances that often lead to explosive returns. Because of their scarcity, these unique situations only come about a few times per calendar quarter.

As you will see in "How to Spot Major Global Inflection Points" in the book's Appendix, I am rarely swayed by mass-media induced public opinion at key market junctures. At these inflection points, I am buying when you are selling and selling when you are buying. By now, I am well aware that the big money is consistently made by going directly against popular opinion. About the only thing that truly sends shivers down my spine is the word "consensus"—especially as it relates to the contagious groupthink pervading the financial mass media.

I have a track record of consistently achieving unheard of 3, 4, and 5-digit returns in short periods of time. I have learned that in order to experience "socially acceptable" smooth returns over time, one must accept a dramatically lower level of portfolio performance. While others are taught to bunt, I am exclusively seeking home runs backed by well- defined risk.

Investing with swagger, my goal as the "trading cowboy" has never been to have smooth returns. In light of this, I have learned from my mentors that it is absolutely essential to develop immense confidence and (gulp) a cocky attitude when in the "trading zone."

For good or bad, I have learned that you have to transform into a selfish, greedy, testosterone-filled, risk-taking gladiator to succeed against your foes. And yes, fellow investors are your foes. Their sole intent is to throw you in the gutter, kick you in the face, and leave you penniless and despondent. Outside of these pages and outside of the trading ring, I think you would find that I am quite different than the character I portray when the cameras are rolling.

As for "luck"—when you put thousands of hours into research and refining your method, you create your own luck. The funny thing is that in general the harder I work, the luckier I seem to get. Luck is all about identifying blockbuster patterns that repeat over and over again throughout history. Luck is all about following the Kelly Criterion (discussed later) and betting big when all of the variables align in your favor.

What about risk? Well, a rapidly growing company with a single-digit price-earnings ratio (PE) isn't inherently risky; it's simply a "bases loaded anomaly" begging to be knocked out of the park for a grand slam. What *IS* risky is investing in a big cap stock like Microsoft (MSFT) that has an equal likelihood of going up 15% or down 15% over any given timeframe. I focus intensely on calculated risks and highly skewed risk/reward scenarios. Surprisingly, I am such a big believer in "fat pitches" that not once in my entire life have I purchased a physical lottery ticket.

I get a big kick out of buying a stock that nobody else will touch with a 10 foot pole. When everybody else is worried to death about what can go wrong, my only focus is on what can go right. There's nothing I like better than going against the herd. It is in these moments that fortunes are made. As you will see in the Appendix, I nailed some of the biggest inflection points in market history while everybody else was paralyzed by groupthink.

I often stay in cash and step away from the market for long periods when stocks aren't acting right; but when conditions are ripe, I stalk stocks like a tiger stalking its prey. When I am in the market, I am a "Position Trader" holding my stocks for weeks or months- as long as they are going *up*. I began my career with the intention of holding my biggest winners for a year or more. I learned the hard way many times over that blockbuster stocks and long term capital gains are as compatible as fire and ice. Thus when technical conditions and sentiment hit frothy extremes, I sell at a moment's notice.

There is no need to ever consider making my accountant feel all warm and fuzzy inside by achieving long term capital gains. When I'm risking precious capital, I'm in the market for one reason and one reason only: to achieve spectacular returns by exploiting irrational market behavior.

Out of the 15,000 stocks in the U.S., and some 63,000 stocks worldwide, my sole purpose is to discover the one or two biggest future winners that have the ultimate risk/reward characteristics of undervaluation, rapid growth, solid technical base, inspiring theme, and "It Factor"—all of them ideally supported by recent insider buying. These special situation stocks typically have a powerful and contagious story to tell. The really big money is made while surfing the waves of emotion generated by these game-changing stocks. I have succeeded in discovering these rare beasts consistently over the years, and I now consider myself to be *the* expert on what I like to call... "Superstocks."

Over several years at the start of my career, I had separate account drawdowns (trading losses) of 61%, 64%, 65%, 100%, 100% and 106%. Unbelievable? Yes. After each setback, rather than crawl to the safety and stability of an office cubicle, I returned to the market with an absolute vengeance.

After these and other significant setbacks over the years, in entirely separate time periods, I've seen my personal portfolio surge 111% in 4 weeks, 117% in 4 weeks, 156% in 8 weeks, 264% in 12 weeks, 273% in 16 weeks, 371% in 10 weeks, 1,010% in 17 weeks, and 1,026% and 1,244% in 29 and 46 weeks respectively (same time period).

Once every few years, we hear stories of somebody who turns his modest college savings into a million dollars within a short time period. Outside of the internet bubble of the late 1990's, what are the odds of somebody achieving this type of return just *one time* in his investment career? 5 million to one? 10 million to one? What are the odds that somebody could achieve such extraordinary returns over and over and over again? I dare say only a small handful of people have ever had short term returns similar to mine. By sticking with my principles, I repeatedly put myself in a position to achieve what very few others have ever achieved before.

Recording record-beating returns doesn't guarantee future performance, but it certainly establishes the credibility of the method I employ: a simple method that you can master through hard work and discipline.

As investors, it is one thing to discuss investment theory and to dream of extraordinary returns, but another thing entirely to experience such explosive returns firsthand. This fact alone separates this book from the other 98,342 investing books in the public domain.

I am well aware that not everything I say in this book will be applicable to your situation. I also don't want to sugarcoat things by saying that this book guarantees riches. The likelihood of anybody achieving similar 14,972% returns in 28 months is slim. Look, I have traded a couple billion dollars worth of stock and I have spent (lost) millions on my market education. It is my objective that you will be able to learn from the rules I developed during and after my numerous successes and failures. My ultimate goal is to provide you with a good deal of quality actionable information to help you significantly outperform the major market averages over time.

To supercharge your returns, we will work together to try to shift your focus and your efforts from the abundance of activities that *DON'T* contribute to investment success to the few activities that *DO*. You will learn to actively question each and every one of your habitual investment activities. Frankly, a majority of these activities need to be thrown out. You will learn that by doing *EVERYTHING* differently you can put yourself in a position to achieve massive returns. Most importantly, in some small way, I hope this book will help you develop a "Millionaire Mindset" that will inspire you to take immediate action to achieve your dreams.

I would like nothing more than to increase your level of happiness through your future investing success. I've proven that I can beat all odds time and time again. It is now my mission to help you beat the odds without taking on the level of risk that I occasionally took on.

From the bottom of my heart, I welcome you with open arms and thank you for joining me on this unique journey. This book will turn everything you've ever known about investing on its head. Pack your bags; you're in for a wild ride!

## *MY MOTIVATION FOR WRITING — WHY NOW?*

> *"There's a moment where you're not a kid any more, when you realize time is finite."*
>
> Salman Rushdie

Many people will ask the obvious question: "If you are so good at trading, why are you writing?" Well, I initially had designs to write this book way back in 2006. However, the timing just wasn't right for me. The inspiration to write simply wasn't present and there would prove to be much more for me to learn about the markets in the future. During time away from the market, I started experiencing feelings of guilt and restlessness over not writing the book. It was during a period of reflection in Indonesia in 2011 when several waves of inspiration finally took hold of me. I concluded that the time was finally right for me to start the second chapter of my life. This book had been my dream for far too long, and as we know—there's a huge price to pay if we don't live our dreams.

In the days that followed the decision to write, I dug out all of my old trading notes and I performed a complete audit of my entire investment history from start to finish. It wasn't until I conducted the audit that I realized the full extent of my success. Prior to that, I had never been fully conscious of exactly how much I started with or precisely how much I had made. During my research, I was surprised that I couldn't find anybody else with a better personal portfolio return during the post internet bubble modern era. This finding provided me with even more motivation to write.

As I conducted my audit, did I find that all of my trades worked out? As you will discover, the answer would be a big resounding *NO!* In fact, a *MAJORITY* of my trades didn't work out as I anticipated. Fortunately, it became apparent that as long as I cut my many losses short, my few winners carried my account.

As I looked at similar investment books, I became disturbed by how most of them made investing success sound so easy. From my experience, nothing could be further from the truth. Like anything else worthwhile in life, it takes hard work, determination, and massive trial and error to achieve success. I also noticed that most of the best-selling books and newsletters were written by the slickest marketers who had run-of-the-mill track records. Taking advice from many of these guys is akin to taking healthy lifestyle advice from Dick Cheney.

By nature, people assume that if somebody appears on television or in print, they have an outstanding investment record and are great at what they do. In practice, nothing could be further from the truth. I wondered why people spent their hard earned money on books written by professional writers who know plenty of theory but have never achieved a high level of success. One of the top selling investment books I looked at was written by a 26 year-old professional writer with a degree in literature with no investment success to speak of. But boy, the book sure sold a lot of copies and looked great. Our culture is all about psychological manipulation (marketing)—be it Coke, Budweiser, Nike, or McDonald's. It became apparent to me that the world of Finance is no different. I just had to write this damn book to tell it like it really is.

You will find the best traders are the ones who spend every waking hour in front of their monitors. They are the dull ones. I wanted to give a voice to those of us who have spent a majority of our time trading in the trenches 100% outside of public view.

Furthermore, I was inspired by a common complaint that I saw among Amazon.com book reviewers—that investment authors consistently covered up their failures. The accepted norm is for authors to move swiftly from one victory to the next while conveniently skipping over their failures. I don't care who you are; everybody fails at some point. Readers are well aware that the majority of what we learn in life comes from our failures. Why hide them?

I would be untruthful if I implied that I had no financial incentives in writing this book.

Given my volatile trading history, I thought it would be useful to have a separate stream of income that might provide a level of emotional and financial stability. It took me far too long to realize, but this lack of financial stability was causing havoc with certain aspects of my life.

> *"If you're not making someone else's life better, you're wasting your time."*

Actor Will Smith

There were several other equally important reasons for taking a stab at writing. As I spent a Sunday afternoon earlier this year in beautiful Parque San Martin in Mendoza, Argentina, I sat in contemplation and began jotting down the many reasons for writing this book.

I realized that by trading in total isolation for so long, my career had lacked meaning. My energy was not being shared with others, but instead was being focused inward. I found that working by myself and for myself, had caused a low energy burnout that led to a "mini-retirement." Trading alone lacked value and I wasn't enriching the world around me in any meaningful way. In my self-absorbed selfish pursuit of market domination, time was beginning to lose its importance as each new day morphed into the next.

I reflected on reaching "adulthood" and the newfound inner urge to leave a legacy. Something ever-lasting that not only documented the journey of my trading life but would teach others in the process. By writing, I could bring more creativity into my life. As I grew tired of consuming and constantly "taking" from life, I wanted to give back in some small way by sharing this knowledge and passion.

I knew that by teaching others, I would learn more about investing, so it's a win-win of sorts. By sharing my passion, I thought I might empower and inspire others to define and shoot for their financial dreams. As a by-product of writing, my hope was to meet people with similar interests and similar stories.

Taken together, the reasons were an overwhelming signal for me to take action to begin my second act in life.

But why now? People think I'm crazy for releasing the book now. They say that books need to be released during periods of heightened social mood and market frenzy. I disagree. I believe that for the benefit of the reader, those are the worst possible times to release a book. My belief is that the best time to read a book of this nature is during universal pessimism. It is my hope that readers will be able to utilize what they have learned in these pages to eventually crush the market when social mood begins to turn (if not well before).

Look, we have massive unemployment, trillion dollar government bailouts, the "Occupy Wall Street" movement, the "Fiscal Cliff," the multi-trillion dollar U.S. debt bubble, the "2012" end of civilization, the crash in China's economy, the debacle in Greece, Spain, Ireland, Portugal, Italy etc., the "end of the European Union," the "end of the Euro currency," economists calling for an imminent recession, and Goldman Sach's call for a possible 2012 25% drop in the S+P 500.

Did I mention that there are about 10 countries today in the Middle East that are threatening to take down the entire planet? The media couldn't build a higher "Wall of Worry" if it tried.

As you will see, the largest market advances in history happened when we least expected them to happen. The largest market advances happen *in spite of* the prevailing Wall of Worry (negative groupthink). In short, market advances *NEED* a gigantic wall of worry to keep as many people as possible on the sidelines.

It is my belief that the 30-plus year bull market in treasuries has ended. This in combination with infinite global "quantitative easing" could provide the hidden fuel for literally years of great investment opportunities to come. Call me crazy, but it is my belief that it makes sense to help readers prepare for and to be ready to knock the cover off the ball when winter turns into spring. The last time I checked, winter *ALWAYS* turns into spring.

## THE JOURNEY AHEAD

In my very biased opinion, one thing that truly sets this book apart from all the others is the fact that I have chosen to show real-life examples from my trading history. It is rare to see a book that shows an investor's thought process prior to entering a major trade. It is oh-so-easy in hindsight to analyze a successful stock that you never owned. The ability to control your emotions is 90% of investing. Emotions never enter into the equation when you analyze stocks you never owned.

In this book, I try to provide exactly what I saw technically and fundamentally prior to establishing my positions. I even include several old "email alerts" and stock postings that describe exactly what I saw before stocks and markets made their major moves.

Broadly speaking, the first part of the book details my investing journey over the years. Some of it is deeply personal. I hope you find it interesting. Beyond that, we will discuss how *YOU* can become a successful investor. There will be much discussion about the media, independent thinking, sentiment, psychology, and achieving "Flow" as it relates to your success.

I devote quite a bit of the book's real estate to emotion because whether you like it or not, emotions drive markets. You may find some of these sections to be tedious or boring, but they are absolutely essential to mastering the market. We will also spend some time on instilling confidence and developing a "killer instinct" as it relates to the market. Such traits are vitally important because quite simply, the timid are absolutely *CRUSHED* in the market. Finally, we will transition into everything you want to know (and then some!) about Superstocks.

Lastly, the Appendix is a collection of my old alerts discussing exactly what I saw before major stock market inflection points. I also include my recent "annual outlooks" (2010—"Do Absolutely Nothing," 2011—"Priced for Perfection," 2012—"Face-Ripping Market Smorgasbord," ,2013—"Global 200%-500% Anomalies") which help show how I formulate my long-term market outlook. If you enjoy reading my alerts and find them educational, feel free to contact me to be added to the friends and family list. At some point, I intend to put a much larger collection together in a .pdf format for posterity.

The book includes many charts. I urge you to spend time studying them and to really *THINK* and try to understand them. The charts convey absolutely *EVERYTHING*. If you can't become "one" with a chart, there is simply no way to succeed on a massive scale in the stock market. A majority of the book's charts are actual holdings from my 28 month historic portfolio advance. A few others are some of my favorite holdings from 2006-2008. Lastly, in order to freshen things up a bit, a few charts are from the past year or so.

Let me ask you a question before we move on. Currently, are you investing in stock prices because they will go up and will thus maximize personal wealth creation? Or are you investing in an emotionally satisfying and comforting *"STORY"?*

By the end of this book, I think your initial response may surprise you.

A great deal of the book will deal with doing things that are *NOT* comfortable to you. Most investors are destined for mediocrity because it is literally too daunting for them to leave their comfort zones. We will discuss the importance of actively questioning your status quo while focusing on really stretching to do things others simply cannot do. I guarantee that in practice it will be emotionally *VERY* difficult to follow parts of my philosophy.

This book is not a "system" that so many other books claim to be. It is all about solid research that will forever stand the test of time. As you read the book, in order to better understand its concepts and to increase your comprehension dramatically, it may help if you visualize yourself as a professional trader or investment manager (if you are not one already). I say this because there have been numerous "commitment studies" demonstrating that people with a long term commitment learn at an accelerated pace. People who truly "believe" that they will be doing a particular activity for the rest of their lives will learn 2-3 times as much in the same period of time as those who do not have a long-term commitment.

I also want to add that I apologize if my tone seems to be too optimistic or "Ra-Ra" at times. My intention is to instill within you the right confident attitude to aid your success over the long term. As I ask later in the book, when was the last time you saw a pessimistic billionaire?

But now, I want to tell you a bit about how I got started in this field. My romance with the financial markets began some 17 years ago. Let me tell you- the beginning was certainly anything but easy for me. Given my guarded nature, a majority of what will follow is not known by anybody else. *UNTIL NOW...*

# CHAPTER 1

# *My Story*

*"It's one thing to study war and another to live the warrior's life."*
Telamon of Arcadia, mercenary of fifth century B.C.

I have always believed that life will pay you whatever you ask of it. As the saying goes, "Ask for a quarter and you will get a quarter, ask for unbelievable success and you will get unbelievable success." Following Jim Carrey's famous example, I wrote myself a check for $1 million dollars in 1997. My impossible goal was to be able to cash the check on my thirty-second birthday in 2007. By saving every penny of a potential $50,000 salary combined with 20%+ annual investment returns, I figured I could reach my goal of a million dollars by age 32.

At the time, it was certainly an outrageous idea that was highly unlikely to materialize, but you have to think *BIG*—right? A few weeks later, I placed the check in storage with some old bank documents and forgot about it entirely for 15 years. I stumbled upon it again as I began researching old trading documents for this book. In hindsight, perhaps I just didn't dream *big enough.*

## THE EARLY YEARS

Growing up, I can't say that I had any interest in going into Finance. Frankly, I really didn't know anything at all about the field. What I did know for certain was that I was passionate about NOT going into Law. Seven members of my immediate family worked as attorneys or worked in other capacities at law firms, and the prospect of having to repeat the same boring dinner conversations while speaking the same legalese did not interest me in the least. I knew exactly what I *did not* want to do. I just had no clue about what I *did* want to do.

While attending Emory University in Atlanta, GA, I decided to pursue Economics as a major. The decision required a little coaching from my father, but after several years of flip-flopping I had finally picked a path to pursue. As I studied Economics 101 during my sophomore year, I found myself becoming more and more interested in the stock market. I suppose that this interest developed primarily because of the potential of making a fortune by investing in stocks.

As a requirement for this class, I started reading the *Wall Street Journal* every morning. I immediately found myself attracted to the "Money and Investing" section and more specifically to the listing of the daily "biggest gainers." I had always viewed the market as a place where you deposit your savings and watch your nest egg grow very slowly over many, many years. Yet I found it incredible that the people investing in the "hot" companies were making 50%, 100% or more in a single day. By finding these big gainers before they made their moves, would it not be possible to make a fortune in the stock market? To me, the implications were incredible.

From that point forward, I began "paper trading" (trading on paper without money) with the daily help of the *Wall Street Journal*. Since the internet had yet to dominate our lives, I would highlight the stocks in the newspaper that I believed would make the largest advances. Following the Peter Lynch model, my picks were typically the companies that I was most familiar with: Coca Cola, Delta Airlines, Nike, automobile companies and various fast-food franchises. Since I was totally in love with "Boston Chicken" and "Pollo Tropical" and frequented them a few times per week, I figured that it was inevitable that these would prove to be home run stocks.

Over time, my paper-trading results proved to be nothing to write home about. I am not sure if I was even able to beat the general market. Surprisingly, in the years since, I discovered that the only way to extreme success in the market is *NOT* to invest in what is *familiar,* but rather to invest in the *unfamiliar.* We will discuss this concept in greater detail later.

As I continued to entertain myself through paper trading, I was introduced to a fellow student who was an intern for Merrill Lynch. He informed me that he was intimately familiar with a developmental-stage biotech company that had a drug in its pipeline that would "cure blindness." Unfortunately, I can't recall the name of the company this many years later. My new friend suggested that this firm's drug would be approved by the FDA within a few weeks and it would become a billion dollar company.

He speculated that their $0.20 stock would catch fire and shoot to $10 or $15 once the news was released. Well, I had never been so excited in my life. I promptly thanked my new friend and immediately drove to the nearest brokerage and opened up an account funded with my $2,000 savings. Minus the outrageous $75 commission, I purchased as many shares as I could. I thought it was simply a matter of time before this stock made me rich.

After watching this biotech stock slowly tick lower over the next several weeks, I picked up the phone and called this big shot Merrill Lynch intern to ask him if he had any news for me. He reassured that everything was still on track. Like a good broker should, he reassured me to continue holding the stock as everything would turn out just fine.

As the weeks and months passed, my penny stock continued to drift lower. It continued down this depressing path until one day the big news finally came out. The drug had been... *REJECTED* by the FDA! I was pretty certain that the stock's reaction would not be good. After the news hit, the stock dropped off a cliff and was virtually worthless overnight. Thanks to following my first "hot tip," I had lost my entire savings in this bio-wreck! I admitted defeat, closed my account, and it was back to my studies for me.

After graduating two years later, I moved to Vancouver, B.C. and interned for a small technology company. It was my responsibility to transfer their shares from the Vancouver Stock Exchange to the NASDAQ (yeah right!). After working there for several weeks, I became enamored of their technology: devices that monitored natural gas and water flows for utility companies all over the world. As every good CEO is taught to say, my boss told me that *BIG* things were on the horizon for the company. He informed me that their $0.30 stock would be a great long term investment.

My fellow co-workers also seemed to think that the company would do well going forward. I drank the Kool-Aid and decided to follow my co-working herd into the stock. That evening, I somehow convinced my highly skeptical father to give me $3,000 to invest in the company's stock. I suppose he figured that $3,000 was a small price to pay to teach me that penny stocks were a loser's game. Within days of opening a Canadian brokerage account, I was the proud owner of some 10,000 shares of my employer's stock.

The longer I worked for the company, the further their stock declined. Perhaps the stock's decline was a reflection on my performance within the firm? I began to take notice that the CEO was much more focused on trying to raise capital than actually expanding the business. From time to time, he would try to reassure me that the stock was still a good long term investment. This lowly intern continued to believe his sales pitch.

I found myself transitioning into the "buy and hope" mentality as I watched the stock trade lower in a straight line over the next several months. I certainly wasn't making any progress moving the shares to the NASDAQ. Why wouldn't the NASDAQ national market want a penny stock from Vancouver?

As I pursued other ventures over the next several months, I forgot about the stock altogether. A year or so later, I noticed that the stock had been delisted and was worthless. On the bright side, I didn't have to pay an exorbitant commission to sell it. I had lost everything yet again. Fortunately, I finally learned the lesson that investing in penny stocks is a sucker's game. The score was now Mr. Market 2, Jesse Stine 0.

In 1998, I returned to Atlanta to start a student laundry service. This happened to be just months before the kick-off to the most extreme vertical stock market move the world has ever seen. As stock euphoria took hold, and as CNBC transformed into "must watch" television, I decided that I should get back in the game. I took the $10,000 I had saved from my business and opened up an account at online broker Ameritrade.

I followed Peter Lynch's advice yet again—to invest in what you know best. In those days, I not only used America Online every day, but I received one of their "free starter kits" in the mail just about every week. Around the same time, I was smitten with the AOL ticker symbol as it scrolled continuously along the bottom of the CNBC screen all day, every day. I decided to take the plunge yet again and I put some money into AOL. After some initial success, I decided that the smart thing to do would be to hop on board the phenomenon that was sweeping the nation—I would become a bona fide "day trader" like millions of others.

Just like real estate agents in South Florida in 2005, it seemed like just about everybody in

Atlanta was now a bona-fide "day trader." Remember Mark Barton? Anyway, for the next couple of months, when I wasn't coordinating the laundry business, I sat in front of my computer screen all day long Monday through Friday trying to time the market's intraday moves.

To magnify my gains, I learned that I could magically borrow money from my broker at the touch of a button using "margin or "leverage." Utilizing a margin account seemed like a surefire way to make a boatload of money. I ended up leveraging into AOL, AMZN, EBAY, CMGI, MSFT and several other .COM highfliers. The daily fluctuations were exhilarating. The profits were more addictive than anything else I had ever experienced. It seemed like anybody could do what I was doing. It was so easy. So easy, that is, until the Asian Financial Crisis hit like a ton of bricks in the fall of 1998.

Within six weeks, the NASDAQ plummeted 37% while most of the .COM bubble stocks fell some 50-70% apiece. Adding more and more margin as I tried to vengefully dig myself out of a hole, I found myself wiped out yet again within weeks. My aspirations of day trading full-time ended in the blink of an eye. I had lost everything....*AGAIN*. Remaining hitless, I now stood 0 for 3. I made the decision that I would never invest or trade again. I thought the market was simply rigged for the average investor to lose. For me, my focus returned to the laundry business.

For the next three years, I didn't think about the market at all. Even though I missed the greatest advance in market history, I didn't miss trading for a second. During this time, I shut down my business and returned to school to pursue a Master's degree in Business. To make ends meet, I worked as a manager for a valet parking company. I was in my mid 20s, back in school, making good money, and I was living it up with fellow students and co-workers in the evenings. Life had never been better for me.

As life tends to go in cycles, the good times changed on a dime on December 12th, 2001.

## 12/12/2001

On that December morning, I awoke with what could best be described as acute confusion or "brain fog." Without any warning, I found myself having a terrible time trying to process information. My cognitive abilities had inexplicably vanished overnight. In the ensuing days, one thing after another started happening to my body and my mind.

Early in the ordeal, my right thigh began twitching and continued to twitch for weeks on end. I then experienced intense vibrations in my lower back that felt quite similar to the sensations from an electronic hand massager. To make matters much worse, I found it terribly difficult to maintain my balance which made it impossible to maintain my daily running routine. Performing simple tasks like counting money or inserting a key into a lock became challenging beyond belief. Previously insignificant tasks like these suddenly required several if not dozens of attempts.

I found it so challenging to formulate speech that I pretty much stopped talking altogether. After taking a shower, I would become so overwhelmed with exhaustion that I would collapse onto my bed for at least fifteen minutes afterward to regain my strength. As my systems were progressively shutting down one by one, my life was rapidly unraveling in front of my eyes. I felt like I had been blindsided by a speeding freight train.

By far the most unsettling aspect of the entire ordeal was the inability to comprehend what was going on around me. I would sit in class with a feeling of helplessness as I understood very little of what the professor was saying. I couldn't even make sense of a simple television show. I vividly remember watching *Friends* one evening and not being able to follow the program at all. In that moment, there was no way for me to control the tears.

As I tried to put the pieces together, I remembered that I had vision problems in my left eye for a few months during the previous summer. Were my vision problems related to my current condition? Outside of colds and the flu, I had never had any health issues in my entire life. I was only 26 years old. Why was this happening to me? I was completely in shock. The only diagnosis that I could come up with was that I was having some sort of early stroke.

The days and weeks that followed were spent in and out of emergency rooms and doctor's offices. The doctors performed every test known to man. The fear was that Multiple Sclerosis (MS) was the culprit. As is often the case with MS, after weeks of testing, nothing came back conclusive. All the while, I truly felt like I was rapidly dying. Scared would be an understatement.

Around 8:30 one evening during the second week of February in 2002, as I sat listening to George Winston, I became overwhelmed by a sudden ability to "comprehend," to "hear," and to "feel" music for the first time since this horrific episode began some two months earlier. After being an isolated prisoner of this intense fog for so long, I was exhilarated to regain just a tiny bit of my cognition. From that moment on, more and more of my symptoms began to subside over the next several days. Within 2 weeks, I returned to about 80% of my former self.

Over the next year or so, one or two symptoms at a time would randomly surface for small stretches of time but they proved to be much less debilitating. The good news is that over a decade later, I'm in great health. As you will see in the chapter titled "Become a Better Trader," I take every possible effort to maintain excellent health.

## *FROM DESPERATION COMES INSPIRATION*

They say that every cloud has a silver lining. In the midst of my health crisis, I spent hundreds of hours researching everything I could find about Multiple Sclerosis. Over those two months, I became an expert on every Multiple Sclerosis drug and therapy in existence. What I quickly discovered was that the handful of drugs on the market at the time didn't do much of anything for MS patients. I spent my days on multiple sclerosis message boards trying to find out if there were any potentially effective therapies on the horizon. A couple of drugs seemed to subtly suppress the symptoms but they didn't help reduce the number of attacks or the severity of the lesions in the brain. Although the drugs on the market barely worked, patients were willing to spend billions of dollars a year on them. It quickly became apparent to me that because the disease is so debilitating, those suffering from it are willing to spend whatever it takes on drugs that only slightly reduce the symptoms.

I thought to myself that if those afflicted with this dreadful disease were willing to spend billions on drugs that really didn't work, what would be the potential market for a drug that actually did work? Whoever developed such a drug would win the sweepstakes and virtually control the entire market overnight. In doing so, the victor could charge virtually any price for the drug.

In my research, one drug continued to come up in chat room discussions over and over again. People speculated that in early clinical trials this drug eliminated some 90% of the MS brain lesions. Apparently, the drug led to both a substantial decrease in symptoms and a significant reduction in the number of attacks. Such a miracle drug would truly be the Holy Grail for MS patients I thought. The name of this potential Superdrug was Antegren. It was being tested in clinical trials by an Irish drug company named Elan Pharmaceuticals.

A few months after my illness subsided, I began studying everything I possibly could about this drug as well as the company. What really grabbed my attention was that Elan's stock had fallen from $63 to $1 over the previous few months. The stock had been hit hard by a setback to another drug in combination with accounting irregularities pertaining to "off balance sheet transactions."

Allow me to digress for a minute. Don't ask me how or why, but after my eight week brush with physical and mental disability, I somehow developed a keen ability to visualize future chart patterns before they emerged. I had never paid much attention to stock charts or technical analysis in the past, but out of the blue, my mind was suddenly drawn to chart patterns. Chart patterns would become an obsession of mine from that point forward.

Based on Elan's (ELN) chart pattern, I had a strong visual sense that the stock would create powerful "bases" (periods of consolidation/resting spots) that would propel it to much higher prices going forward. In the decade since then, I have relied heavily on this "sixth sense" whenever I look at a new chart pattern. This subconscious ability keeps me from overanalyzing technical indicators which tend to confuse me more than anything else. I have found that this ability certainly is not unique to me. It is something that many traders naturally develop over the years as they hone their craft through trial and error.

I now return to the story. If Elan's Antegren was just 20% as effective as some of the data being published suggested, it was my strong belief that the drug would dominate the market and command upwards of $5 billion per year in high margin sales. Due to the severity of MS symptoms, I believed that there literally could be no side effects severe enough to derail the drug from coming to market.

Meanwhile, there was considerable skepticism throughout the analyst community regarding the drug's odds of success. They were doubtful that this drug could make it through the pipeline let alone make serious money if approved by the FDA. Many analysts were giving it less than a 50% shot of success. I simply did not agree with their assessment. Going through what I had gone through with MS-like symptoms, I knew deep in my heart that there was no way they could take this wonder drug away from the MS community.

I found myself seduced by a $1.25 stock with a $500 million market cap (a much larger market capitalization than a penny stock) that was developing a drug that I was fairly certain would eventually bring in $5 billion in annual sales. I figured the drug's gross margin would be upwards of 90% resulting in well over $4 billion in annual profit. Altogether, excluding the other potential blockbuster drugs in its pipeline, I believed that Elan's market cap could ultimately reach $80 billion—some *160 TIMES* its $500 million market cap at the time.

It seemed entirely illogical to make such an absurd projection, but just a few months earlier, the stock was trading some *30 times* higher than where it currently stood. I thought, why couldn't it return to those levels again? To cap things off, the CEO had just filed in Ireland that he purchased several hundred thousand dollars worth of shares in an open market buy.

I was staring at a stock that I believed had 80 to 160 upside potential, compared with a downside of only 1. Saying the risk/reward ratio was skewed heavily in my favor was an understatement. So after a reinvigorating four year vacation from the market, I took my $22,000 in savings (yes, I was one frugal S.O.B.!) and put it all into ELN at $1.25 in October of 2002.

Over the next 3 months, I watched in awe as the stock surged from $1.25 to $4.50. My $22,000 initial investment had appreciated to roughly $80,000. At 27, this was my first real taste of success in the market. But according to my calculations, the stock's rise had only begun.

As the market Gods would have it no other way, Elan announced an Antegren setback 2 months later. I watched in horror as the stock dropped by almost 60%. I was in total disbelief. I was now 0 for 4 in my efforts to crush the stock market.

Since I wasn't leveraged, I still had about $35,000 (yes, I had actually made a little after all was said and done) worth of the stock and decided to let it ride as I stood by my thesis. From the lows of the day of that announcement, the stock rarely had a down day for the next 10 weeks. Elan embarked on a monster run from $2.25 to $9. After transitioning over to TD Waterhouse and trading in and out of the position and adding more shares on margin, my $35,000 investment turned into $165,000 within 10 weeks. Thanks to ELN, I now had a higher net worth than anyone I knew within my age bracket. My 28th birthday was quickly approaching and I couldn't wait to celebrate my newfound wealth with my friends.

On the morning of my 28th birthday on June 26, 2003 I fired up my computer to see if there was anything exciting to do on my birthday. As I turned to a financial site, I quickly discovered a major headline for Elan. The company stated that it had discovered that a lethal brain infection was occurring in a small number of patients enrolled in the Antegren clinical trial. Certainly this news could not be good for the stock or for me. Since the company's fortunes now relied almost exclusively on this single late-stage drug, the stock was completely destroyed that day.

Due to the leverage I employed, I was nearly wiped out on my birthday. From its height a couple of weeks earlier, my account instantly plummeted from roughly $165,000 to around $36,000. I found myself again right back where I started. I couldn't believe that this was happening to me yet again—and on my birthday, no less. I was in complete shock; completely shattered and destroyed. I sold my entire stake that morning. I had lost just about every penny that I had made. I was now 0 for 5 in my quest.

Note: ELN eventually partnered with Biogen to market Antegren. The drug is now known as Tysabri. It is currently on the market and analysts project the drug to do $3 billion in annual sales by 2016. After I sold the stock that day at $5, ELN steadily advanced to $30 over the next 12 months.

## THE PERIOD OF ACCELERATED LEARNING

Although I was dazed after my most recent stumble, I now knew first-hand that through proper research it was entirely possible to make a relative fortune in the market in a short period of time. Clearly, due to my medical scare, I had stumbled upon Elan by "accident." I recognized that it would be very difficult for me to find big winners in a similar fashion going forward.

After 3 crash-and-burn episodes with biotech stocks, I certainly wanted to focus my attention on other less risky sectors. The burning question keeping me up at night was whether or not there was a reliable method to spot the big winners *before* their advances? That brief encounter with success ignited a passion inside of me that will burn brightly until the day I die.

As I recovered from the Elan episode, it became my sole mission to discover "the secret" to finding the market's next big winners. I had finally found my calling in life. From that day forward, I wanted to be the best investor that I possibly could be. I wanted to be better than anybody else. I read anything about trading and investing that I could get my hands on. I spent my days at the library and my evenings online searching through financial websites for investing wisdom.

I literally inhaled investment classics like *How I made $2,000,000 in the Stock Market* by Nicolas Darvas, *Reminiscences of a Stock Operator* by Edwin Lefevre, *Market Wizards* by Jack Schwager, *A Random Walk Down Wall Street* by Burton Malkiel, *Beating the Street* by Peter Lynch, *The Successful Investor* by William O'Neil, and several others. I found the best resource of the bunch to be O'Neil's *The Successful Investor*. His method appeared to be quite simple and the book seemed to identify most of the market's biggest winners before their major moves.

Several years earlier during a "Semester at Sea" visit to Cape Town, South Africa, I stumbled upon a book titled *Unlimited Power* by Anthony Robbins. A key theme of the book was the magic of modeling excellence in human behavior. Robbins asserted that in order to achieve ultimate success in any aspect of your life, you must model the absolute best in others. This necessitated seeking out the most successful people in your field and using them as blueprints for your own eventual success. I decided to take Robbins' advice and I set out to find the absolute best traders in the market. Specifically, I wanted to seek out traders who had mastered William O'Neil's principles.

I scoured the internet in an attempt to find the absolute best traders in the business. After mediocre initial success in this vast search, I somehow eventually stumbled upon trading gold—I had finally found my mentors. I will go into further detail about this group of traders in the "Mentors" section of this book. Looking back, this intense period of self-education changed the course of my life forever.

Based on my newfound knowledge, I developed a specific list of criteria to look for, based upon the qualities of past big gainers. I then combined this checklist with specific powerful chart patterns that I deemed to be "investable." I told myself that I would focus my efforts exclusively on the select stocks that met both the highest technical and fundamental standards. Over the next couple of months, I invested in a few stocks that met many but not *all* of my strict criteria. There wasn't much to write home about until...

## THE "STAIRCASE" THAT CHANGED MY LIFE

In late September, 2003, while scrolling through a new batch of charts, I noticed a chart pattern that I had never before encountered. The stock had traded down from over $20 a year earlier to just $0.25. After hitting bottom around $0.25, it then consolidated in a sideways "base" for a few months. Once the stock broke out of its base, it shot up to $0.75 where it sat perfectly still for several weeks. It then shot up to $1.50 where it repeated the pattern and sat quietly for a period of time. This process repeated itself around $1.50, $2.50 and then just under $4. The stock was carving out what I called a perfect "Staircase" pattern (an example of this can be seen in Chapter 12). This was the most powerful looking chart pattern that I had ever seen. The company was TRM Corporation (TRMM).

Next, I dug into TRMM's fundamentals and was floored by what I discovered. What first caught my attention was that the company had earned $0.16 per share in the most recent quarter compared to a loss in the same period a year earlier. After digging through hundreds of pages of the company's 10q and 10k SEC filings, it became evident to me that the company would be profitable on an ongoing basis.

I projected that TRMM would earn upwards of $0.30 per quarter starting sometime in the next two or three quarters. But the biggest shocker was that virtually every company executive was buying shares on the open market—at *ever increasing* prices. It seemed as if a brand new insider buy was filed every few days. I had never seen anything quite like it before.

Here was a $4 stock with a picture perfect chart pattern backed by future earnings that could support a $24-$36 share price within the next few quarters.

After concluding my research, I bought several batches of the stock over the next two weeks. Given what I believed to be an extremely favorable risk-reward profile, I bought the stock without any fear or hesitation whatsoever. I had every expectation that this Portland, Oregon-based ATM and copy machine stock would evolve into a blockbuster. As the stock climbed above the $5 threshold, my confidence grew and I added to my stake on margin.

Over the next 2 earnings reports, my initial thesis proved to be correct. TRMM reported $0.20 earnings per share (EPS) and $0.31 EPS sequentially over the next two quarters. As the stock marched higher, I continued to add more shares on margin after every pullback. The stock continued to march higher within a defined channel at a roughly 45 degree angle out of its initial base. After several months, the chart pattern broke to the upside out of its channel and turned parabolic (a much steeper angle, almost vertical) sending the stock above $27.

In a little over seven months, my initial account value of just under $46,000 now exceeded $800,000. My self-education and research was paying off in a *BIG, BIG way.*

As one might expect, the stock's parabolic ascent had sent shareholders into a total frenzy. Although the stock had reached my price target, there was a general feeling that the company's future would only get brighter. The consensus (a dirty, dirty word) on the Yahoo message board was that the stock would hit $60 sometime over the next few months. The shareholder environment was truly euphoric. Every day was a party.

Today, I know an awful lot more about price targets, stock euphoria, and parabolic chart patterns. I know all too well what takes place shortly after a euphoric parabolic run. At the time, however, I knew very little about these things and I just surfed the waves of excitement and emotion with a huge grin on my face.

In the days following the stock's breach of $27, I flew to Las Vegas to meet up with my family. As you might imagine, after TRMM's epic advance, I was on cloud nine. The timing of the Vegas vacation could not have been scripted any better.

*Or so I thought.*

On May 17, 2004, on the second day of my trip, I awoke to see that TRMM was in the midst of a massive selloff. After its vertical thrust, its chart had simply imploded in spectacular fashion, very similar to what happens to old Vegas hotels. As I sat in shock in my hotel room, I was forced to liquidate a majority of my position at unfavorable prices. Because of my non-judicious use of leverage, my $800,000 account value plummeted to the measly sum of $150,000 in a single day. After the biggest debacle of my career, the rest of my vacation was a total bust.

If you are still counting, I now stood 0 for 6 in my mission to conquer Mr. Market. As my career progressed, each portfolio surge was more dramatic than the previous ones. Unfortunately, each subsequent collapse had become more spectacular in scale.

In spite of my most recent loss, I now had firsthand knowledge of what types of stocks provided the biggest returns. More importantly, I now had utmost confidence in myself and my investing ability. Similar to past episodes, I took a couple weeks off to reflect and to regroup. However, I knew deep inside that I would bounce back with a vengeance yet again.

## HISTORY BEING MADE

Emerging from that dark day in May, 2004, I continued to relentlessly focus on the principles that I knew would uncover the biggest winners going forward. I spent virtually every waking moment in front of my computer screen for the next 2 years. Consistently working ninety hour weeks, I uncovered a majority of the biggest gainers in the entire market. In the twenty months following the TRMM debacle, I embarked upon a run unlike any other.

This rewarding period was anything but easy as I endured several more serious account drawdowns along the way. In spite of these setbacks, my personal portfolio cash value surged from $152,000 (06/04) to $267,000 (10/04), to $586,000 (12/04), to $1.23 million (02/05), to $2.13 million (05/05), to $4.46 million (07/05), to $5.8 million (09/05), and ultimately to over $6.8 million by January of 2006. During this period, I had no other sources of income. As one might imagine, it was a truly exciting time.

The most difficult part for me was to resist every natural temptation to sell or become complacent when my account reached significant million dollar milestones. It was not easy in the least to hold on. I now know firsthand what they mean by "let your winners run." It is definitely something that does not come naturally. I had to cultivate a *tremendous* level of confidence to enable me to do so.

I will go into detail about some of my biggest winners from this period in Chapter 12.

## THE MONEY

I vividly remember the day in 2006 when I first walked into my new accountant's office in Palm Beach, Florida. After a few minutes of small talk, he informed me that due to the demand for his services by high net worth individuals, it would probably make more sense for me to seek the assistance of an inexpensive national firm like H&R Block. After listening to his introduction, I handed him my statements from the past few years. I will never forget his reaction after he thumbed through a few pages. He looked up and yelled "Are you kidding me?!" He immediately stood up and walked over to his office door and shut it for privacy. He enthusiastically exclaimed "I have never seen or heard of anything like this." Needless to say, he took me on as a client.

Money to me has always been about time, freedom, and fulfilling experiences. Although beating the market has always been my primary motivation, I certainly did not complain about the money once I had it. Here I was at the age of 30 with millions of totally liquid assets at my disposal and virtually no overhead. I thought it was about time that I reward myself and others for my intense efforts.

The number of commas in my account balance allowed me to do things I had only dreamed of doing before. I was able to buy the cars I was obsessed with as a kid, train to be a pilot, buy my dream condo, travel the world, host gourmet dinners, contribute to charitable causes, and to give a motivational speech or two. For the following two years I continued to enjoy discovering future winners, but more than anything else I was enjoying my winnings and living life to the absolute fullest.

* In all honesty, the money certainly did not change my outlook on "shopping" in the least. To this day, it's *one* trip to the mall every year or two and that's all I can stand. Personally, I can't think of a more unpleasant way to spend my time. I continue(d) wearing my Old Navy clothing purchased in the 1990s and I continue to be totally fine with that.

## THE BET

Now, let me fast forward to 2008. Yes, *THAT* 2008. During the middle of a horribly lengthy and painful break-up with my girlfriend at the time, I watched from the sidelines as world markets declined swiftly into the fall. Given the extent of the 2008 market crash, I stipulated that the few traders who were still solvent would pick up the pennies and make a fortune. I monitored dozens of time-tested indicators daily as I looked for advantageous risk/reward set ups where I could ride the large snapback rally that was sure to arrive. After several weeks, the technical and sentiment readings were screaming that the market was more oversold than at any other point in its history.

Everything I monitored seemingly indicated that it was safe to return to the market. The nature of the oversold conditions indicated to me that the mean reversion bounce-back rally would spring the market some 15% or 20% higher within a matter of days. Being the calculated risk taker that I've always been, I put my proven "bread and butter" Superstock strategy aside as I returned to the market. It was a bold attempt to time the bounce. Given the historical magnitude of the global decline that had already transpired, I went in heavier than ever before.

To maximize my leverage, I bought call options and triple-long exchange traded funds (ETF's) on margin. Given the compounding effects of my holdings, if the market bounced 20%, my portfolio would have doubled or tripled. I truly believed that it was inevitable that history would ultimately repeat and the market would embark upon a vicious rally to the upside within days of my entry. I was confident that this would prove to be the defining trade of my career; the trade that sent me well on my way to a nine-figure net worth. I put everything on the line. I was absolutely certain in my conviction.

The days that followed were days I will never expose myself to again. In pursuit of the trade of a generation, I had abandoned every single one of my trading rules. As anybody who has lived through 2008 now knows, I was wrong—*dead* wrong! Due to call options and the extent of the leverage utilized, I lost about 75%. I took a several million dollar hit within a matter of days. Millions that I had worked so hard to accumulate had simply vanished in the blink of an eye. I committed a series of fatal mistakes: over-leverage, utilizing options, catching falling knives, trading the general market, trading without stop-losses... the list goes on.

Previously, my winning strategy had been uncovering undiscovered Superstocks fueled by insider buying. Had I let the turmoil of my relationship affect my judgment? Did I simply become too greedy? Who knows? What I do know is that because I violated every one of my rules, I was well-deserving of every ounce of the punishment.

## THE REAL JOURNEY OF A LIFETIME

Having been inspired by Tim Ferriss' book *The 4 Hour Workweek,* in the aftermath of my latest debacle, I figured there would never be a better time to embark upon my first real "mini-retirement." This hiatus would be a much longer version of the ones in the past that proved to be so personally rewarding and re-invigorating.

At the time, it was universally believed that the world was falling apart as we entered the first phases of "The Great Depression 2.0." I figured that if ever I was to step away for an extended period, there would certainly never be a better time to do so.

Without much of a plan, I shut down my trading operations and moved all of my possessions into a 10' x 10' storage unit in Atlanta.

After winding down my personal obligations, I embarked upon the journey of a lifetime and never looked back. At the age of 33, I had absolutely nothing holding me back. I was now officially "mini-retired."

With five shirts, two pairs of pants, two pairs of shoes, two pairs of shorts, seven boxer shorts, an iPod, a laptop, and as many books as I could cram into my small backpack, I left the United States without an agenda. Over the next three and a half years I traveled extensively throughout Laos, Colombia, Peru, Ecuador, Chile, Argentina, Uruguay, Australia, Thailand, Macau, Malaysia, Singapore, Hong Kong, Indonesia, and China. My travels took me through twenty-three of China's thirty-three autonomous regions. I even managed to squeeze in Canada and thirty of the United States on two separate camping trips when I returned.

The time away was an essential journey of self-discovery. I threw out my watch, watched absolutely no television, read and summarized dozens of books on human behavior (not books on trading, as I'll explain later), studied Buddhism, and ran two half marathons. I drank "cat shit coffee" in Laos, slept in jungles and on beaches, met some of the world's foremost computer hackers, and went through four unreliable laptops. I even found myself selling gourmet chocolate from Kazakhstan at one of the world's largest trade shows in Chengdu, China.

During my travels, I was held up at knifepoint in Ecuador, had $850 stolen while riding a bus in Thailand, motor-biked across Indonesia, went without hot showers for months at a time, and was roughed up by corrupt police officers in a small shack in Southern Colombia. I sampled a "happy shake" in Thailand, saw dogs slaughtered for meat, climbed several 8,000-12,000 foot mountains all over the world, and was abandoned in China by a rogue bus driver who kept every last one of my possessions. I even lived among chickens, roosters, and pigs for long stretches.

Having spent much of this time in small villages, I can honestly say that a majority of the people I encountered in the developing world had a level of contentment and happiness that easily surpassed that of most of us in the United States. I found that the formula of a simple lifestyle + no debt + independent communities + sunshine + close family + daily involvement and interaction with nature = one heck of a consistently *BIG* smile.

It was not until four days before my most recent flight to the States that I came to the startling realization that I would be unable to return. After thumbing through my passport, I noticed that I did not have a single inch of space remaining for an exit visa. Over the next three days, I became intimately familiar with the U.S. embassy and its staff in Buenos Aires. As another demonstration of bureaucracy at its finest, the simple process of having pages added to my passport turned into a multi-day fiasco. Luckily, everything worked out in the end and I was able to return home.

In the last year of my "retirement" alone: I flew some 78,000 miles; personally drove 16,000 miles; spent close to 200 hours on trains, 300 hours on buses, and countless hours on motorbikes. Although I rarely placed trades during my retirement, I followed the market closely. I often sent out email market updates to friends and family or posted in public stock forums. Despite my psychological and physical distance from the market, I found that I certainly had not lost my touch or my enthusiasm for investing.

During this time, I sent out dozens of emails highlighting the occasional special situation stock—but mostly alerts predicting sector or general market inflection points. Not wanting to be enticed to trade during my hiatus, most of the time I tried not to look for Superstocks. I focused primarily on global markets, sectors, and themes.

Although there was no personal financial gain, I truly enjoyed composing and sending out my market commentary. This practice kept me involved in the market and allowed me to stay in touch with my network of trading contacts. Surprisingly, composing these updates gave me more satisfaction than the act of trading had previously. To receive my commentary, feel free to contact me.

In the end, the time away from family, friends, markets, and country was essential for me to gain a new perspective on what is truly important in my life. The time off was truly a once in a lifetime period of reflection and growth. I now try to focus on the most important things in life: gratitude, friendship, family, happiness, and health.

Realizing just how precious life outside of trading is, I now consciously go out of my way to try to create in every moment, to never cease learning, to live outside of my comfort zone, to be more disciplined, to improve my thinking, and to live and act in every moment. But perhaps most importantly, I now realize that we *don't* have all the time in the world. Because of this, I now always try to take the *road less traveled*. I emerge from my retirement with an entirely new vantage point, ten times more energized and motivated than ever before.

## A NOTE ON DRAWDOWNS

> *"An expert is a person who has made all the mistakes which can be made in a very narrow field."*
>
> Physicist Niels Bohr

There's an ever-so-slight chance that you may have noticed the words "loss" or "drawdown" mentioned throughout my trading history. The immense account drawdowns and subsequent dramatic comebacks that I have endured in my career have been nothing short of breathtaking.

Clawing my way out of the abyss each time, I have broken the odds time and again. They say it is not how many times you get knocked down, but how many times you get back up. If I didn't truly live and breathe trading, I would certainly be doing something entirely different today as a result of these drawdowns. If I have learned one thing through all of my ordeals, it is that the only sin in life is to punish yourself over past failures.

Fortunately, I have learned to view losses as part of the cost of my trading education. Each separate experience has certainly allowed me to hone my craft. I am comforted in knowing that I am not alone in my experiences. In fact, many of the great investors that I have studied have lost their fortunes on several occasions.

Hedge fund Billionaire John Paulson has endured drawdowns in excess of 50%. Famed penny stock trader Timothy Sykes lost most of his fortune by the time his hedge fund collapsed in 2007. Energy hedge fund magnate T-Boone Pickens has said "I have been broke three or four times. But fortunately for me I'm not an MBA, so I didn't know I was broke." Similarly, world-record holder Dan Zanger said that he lost his entire account "three or four times" and lost over 50% in the months following his record-setting performance during the internet bubble. Investment legend Jesse Livermore lost his *entire* trading fortune on at least five occasions.

Curtis Faith of "Turtles" fame said, "Unfortunately, you cannot make the 100 percent plus returns we did as Turtles without drawdowns at these levels. I think my worst drawdown was something in the order of 70 percent. I don't know many people who can sustain that level of drawdown. It is very difficult on most people's psyches."

Extreme account drawdowns could almost be considered a prerequisite for massive trading success. Against all odds, the most successful traders just never surrender; their suffering capacity defines their greatness. Like many aspects of life, it is only when we hit absolute "rock bottom" that we decide with every fiber of our being that we simply *must* do *whatever it takes* to succeed on a massive scale. Likewise, in my personal life, it was only after gaining weight and feeling like complete garbage that I found the motivation within to radically change my lifestyle. Without hitting rock bottom, it can be difficult to cultivate the necessary passion within.

It has been said that formal education will make you a living, but self-education will make you a fortune. Extraordinary drawdowns certainly have given some of the world's best traders a priceless self education.

Like many others before me, it was during my own visits into the portfolio abyss that my trading methodology and resilient psychological makeup evolved. I never would have posted such returns had I not endured such extreme emotional and financial extremes. I learned that absolutely *no loss* is insurmountable.

Necessary learning experiences? You better believe it. The key is not only to learn from them but perhaps more importantly to find the courage and motivation to strike back.

Having said all that, would I recommend that anybody endure similar episodes? Absolutely not! Not in a million years. Those aiming for the record books take on levels of leverage and risk that inevitably backfire. Although I continue to search high and low for the next big Superstock, I now utilize an approach based upon maximizing gains within the confines of constant risk-reduction and well-defined risk/reward. That being said, I would *NEVER* avoid a potential blockbuster stock in pursuit of risk mitigation.

My wish for you is to maximize your potential profits while limiting risk. Utilizing lessons learned from my failures, I outline a rules-based approach later in the book that will help prevent you from making the same stupid mistakes that I did.

# CHAPTER 2

# *Today is the Day to Divorce Yourself from Mediocrity*

*"You are much better off going into the market on a shoestring feeling that you cannot afford to lose. I would rather bet on somebody starting out with a few thousand dollars than on somebody who came in with millions."*

Jack Schwager

As detailed in my personal journey, investing in the stock market is one of the few areas in life where an average person with little experience can make a fortune. Although I have a few "traditional" qualifications to be a trader—an undergraduate degree in Economics, a Master's degree in Business, the experience of starting a couple businesses, and preparation for the Series 7 stockbroker exam—I feel very strongly that not only are such credentials not required for trading success, but they actually inhibit it.

Some fifteen years ago, thinking I would become Wall Street's next Gordon Gecko, I applied to every major investment bank on Wall Street. I was flat out rejected by each and every one of them. Goldman Sachs, Morgan Stanley, Merrill Lynch, and others—they all rejected my application. Looking back, I consider myself extremely fortunate that I was not hired. In fact, to this day, I keep those rejection letters as a reminder of just how lucky I am.

Had I been forced to adopt the traditional Wall Street rules and groupthink, there would have been no chance for me to achieve the independent perspective I have worked so hard to develop. I know several people who have been classically trained on Wall Street. Frankly, their ability to think independently and spot big trends and make big money leaves much to be desired.

Outside of the need for a few thousand dollars of start-up capital, there are virtually no barriers to entry for somebody wanting to take a swing at investing. Heck, you don't need a degree, you don't need to be good looking, nor do you need any experience (well, you do to be successful). Assuming you have a laptop, some savings, and some time, you can literally set up your office in any coffee shop the world over. As a trader, you have total freedom, no boss looking over your shoulder, no deadlines, unlimited time off and a potentially limitless supply of wealth provided by the tailwinds of unlimited global quantitative easing.

Despite its appeal, very few traders achieve resounding success in this business. The boundless freedom the trader is faced with requires the utmost in self-discipline (a never-ending quest for me) which very few people possess. Furthermore, most traders are controlled by fear and second-guessing which ultimately leads to missed shots when presented with the opportunity of a lifetime. Discovering a huge winner means absolutely nothing if you don't have the courage to buy and the confidence and conviction to hold for the duration.

## GO BIG OR GO HOME

> *"With speculation, the risk of loss is more than offset by the possibility of a huge gain; otherwise, there would be very little motivation to speculate. While it is often confused with gambling, the key difference is that speculation is generally tantamount to taking a calculated risk and is not dependent on pure chance, whereas gambling depends on totally random outcomes or chance."*
>
> Investopedia

Of the 15,000 or so publicly-traded companies currently trading in the United States, about half are traded on the major exchanges. Our goal together is to learn how to find the one or two jet-fueled Superstocks out of those several thousand that have the potential to change your life forever. We are seeking an undervalued stock that has the ultimate technical setup backed by world-class fundamentals. The idea is to purchase these stocks at such a point when the potential upside outweighs the downside by a substantial margin.

As we move forward, we will shed light on the specific criteria and signals to look for when buying and selling. Believe me, it truly only takes a few of these stocks during your investment career to propel your portfolio into another stratosphere. One big gainer literally makes up for dozens of the inevitable losers.

You might be asking yourself: "But how difficult is it to find these rare stocks?" Well, aside from the time required, it really isn't all that difficult for the average person to identify these hidden gems well before the rest of Wall Street. I have to be honest though—identification is just the tip of the iceberg.

The optimal buy point and sell point, and the psychological preparation that go into a major trade are much more difficult to master. If it was easy, everybody would be making money in these stocks, right?

You might agree that the stock market is more or less a glorified casino for financial heavyweights. The difference between a casino and the stock market is that it is much easier to win big over time in the stock market. Unlike a casino, by being highly selective when picking stocks, you can stack the odds heavily in your favor thus vastly increasing your likelihood of success.

Although the process of discovering these stocks can be quite exciting, you will learn that successful trading can be downright boring as you might not execute a trade for extended periods of time.

## CALCULATED RISKS

*"Risk comes from not knowing what you are doing"*
Warren Buffet

*"Instead of employing a statistical thinking toward market decisions, the general public keeps investing based on impulsive "feelings," letting an assortment of emotional biases rule their lives. In the end, to their detriment, people are always risk-averse toward gains, but risk-seeking toward losses. They are stuck."*
Author Michael Covel

The most successful *long term* stock market investors are those who have mastered the fine art of taking large CALCULATED risks. These rare traders take immediate and decisive action when they see great potential reward in combination with minimal and well-defined risk. Such a one-sided situation is what I like to call a "Fat Pitch."

Successful investors use their high self-esteem and massive confidence to their advantage, because they are ready and willing to fail in the pursuit of the big trade. As my editor says, "Scared money never wins!" They understand that in order to succeed, they need to actively pursue and take on calculated risk over and over and over again. In the end, there are three types of investors in this world: those who make things happen, those who watch things happen, and those who wonder what happened. Which one are you?

As easy as it might sound to take on the required risk, our society is imprisoned by the concept of risk mitigation *at any cost*: guaranteed rates of return, living in the same town we were born, working for a stable corporation, long-term contracts (mortgage, marriage, employment, cell phone, cable, internet etc.), insurance for just about everything, and so on. Because of this cultural hypnosis, most of us find it emotionally unappealing to accept the required risk when the payoff could be huge.

I can't tell you how many times I've been around risk-averse investors who simply could not motivate themselves to pull the trigger on a "risky" stock that appeared to have well-defined

10 to 1 upside. They couldn't even get themselves to risk 1% of their capital on such a trade. If the stock isn't in the S&P 500, or if a "highly qualified" television snake-oil salesman didn't recommend it, forget about it.

By all means, if you want to be like everybody else—if you want an average life and average rates of return—you must avoid risk at any cost. If you want to avoid risk, the next time you find yourself at a bar (if you are single), I urge you to never even consider striking up a conversation with the beautiful guy or girl of your dreams. If you were to ask somebody on their death bed what their biggest regret in life was, I can almost guarantee that their big regret was not taking more calculated risks along the way. To me, life without some level of risk just isn't worth living. There's no point in living if you don't feel alive.

The question I must now ask of you is whether you are satisfied with your past investment returns. If so, I sincerely applaud you for a job well done. If not, are you willing to recondition your mind, to burn all bridges, to step out of the crowd, to re-write your story, and to do things a little differently in order to succeed? Perhaps to succeed on a scale you never thought possible?

> *"Twenty years from now you will be more disappointed by the things that you didn't do than by the ones you did do."*
>
> Mark Twain

## ARE YOU CRAZY?

> *"A prophet is not someone with special vision, just blind to what others see."*
>
> Nassim Taleb

Everything worthwhile in life is just a few feet outside of our well-defined comfort zones. Winning at trading must be learned, and is definitely *not* within our comfort zones.

Please allow me to ask a few more questions of you. Do you have the drive, determination, passion, and time required to break free of investment conditioning? Are you hungry to learn? Do you have an incredible belief in what is possible? Do you have a high tolerance for calculated risk and the emotional ability to endure the inevitable ups and downs? Will you be able to nurture an open mind to spot the obvious? Are you willing to implement self-discipline in every aspect of your investing? But perhaps most important of all: are you willing to take a huge step forward to take action to destroy your bond with investment mediocrity?

These are all very important questions to ask. Frankly, if you are missing any of these essential ingredients, you may be best served by turning your savings over to an "investment professional" then focusing on the more important things in life. There is absolutely nothing wrong with that. In fact, if investing isn't fun for you, cut your losses short and put this book down immediately. Life is simply too short to spend time on things that don't energize and excite you.

You must be brutally honest with yourself and ask yourself "why?" Why do you want to try to beat the market? If future possessions are truly all that matter to you, I am afraid that you may be sadly disappointed in the end. From firsthand experience: after achieving fortune, things may appear great at first, but as the saying goes, "the more things change, the more they stay the same." It is referred to as the "hedonic treadmill." The more we try to improve our lives by accumulating more "stuff," the more we become accustomed to that stuff and the more our lives tend to stay the same.

Yes, more money certainly offers you the chance to improve yourself, which can radically change your life for the better. But the sad truth is that 90% of people who gain fortune simply stay the same and life goes on as it always did before.

It becomes a whole lot easier to achieve outsized returns if your mission and vision for your life are more than just the hedonic pleasures provided by the dollars and cents.

Yes, it takes a very special breed of person to step outside of his comfort zone to do what's necessary to achieve abnormal returns. Some call these people crazy. They might be right. You may remember this dialogue from an Apple television commercial from many years ago: "Here's to the crazy ones, the misfits, the rebels, the trouble makers...they changed the world, they pushed the human race forward. While some may see them as the crazy ones, we see genius. Because the people who are crazy enough to think they can change the world are the ones who do."

I am not implying by any means that you will change the world after you've read this book. But by taking calculated risks, by thinking outside the box, by seeing things from a new perspective, and yes, by being a little crazy, you can certainly change *YOUR* world.

## THE 1%

> *"Don't let the noise of other's opinions drown out your own inner voice and most important, have the courage to follow your heart and intuition."*
>
> Steve Jobs

As you probably know, the market is a zero sum game. Every time somebody wins, inevitably somebody else loses. Over time, money flows from the many to the few. The reason most investors underperform the market is that they spend a vast majority of their time studying the same concepts and techniques that 99% of other traders have studied before. They read the same books, surf the same sites, and watch the same people on television.

One of the most important lessons I've learned in life is that what everyone knows isn't worth knowing. What the investing public fails to realize is that fortunes are made from the discovery of quality outlying information and fortunes are lost by relying upon well-dispersed, well-known mainstream information. The 1% of people who accumulate all of the market wealth are those who do absolutely everything differently. They focus on the one or two game-changing variables that truly make all the difference.

I find that the majority of investors spend a great deal of their time scouring through every possible resource to dig up any information to support their investment thesis. They desperately search for *ANYTHING* that remotely supports their thesis—in analyst reports, on *Zero Hedge, Bloomberg, Seeking Alpha, Barron's, Financial Times, Yahoo Finance*...the list goes on.

To make matters a great deal worse, they then share their discoveries with like-minded people in an attempt to receive even more positive feedback to further strengthen their conviction. This is typical human behavior for you. They sink so much time and effort into this pursuit that the sunk emotional costs leave them no choice but to marry their stocks. Once all of that energy has been put into "research," it then becomes "till death do us part."

Later, you will discover that there are a limited number of variables that you should study prior to taking a position. All other attempts at "research" should be left to market novices.

I will go to my grave believing that this insane pursuit of financial validation is a total waste of human resources. In this endeavor, time, talent, and intellectual horsepower are thrown away on an infinitely massive scale.

## RIGHT OR RICH?

I know this will come as a surprise, but you will find that the 99% receive much more psychological satisfaction from being right than from getting rich. 99% of traders are forever prisoners to their ego. For them, the emotional satisfaction gained from being right on a handful of 0.5% trades far outweighs the satisfaction from one 300% monster trade that may slowly unfold over several months. You can see this play out every single day in online message boards or in chat rooms. Joe Six-Pack boasts that XYZ corp will shoot up 200%. An hour later, Joe enthusiastically exclaims to the board that he sold XYZ for a 1% gain. Two months later, XYZ does in fact move 200% higher. Joe inevitably watches from the sidelines in disbelief.

At the end of the trading day, if Joe Six-Pack is able to demonstrate to everyone in the group that he was correct on a majority of his predictions, his ego absolutely explodes. He feels validated, and to the others he is *the man!* If he did absolutely nothing but sat on his big, hairy Superstock for four months, he would have very little to show for it from a group perspective. The majority of investors feel it is absolutely essential to be part of the safety of the group and they sabotage their investment returns to do so. You absolutely cannot afford to be around traders whose egos have a need to be right.

## DEVELOP INDIVIDUAL THINKING

*"Whenever you find yourself on one side of the majority, it's time to pause and reflect."*

Mark Twain

*"I believe that the public wants to be led, to be instructed, to be told what to do. They want reassurance. They will always move en masse, a mob, a herd, a group, because people want the safety of human company. They are afraid to stand alone."*

Jesse Livermore

Over the years, I have found that the best way to spot big future trends is to cultivate individual thinking by trading in complete isolation far from the corrupting effects of groupthink. Outside of my initial "training period," my returns suffered immensely whenever I returned to a group setting over the years. There certainly is a time and a place for group collaboration, but it must be carefully structured in such a way to eliminate "news," "high frequency trading," and groupthink.

Navigating the market in isolation isn't easy for most people to do because human nature dictates that we seek the safety of the herd in order to simplify or eliminate the thinking process. We are controlled by the urge to be in agreement with and to be constantly connected to the viewpoints of others. We seek out "consensus" views so as to feel like we are part of a community of like-minded investors. If we end up on the wrong side of an investment, it feels much better to go down with others. If you follow the herd—your friends, your broker, and the media—you don't have to think at all. How wonderful is that?

A common theme throughout this book is to stand alone. To make your own investment decisions outside of the influence of others. From the beginning, the world's best traders have always been the independent ones, the isolated ones, the loners, the ones willing to discount other's opinions; the few brave souls who shunned the overzealous crowd and shorted Facebook stock on the day of its initial public offering. I want you to develop the ability to see the truth in spite of prevailing wisdom. I want you to become one of the very few willing to stand alone. I want you to become what we in the trenches refer to as the *"smart money."*

## CULTIVATING IDEAS IN ISOLATION

It has been scientifically proven that the quality of the ideas generated in isolation is generally far superior to those generated during brainstorming sessions.

According to Jonah Lehreror in his *New Yorker* article "Groupthink—The Brainstorming Myth," "The first empirical test of Osborn's (Alex Osborn- author of *Your Creative Power*) brainstorming technique was performed at Yale University in 1958. Forty-eight male undergraduates were divided into twelve groups and given a series of creative puzzles. The groups were instructed to follow Osborn's guidelines. As a control sample, the scientists gave the same puzzles to forty-eight students working by themselves. The results were a sobering refutation of Osborn. The solo students came up with roughly twice as many solutions as the brainstorming groups, and a panel of judges deemed their solutions more 'feasible' and 'effective.' Brainstorming didn't unleash the potential of the group, but rather made each individual less creative." Lehrer goes on to say "Decades of research have consistently shown that brainstorming groups think of far fewer ideas than the same number of people who work alone and later pool their ideas."

Cultivating independent thinking is next to impossible for most people as they will do just about anything to avoid being mentally alone. Because they are scared to face their reality and scared of what they may encounter in isolation, they construct their lives around things that will distract and perform the thinking for them. We see this in the explosion of Twitter, Facebook, smartphones, and reality television. As we allow our minds to be controlled by these outside influences, compulsive thinking displaces directed thinking resulting in wandering minds that manufacture anxiety, negativity, and depression. None of these destructive emotions can ever lead to successful trading. In silent isolation, we hear the truth and we see immense possibility.

# CHAPTER 3

# *The Most Potent Drug the World Has Ever Seen*

*"The credibility of any item in finance is inversely proportionate to the amount of publicity it receives."*

Michael Scott.

*"As difficult as it may be, let the federal government and mass media do what they do, which is to spend a ridiculous amount of time and energy attempting to justify their respective existence by providing information for the consumption of the knowledge-hungry masses. If one wishes to be wise, however, one will acknowledge one's own ignorance, observe the herd from a distance, and perhaps shrug in amusement."*

Kent Thune

Please forgive me if I rant a bit in the following sections. Please bear with me as these are subjects that I am quite passionate about.

In my earlier years, I must admit that I was a hard-core news junkie. I had *CNBC* on all day, every day. I simply could not get enough of the non-stop action. The numbing effects of not having to think for myself were quite addictive to me. After eventually recognizing its negative effects on my trading and overall level of happiness, I consciously stepped away from the news cycle several years ago. I admit that I am not 100% perfect in this regard. I exposed myself to the negativity during the 2009 rebound and during the "Fiscal Cliff" of 2011. Neither instance affected me financially but they certainly had a negative effect on my outlook on life.

Although I abhor processed, pre-packaged news these days, I am still a sucker for one-on-one interviews with the right people. I never pass on an opportunity to learn from the best in any field of expertise. I'm embarrassed to admit it, but I get most of my "news" fix from ESPN.

In order to stick to my decision and shield myself from groupthink and manipulation, I do not watch CNBC, Bloomberg or any other form of financial entertainment television. If I am out in public and see this financial entertainment on a television monitor, I simply turn the other way. As a side note, I find it really amusing whenever a friend of mine refers to a popular CNBC entertainment performance as the "Lose Money Fast in an Hour" show.

I no longer surf over to *Forbes.com, Zero Hedge.com, Minyanville.com, TheStreet.com* or to other "financial news" of any sort from any mainstream source. Although I crave the *"media high"* like anybody else, I have made a firm decision to avoid it like the plague. I can't stress just how important it is to follow the 1% and completely abandon this mass-media processed "fast food."

The mass media is structured in such a way as to purposely confuse the hell out of 99% of the investing public. This is done in order to quietly funnel the public's savings over to the "smart money" investors who just happen to be the ones actively manipulating the media in the first place.

"News" is one of the most potent and addictive drugs on Earth and has absolutely nothing at all to do with making money in the markets. In fact, "news" is a powerful money-making deterrent. The investing public has been groomed to become so entirely dependent on the news cycle that giving it up for even a week is akin to a meth addict going to rehab. The instant we turn on the "idiot box," our mind immediately shuts off and the ability to think critically and independently ceases as propaganda gradually seeps in.

I dare say that nobody on this planet consistently makes money by following what they read and see in the mainstream media. If you cannot find a single article in favor of your investment premise, I can almost guarantee you that the trade will ultimately be a winner for you. If you can only find your particular investment theme on obscure blogs, it very well could be a winning idea. If you start seeing your idea in the mainstream press, it is probably time to sell. And God forbid, if you start seeing your theme in books, it is time to sell short.

Go to your local bookstore (if one even exists) and take a look at any "forward-looking" finance book written over the past several years. Take note of the publishing date and its "financial prediction." I can almost guarantee that several years later, the book's prediction never came to fruition. For example, look up David Elias's book *DOW 40,000* (published in 1999) or Harry Dent's book *The Great Depression Ahead: How to Prosper in the Crash Following the Greatest Boom in History.* Can you guess when this one was published? January, 2009—just weeks ahead of perhaps the greatest market bottom in history.

Read these books to learn, read them for entertainment, but don't read them to make money.

I am convinced that the more you consume information on the latest scandal, the latest political controversy, the latest economic crisis, and the latest round of credit and equity downgrades, the worse your investment performance will be over the long run. The sad fact is that scare tactics increase viewership and sell newspapers.

The mass media tries everything in its vast arsenal to turn you into a pessimist. Do you know of any self-made multi-millionaires or billionaires who are pessimistic?

## MEDIA NOISE LEADS TO INCREASED TRADING

As we will discuss further, the vast amount of wealth is accumulated while sitting... while waiting patiently. CNBC, Bloomberg, Yahoo Finance, *CNN Money, The Wall Street Journal, Marketwatch,* Twitter etc. are all screaming at you to trade, trade, and trade some more. In life, the right thing to do 99% of the time is the *hardest thing* to do. The hardest thing to do is to avoid all the noise, to perform your own unbiased research, to make your own judgments, and to come to your own conclusions. Simply walk away from the noise.

Remember that the biggest gainers in the market will be the stocks that absolutely nobody is talking about. I guarantee that nobody in the mass media will lead you to any of these stocks in their initial stages. Always remember that journalists are anything but professional money makers. They write for a living. They are required to publish several new articles a week whether the pieces are actionable or not.

## MEDIA MISDIRECTION

The media has a remarkable tendency to focus on what has already happened. If any members of the mainstream financial media were even slightly adept at predicting what would happen in the future, I guarantee you that they would be on an entirely different career path. Right when it becomes abundantly clear to me that a stock or sector is on the brink of a major long-term powerful reversal, the media rush in to publish competing pieces directly contradicting all my unbiased research. In the markets, financial media is the primary creator of crowd psychology. As we know, crowd psychology is *ALWAYS* wrong at critical market turning points.

## MEDIA FOCUSES ON A DISMAL PAST,
## FORTUNES ARE MADE ENVISIONING A BRIGHTER FUTURE

Here are a few examples of media misdirection:

- In the spring of 2003 the financial media wrote article after article about the imminent demise of the steel industry. The media published data showing that a good chunk of the industry would declare bankruptcy. While the media was preoccupied with prognosticating the death of an industry, the charts of all of the major steel makers were setting up in beautiful basing patterns. The charts were loudly contradicting every fluff piece the media was publishing. Of course, the media would never consider such an esoteric thing as a chart to predict the future of an industry. From the point of maximum media focus, the largest steel producer, U.S. steel, gained *2,000%* over the next four and a half years. Over the same time period, ArcelorMittal steel gained a mind-boggling *3,500%*.

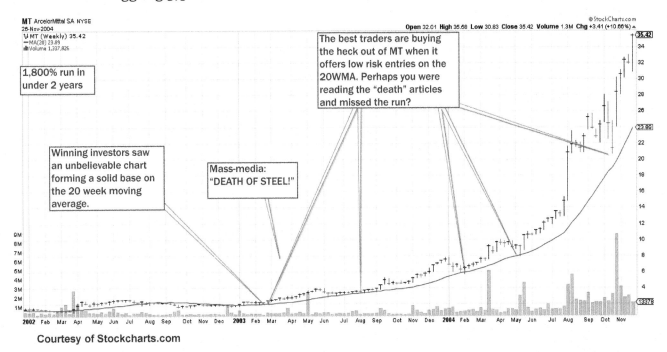

Courtesy of Stockcharts.com

- In July of 2008, media coverage of a "bankrupt airline industry" reached a crescendo. Article after article suggested mass bankruptcies were imminent. From the point of maximum media focus, the airline sector gained 130% in nineteen trading sessions.

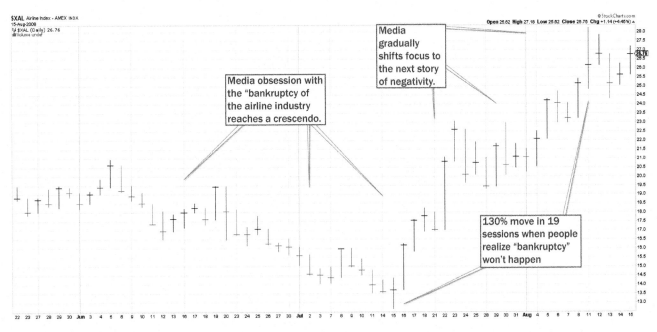

Courtesy of Stockcharts.com

- Remember March of 2009? The media did not publish one single fundamental reason to invest. More accurately, they called for the end of civilization as we knew it. It proved to be the greatest investing opportunity of our lifetime. This is the Dow Jones daily chart from that period.

Courtesy of Stockcharts.com

- Also in March of 2009, the media cried about a "nationalization of the banking system." At this precise moment, it was becoming increasingly clear to me that banks would soon be allowed to creatively adjust the value of many of the assets on their balance sheets. Stocks like Citigroup were setting up in powerful low-level base reversal patterns. From that point forward, the entire banking sector tripled in six months. Here is the Philadelphia Bank Index (BKX) daily chart from that period.

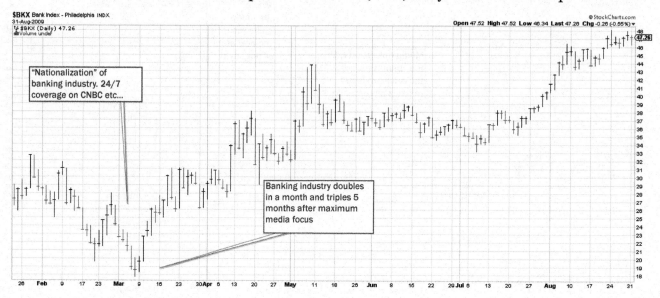

Courtesy of Stockcharts.com

- In April of 2012, article after article focused exclusively on the "sea of excess natural gas." The media suggested that it would take years to work through the excess capacity in storage. They were suggesting that to make room for future production in the pipelines, the industry would have to give natural gas away for free. They were saying that the price of natural gas would go to—gulp—ZERO! Within 10 weeks, the commodity was up 60% from $1.90 to $3 per btu. (See my natural gas analysis from April in the Appendix). Here is the natural gas daily chart from that period.

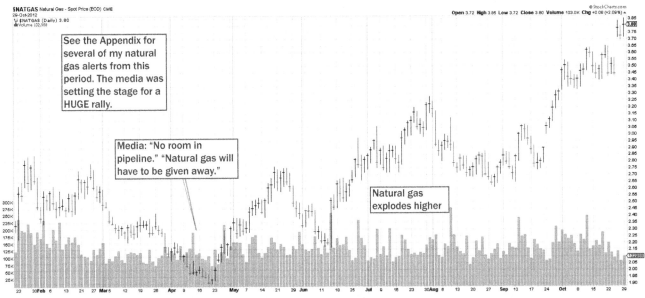

Courtesy of Stockcharts.com

- On June 3, 2012, the media coverage of the massive "European bankruptcy" reached a crescendo with CNBC's Sunday evening emergency special event *Markets in Turmoil*. The S&P futures were pushed lower heading into the show. From the market lows that evening, Spain, Italy, and Greece each returned over 20% within five weeks.

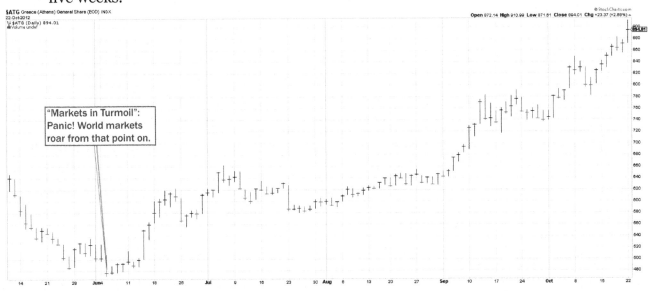

Courtesy of Stockcharts.com

- In August of 2012, the media was saying that "Greece is dead" and there simply is no reason to invest there. As the Greek market closed at 621 on August 15, I sent out an alert titled, "What market could surge 500% post bond bubble?" (see Appendix) In spite of the media headlines, given a variety of technical and fundamental factors, that future 500% market would be none other than Greece. Here is Greece's monthly chart.

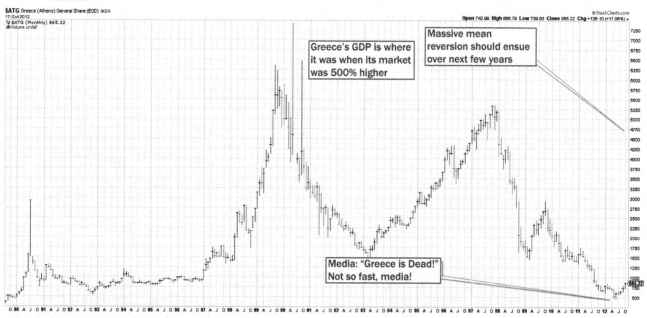

Courtesy of Stockcharts.com

- And last but not least, the media hyper-obsession since 2008 has been the complete and utter demise of the United States as a leading nation. It is now universally believed that the United States has "lost its way." We are no longer the leading power. For five years now, the media has had a diabolical focus on unemployment, the massive debt increase, Federal Reserve money printing, bailouts, stalling GDP, the great political divide, the S&P downgrade, outsourcing etc.

This media groupthink has made its way into the minds of people all over the world. Foreign media has led citizens of other nations to believe that the U.S. is practically a third-world country now. Throughout my worldwide travels over the past few years, I can't tell you just how many people have inquired about just how bad it is in the U.S. these days.

All one has to do is look around and realize that things are just the same as they always were. In fact, since 2008, the U.S. stock market has outperformed virtually every other global market. In light of this global negative groupthink of epic proportions, I would surmise that perhaps the United States is as strong as ever. In fact, perhaps it is the *REST* of the world that has "lost its way."

Contrary to what the media has led you to believe, unless an industry is obsolete (newspapers for example), *entire* industries do not go bankrupt. Generally, a shakeout phase takes place where a couple of the smallest players go out of business. Following the shakeout, as the oversupply condition is corrected, more often than not, the entire industry roars back. Massive sector revivals have happened in the face of media bankruptcy rhetoric throughout history. I have no reason to believe that this won't be the case in the future.

## MEDIA PUMPS AND CATCHPHRASES

- Conversely, in the Spring of 2011, the common media buzzword in the commodity sector was the great "Coal Supercycle." The media became infatuated by the future supply/demand imbalances brought about by increased demand from emerging markets. The media suggested that coal stocks would be in a bull market for years to come. Let me remind you that this was *AFTER* the leading coal stocks had *already* surged 500%-1,000% over the previous twelve months. The charts had gone *WAY* parabolic and were due for a massive correction. But the media continued pumping away in spite of all of the technical warning signs. From the peak of the media "Supercycle" theme, the Dow Jones U.S. coal index collapsed from over 500 to 127 of late.

Courtesy of Stockcharts.com

- In 2007, you could not find an article that did not confidently proclaim that China's market would continue its double digit percentage advances for years to come. China euphoria was everywhere. From where I sat, the Chinese market had clearly gone parabolic in a big way and was simply not investable. As the media was throwing out rosy growth forecasts in the fall of 2007, the Shanghai index began its cataclysmic descent from above 6,000 to 1,700 twelve months later.

Courtesy of Stockcharts.com

The same principle applies to media catchphrases. In late 2007 into 2008, it was nothing but "BRIC," "BRIC," and more "BRIC." It seemed like the media was building another Taj Mahal with all of their "BRICs." The Brazil, Russia, India, and China theme was *EVERYWHERE.* The media proclaimed that you simply *had* to be invested in these countries. Media junkies who followed their advice saw the annihilation of their portfolios. Now that absolutely nobody is talking about these countries, do you suppose it's a good time to invest in them for the long term?

You bet.

Courtesy of Stockcharts.com

The point I want to make is that at the precise moment the media is cheering or crying the very loudest, it is often the case that the charts are signaling a very powerful move in the exact *OPPOSITE* direction. The problem arises when an astute investor clearly sees chart setups in front of him indicating a massive trend reversal and decides to seize the moment. Instead of pouncing on the immense opportunity at hand, the investor usually falls victim to this media groupthink. Being shaken out of his conviction by a bunch of professionally-trained writers, the seasoned investor can miss out on a potential opportunity of a lifetime.

## READ HEADLINES TO GAUGE SOCIAL MOOD... AND TRADE AGAINST IT!

Although I actively avoid all articles from the financial press, I do pay attention to the headlines when conditions dictate. I take notice when major headlines from several distinct media sources all sing a similar tune. Like the rest of us, the media is highly susceptible to crowd behavior and mental contagion. Paying attention to the headlines while avoiding the influence of the articles helps a great deal to gauge social mood at inflection points. By having a good feel for social mood, I am much better equipped to formulate a potential profitable contrarian position based on the charts.

The financial media never has your best interest at heart and generally has a well-formulated agenda to get you on the wrong side of the boat. As you will see in the "Manipulation" section, these "misdirection campaigns" are often funded by hedge funds, investment banks, or other institutions with millions at stake. It may be argued that people in finance lie all the time. Charts don't lie!

The smart money moves markets. The smart money does not pay one ounce of attention to the mass media. You must make a difficult choice: to be entertained by mass financial media, or to ignore its lunacy to your advantage. The choice is yours.

## THE "DRUDGE INDICATOR"

The media groupthink described above is best illustrated by "The Drudge Market Indicator" developed by Bespoke Investment Group.

According to Duff McDonald at Fortune.com:

"What Drudge does not do with any regularity is post finance-related links. And here's why that gets interesting: with 30 million *DAILY* views, Drudge is arguably the most widely followed news source on the web. Once financial news stories go mainstream, and pessimism or optimism (it doesn't matter which) seems to have gone all the way down to the last man, then you would best serve yourself by looking in the other direction.

As Paul Hickey of Bespoke puts it, once a financial-page headline has moved into front-page status for a sustained period of time, "It's probably getting close to an inflection point, whether it's a bottom or a top." Bespoke have compiled fifty-day rolling periods of finance-related headlines on Drudge since mid-2003. The day of maximum concentration—that is, the day with the most days out of the previous fifty with a finance headline—was February 27, 2009, with twenty-one. The bear market low happened less than two weeks later, on March 9.

Hickey also points out that there was a day with exactly ZERO finance headlines over the trailing fifty days in the summer of 2008, just before it all hit the fan with Lehman Brothers. No one saw it coming, and so come it did. Drudge's mood, in other words, is something to bet against."

http://finance.fortune.cnn.com/2011/07/08/the-matt-drudge-market-indicator/

Courtesy of Stockcharts.com

# CHAPTER 4

# *Wall Street's Worst Kept Secret*

*"Believe none of what you hear and half of what you see."*
Benjamin Franklin

It is well known throughout the business that the very best traders manipulate markets to enter and exit their positions at the most favorable prices possible. This is nothing new to The Street, as manipulation always has been and always will be an integral part of worldwide markets. Our job is to accept what is, and try to use manipulation to our advantage. Over time, you will find that spotting manipulation will become second nature to you.

## MEDIA MANIPULATION

Here are just a few examples of how financial institutions manipulate the media and 99% of investors for their own benefit. The following quotes are from a television interview with a very well-known trader. I won't name him...just yet. I remind you that the passage is from a television interview and is thus a bit choppy.

### On artificially driving futures higher or lower:

"It's a fun game. A lucrative game"
"It's a very quick way to make money...and very satisfying"

### On shorting a stock like RIMM:

"It's really important to defeat Research in Motion... to get the Pisani's (CNBC reporter) of the world and the people talking as if there's something wrong with RIMM... and then you would call the Journal *(Wall Street Journal)* and get the bozo reporter on Research in Motion and feed him that Palm's got a killer that it's gonna give away. These are all things you must do..."

### On manipulating AAPL:

"...it's very important to spread the rumor that both Verizon and AT&T have decided that they don't like the phone. It's a very easy one to do. Also, you want to spread the rumor that it won't be ready for MacWorld. And this is very easy because the people who write about AAPL want that story and you can claim that its credible because you spoke to somebody at Apple because Apple (can't comment). So it's really an ideal short...the way to do it is you pick up the phone and call six trading desks and you say "listen, I just got off the phone with my contact at Verizon—he has already said listen, we are an LG house, we are a Samsung house, we are a Motorola house, there's no room for APPLE, they want too much, we're not gonna let them (Apple) do what they did to music. I think that's a very effective way to keep a stock down."

This person then discusses how to manipulate a stock by buying put options to "create an image that there's gonna be news next week and that's gonna frighten everybody." In turn, the traders call CNBC's Bob Pisani to tell him about the puts.

He continues: "And these are all what's really going on under the market that you don't see. But what's important when you're in that hedge fund mode is to **not do anything remotely truthful.**"

"...leak it to the press and get it on CNBC, that's very important, and then you have a vicious cycle down. It's a pretty good game."

This well known trader? None other than Jim Cramer on *TheStreet.com TV.* http://www.youtube.com/watch?v=gMShFx5rThI

## THE KINGS OF MANIPULATION: BIG, BAD GOLDMAN

I have seen almost every Wall Street shenanigan imaginable. Bar none, the best mass-media manipulator in the business is Goldman Sachs. In my earlier days, I used to complain that their market manipulation was criminal. Since then I have learned to accept it and use it to my advantage.

Goldman is the best in the business at downgrading a financial entity precisely when its chart is screaming "BUY." On the flip side, they are the best in the business at upgrading an entity precisely when its chart is clearly indicating sell. Their clear objective when issuing a "buy recommendation" is to get the dumb money (retail investors) to buy at the precise moment that their trading department is establishing massive short positions.

On the other hand, a "sell recommendation" induces dumb money to sell while Goldman initiates long positions. This practice goes back decades. Goldman employees make *MUCH* more than I do. They are much smarter than I am. If I can spot these market turning points from a million miles away, there's zero possibility that the precise timing of each and every atrocious call is purely coincidental.

### Goldman Manipulation Examples

For example, in just the past few months, Goldman has been true to form by hand-feeding some historically laughable calls to the media.

Here is an unedited Goldman excerpt from my January 2, 2012 annual market outlook titled "My 2012 market prediction—an explosive, face-ripping, worldwide market smorgasbord":

Goldman Sachs. I will never understand how Goldman Sachs will forever be allowed legally to purposely mislead investors. It is what it is. At the end of 2010, the indexes surged over 20% resulting in an end of year weekly RSI (14) in extremely overbought territory above 70...a level consistently leading to significant market declines or crashes. So...I've seen it over and over and over w/ Goldman (as with many other houses), as they upgrade at unsustainably overbought levels and downgrade at unsustainably oversold levels. Anyway, their forecast for 2011 was for a 25% S&P surge LED BY........ BANKING STOCKS!!!!! Just take a second to look at some banking stocks over the past year (note: bank stocks declined by 35% at one point and finished the year down about 20%)! This brings us to 2012. What is Goldman's forecast??? Any guesses???

"Our 3-month, 6-month, and 12-month forecasts are 1150, 1200, and 1250'!! And how about this: 'We estimate the S&P 500 could fall by 25% to 900 in an adverse scenario in which the Euro collapses. Wow!"

After Goldman's 2011 call of a 25% gain, we saw the great crash of 2011.

After Goldman's 2012 call of significant 3, 6, and 12 month declines, the market surged higher for several months.

Here are some more immaculately timed Goldman calls from this past year:

March 21, 2012—Goldman said "Best time in generation to buy stocks"; the market fell steadily for the next 10 weeks.

April 12, 2012—Goldman downgrades natural gas; natural gas surges 40% over the next 5 weeks.

June 1, 2012—"the measure (S&P) may fall to 1,125"; a multi-month rally immediately ensued.

June 1, 2012—Take this one for what it's worth: Goldman Sachs alum Raoul Pal releases a presentation on "The Biggest Banking Crisis in History" and "The End Game"... "Assume that no one and nothing is safe"; a multi-month rally took hold. ( http://www.businessinsider.com/raoul-pal-the-end-game-2012-6#for-more-on-why-the-economy-is-crumbling-31%23ixzz1wmnMj59I). I wouldn't be surprised if this evidence is taken down by the time you read this.

June 21, 2012—"We are recommending a *SHORT* (very rare call) position in the S&P 500"; a continuation of the multi-month rally immediately ensued.

On August 20, 2012, Goldman called for a 12% decline and warns to get out of stocks before the "Fiscal Cliff"; we will soon see how this one plays out.

Courtesy of Stockcharts.com

These calls from Goldman and others are highly calculated. By no means whatsoever do they have the investing public's best interest in mind. When Goldman issues a recommendation directly contradicting the technical indicators, the rule of thumb is that Goldman's call will fail miserably within one to two weeks of its release. You'll find that their calls rarely fail immediately as there would simply be too much evidence left at the crime scene.

The smart money moves markets. As you have seen, the smart money controls the game by controlling the news. Outside of manipulating "news" for their benefit, the smart 1% do not pay one ounce of attention to the mass media. They know that the only profitable information is tightly held by those in the know. Actionable information never ever makes it into the mass media. If market moving information is leaked to the media, within an instant, the information is no longer actionable.

You must make a difficult choice. The choice is to be entertained by financial media of mass destruction or to ignore its lunacy to your financial advantage. The choice is yours and yours alone. Do you have the required self-discipline?

# CHAPTER 5

# *Becoming a Better Trader*

In this chapter I will help you become a better trader; in particular by helping you better understand your trading psychology. Think of me as a kind of trading "mentor," and let's start there by underlining the importance of having a mentor.

## *MENTOR*

Human beings tend to perform to the level of the people they interact with most often. If you hang out with a bunch of bums day in and day out, there's no question that you're going to become a bum. Similarly, it has been proven that your wealth is closely tied to the people you spend the majority of your time with. The same holds true in trading and investing.

As I briefly touched upon earlier in the book: in 2003 I was lucky enough to stumble upon a now-defunct Yahoo! trading group led by "Lizard King" and "Revshark." I was immediately impressed by the quality of posts in the forum. Perhaps a dozen or so of the traders appeared to be seasoned veterans with vast trading experience. I immediately set my sights on learning as much from this group as I possibly could. I would have to learn as much as I could in a very short period of time, because the group ultimately disbanded six months later.

It was in this forum where I learned much of what I now know about Superstocks. When any of the group members brought up a new stock pick, it was almost a foregone conclusion that Lizard King would bash the pick to pieces. At first, his "arrogant" demeanor startled me, but after a period of time, it dawned on me that this harsh attitude was his way of proving a point. The point being that 99.9% of stocks are a waste of one's time and don't deserve our attention. His behavior also demonstrated to me that the very best traders have a killer instinct that requires a certain level of confidence and cockiness.

I have traded with thousands of traders over the years in several "virtual forums" and, bar none, the six best traders I have ever traded with came out of this group: Lizard King, Meglodon, Babe, Dojowiz, Jon, and Demi. As I only wanted to learn from the best of the best, I didn't focus at all on the second-rate traders of the group. I will be forever in debt to these mentors to whom I owe much of my trading knowledge. The point is that if I had not stumbled upon this group of superior traders, I am certain that I would be in an entirely different profession today.

The importance of a successful mentor or community of successful traders cannot be understated. If you want to be the best, you simply must train with the best. To achieve investing success, you simply must—you simply have to—do everything in your power to put your ego aside and work with people who are better traders than you are.

There are highly successful investors all over the world and all over the internet. It is your job to seek them out and learn as much as you possibly can from them. In seeking a mentor, I also can't stress enough that writing a newsletter, an article, or making an appearance on CNBC does not automatically make somebody a good mentor in the investment realm.

## PSYCHOLOGY OF TRADING

> *"An understanding of mass psychology is often more important than an understanding of economics. Markets are driven by human beings making human errors and also making super-human insights."*
>
> Dennis Gartman

As touched upon earlier, proper mindset is absolutely essential to investing success. Many may disagree, but it is my firm belief that outlook is vastly more important than stock picking ability. If you believe that you can't beat the market, you are absolutely right. If you believe that you can, you are absolutely right. Mindset is paramount to trading success. In this section, I just scratch the surface of this subject. There is a sea of information on this topic and in your quest to beat the market, I urge you to study psychology and human behavior especially as it relates to the market. Perhaps the best book ever written on trading psychology is *Trading in the Zone* by Mark Douglas. It's as good as gold, and I urge you to pick up a copy. Moving on...

## CONFIDENCE IS KEY

> *"Boldness has genius, power and magic in it."*
>
> Goethe

As babies, we are naturally fearless beings. We enthusiastically attempt to do absolutely anything and everything. During our first few years, we failed at almost everything we attempted, but that was fine with us as we knew in our hearts that failing was the only way to succeed.

So what happened to this fearless nature we exhibited in our formative years? According to author and Ph.D Dr. Shad Helmstetter, "During the first eighteen years of our lives, if we grew up in fairly average, reasonably positive homes, we were told *No*, or what we could not do, more than *148,000 times!*" A large part of this is due to the ingrained negativity bias present throughout our culture.

After being told over and over that we can't do things, we begin to believe it. Over time, psychosclerosis sets in, where we become very rigid in our thinking, and we instinctively refuse to pursue what we have been told is not possible. On Wall Street, we have been conditioned to believe that it is simply not possible to consistently beat the market over the long run. The efficient market hypothesis repeatedly rears its ugly head and conditions us to believe that it is nearly impossible to outperform the market as it immediately discounts all known information. Well, whoever formulated that hypothesis certainly never interviewed the best traders.

The product of success in the market is supreme confidence. Paradoxically, one needs supreme confidence in order to become a success in the market. There have been quite a few times when fellow traders have followed me into a very big trade but were unable to hang on due to improper mindsets. Likewise, there have been dozens of times in my own trading history when I lost that winning edge and watched in disbelief as a recently discarded stock increased many fold without me.

Since the stock market is nothing more than global psychological warfare, and human emotion is reflected in the form of market prices, learning to master your emotions is absolutely essential to compete effectively.

## VISUALIZE YOUR STOCK

Upon initiating a new position, the very first step I take is to mentally visualize what my response will be should the stock move lower. In fact, I first mentally visualize the very worst scenario I might face. What if the stock were to drop 40% overnight? This helps my subconscious understand just how precarious the outcome of each trade really is. Close your eyes and visualize what the chart pattern will look like and how you will feel emotionally if the trade moves against you.

If your stock declines, will you add to your position? Will you utilize a mental or physical stop loss in order to exit? Likewise, how will you react if your stock doubles tomorrow? Having a plan of attack and knowing how you will react in any condition will help instill confidence and remove a huge mental burden from your psyche. Without knowing in advance how you will react, the daily fluctuations can drive you completely insane.

Oftentimes, I am so excited about the future prospects of a stock that I truly want it to trade lower so I can establish a larger position. Other times, when I have less fundamental or technical faith in a position, I dump it immediately if it trades against me. Having a mental plan of attack can have a huge effect on your trading success.

## *SUPERCHARGE YOUR FUTURE MINDSET*

Once you have prepared yourself for the volatility to come, it is time to turn your attention to supercharging your outlook and confidence. You first have to cultivate a future mindset. Not only do you have to train your mind to think of yourself as the person you want to be in a few short months, but you must also train your mind to think of how your stock will look and perform over this same period of time.

Do you have a deep belief (backed by the chart and fundamentals) that your $5 stock will be $10 in three months? In virtually every one of my Superstock trades, I believed with every fiber of my being that they would be substantially higher into the future. If I didn't have this mindset going into each trade, I guarantee you that I would have missed 90% of their ultimate moves.

Once you have completed your due diligence and your stock meets many of the Superstock criteria, you must create a big vision in your mind of your stock literally going through the roof.

If the stock meets your technical and fundamental requirements, you should have a deep inner feeling that the stock will undoubtedly achieve your price target. This will instill within you the required psychological energy as well as a relaxed faith that will support you through the volatility. If you don't have this overwhelming belief in your position, it may be an indication that you need to re-evaluate your stock.

I can't tell you how many traders I've worked with who have had a gloomy, downright pessimistic outlook on virtually everything. Such a gloomy disposition seems to become more extreme as we get older. These gloom and doom traders love to forward the latest article on the destruction of Europe while spending a great deal of their time focusing on such things as why "high frequency trading" or "the plunge protection team" are ruining Wall Street.

Falling victim to this contagious negativity happens to the best of us from time to time. When you find yourself getting caught up in a similar emotional loop in the future, just step away and take as much time off as you need. Your trading account will thank you.

What's important is that we remain steadfast in our daily practice of optimistic "mental floss." If you get stopped out of your position, no worries, it's all part of the game. Just don't let any negativity in the market affect how you see individual stocks. A negative bias will destroy your career. Those with a negative bias are without question the least successful investors.

If you look at the most successful people on our planet, they are almost without exception maniacally optimistic about everything. Take Warren Buffet, Bill Gates, Howard Shultz, Richard Branson etc.; they all have this insanely positive world view. Because of their faith in the future, these are the rebels who remain calm in a crisis and seize the low hanging fruit while everyone else is cloaked in fear. Yes, negativity is certainly everywhere, but to an individual, the biggest successes have all made a conscious decision to focus exclusively on what's possible.

## OVERCONFIDENCE

*"Human beings are perhaps never more frightening than when they
are convinced beyond a doubt that they are right."*

Laurens Van der Post

As we now know, a winning attitude is an essential element of the best traders. However, there is a fine line between confidence and irrational exuberance. If you find yourself taking abnormally large positions or increasing the frequency of your trading, you may have crossed that fine line. If you believe that you are a genius—that you can do no wrong—and have delusions that the market is an ATM, you have *DEFINITELY* crossed that fine line.

According to trader William Eckhardt, "In many ways, large profits are even more insidious than large losses in terms of emotional destabilization. I think it's important not to be emotionally attached to large profits. I've certainly made some of my worst trades after long periods of winning. When you're on a big winning streak, there's a temptation to think that you can afford to make shoddy decisions. You can imagine what happens next. As a general rule, losses make you strong and profits make you weak."

## DISCIPLINE

Psychologist Martin Seligman has postulated that self-discipline is twice as accurate as IQ in predicting student's GPA. Similarly, he suggests that self-discipline is vastly more important than intelligence in achieving success in any other aspect of life. I believe this to be especially true in investing. If intelligence alone were the key determinant in investing success, every professor, rocket scientist, and neurosurgeon would rule the market.

A successful trader needs to develop a consistent and disciplined approach to how he selects stocks, how he enters and exits positions, and most importantly, how he reacts to stock gyrations. A disciplined mind is one that does not react randomly to portfolio volatility. As part of the visualization process discussed above, if one mentally rehearses both positive and negative outcomes in advance, there should be much less of an emotional reaction when those outcomes come to fruition.

Perhaps the greatest thing about self-discipline is that it has a very strong correlation to self-esteem and life satisfaction. In short, if you can weave discipline throughout the fabric of your life, you will not only experience tremendous success in the market, but you will find yourself much happier and fulfilled in every other aspect of your life.

## EMBRACE YOUR LOSSES

*"No one is going to know or care about your failures. All you have to do is learn from them because all that matters is that you get it right once. Then everyone can tell you how lucky you were."*

Mark Cuban

When a stock's pattern starts breaking down for whatever reason, take a step back and ask yourself if on that day you would enter the stock for the very first time. If the answer is no, it is probably best to act decisively and cut your losses immediately. As the sayings go: "trade what you see, not what you think." "Do not hope, Act!" "Sell first and ask questions later."

It is critical that you learn to deal with these losses unemotionally. When the inevitable happens and you exit a position for a loss, it must be viewed as an entirely necessary part of the cost of doing business. As an extension, you must separate your ego from the day to day fluctuations in the value of your entire portfolio. I have found that the more often I glance at my account value, the worse my trading results become. Unless you need to pay tuition tomorrow, my recommendation is that you look at the value of your account as seldom as possible.

Focusing on a declining account value will inevitably make you more prone to enter the dreaded "Revenge Trade." Revenge trades happen when you take a larger than normal position in a questionable stock in an attempt to make back the money that you have lost. Ask any professional trader, and he will tell you that revenge trades almost *ALWAYS* end in failure.

After a loss, don't blame yourself, the "shorts," or the market. Don't dwell on the event, simply accept what is, and turn your focus to the constant stream of new opportunities that lie ahead. A positive mindset and emotional self-awareness in these circumstances will help give you the emotional flexibility necessary to choose how you feel. Without this emotional awareness, you may be blindsided by whatever destructive emotions your subconscious throws your way.

Famed investor Benjamin Graham has said that "Intelligent Investment is more a matter of mental approach than it is of technique." Fortunately for you, most of your competition has never considered analyzing their mental approach to trading. Without disciplining their mind, they are intuitively focused on negativity and fear. As your competitors will do just about anything to avoid making a mistake, they will shy away from the greatest opportunities in the market.

The world's greatest athletes, business people, traders, salespeople (you name it) all have a definitive lack of fear of making a mistake. Like staggering babies, they go out of their way to make mistakes. Knowing that there is a distinct possibility of a failure in any trade, you can greatly diminish trading errors based on fear. In this fashion, you must make it a priority to be fearless in your trading and embrace your eventual mistakes wholeheartedly.

## RELAXED FAITH

> *"After spending many years in Wall Street and after making and losing millions of dollars I want to tell you this: It never was my thinking that made the big money for me. It was always my sitting. Got that? My sitting tight! It is no trick at all to be right on the market. You always find lots of early bulls in bull markets and early bears in bear markets. I've known many men who were right at exactly the right time, and began buying or selling stocks when prices were at the very level which should show the greatest profit. And their experience invariably matched mine, that is, they made no real money out of it. Men who can both be right and sit tight are uncommon. I found it one of the hardest things to learn. But it is only after a stock operator has firmly grasped this that he can make big money. It is literally true that millions come easier to a trader after he knows how to trade than hundreds did in the days of his ignorance."*

Jesse Livermore

This quote by Jesse Livermore is perhaps my favorite trading quote of all time. Absolute truth permeates every sentence. I suggest you read it repeatedly until it is becomes part of your trading DNA.

I would say that successful investing is 1% inspiration (stock picking) and 99% perspiration (handling your emotions). In light of this, once you have 1) selected your stocks, 2) waited patiently until they presented a low risk entry, and 3) visualized how you will react in the future, it is then time to sit back, relax, and become a patient Zen-master trader. As we all know, this is much easier said than done. Daily volatility drives us crazy. How in the world does one cultivate disciplined patience in the chaotic market environment?

Have you ever had a stock soar on you within seconds after you sold it? You think to yourself, "If only I had just a little more patience!?" Or similarly, have you ever had one of your stocks soar within hours or days after totally giving up on it emotionally? This has certainly happened to me. This is due to the Law of Indifference. Success in trading has its own time frame and usually comes when we least expect it. Traders are constantly misled by the darkness before the dawn and give up just before something truly spectacular happens.

To cultivate this critically important art of patience, simply step away from the market during market hours. Whenever I decide to go for a long hike, go to the movies, or even more extreme, leave the country, the mental burden of watching every tick of the market is immediately lifted. I find that once I step away from the screen, I am able to focus on the millions of other things in life that are more important than trading.

I was so confident in most of my biggest winners that I simply refused to watch them during the market day. I don't care how confident I am in a particular position—if I open up Level 2 streaming quotes and watch a stock tick-for-tick throughout the day, undoubtedly, my irrational mind finds an utterly meaningless reason to sell it. It happens every time. The insignificant ticks can drive you crazy. The only way to move beyond this and to let your winners run is to set an electronic or mental stop loss (to be triggered end-of-day or next morning), shut down the computer, and go about living your life.

Even more distracting than watching your own stocks trade from second to second is to watch the compulsive trading action of others. Whether it is in a physical trading room, a virtual trading room, or God forbid, by monitoring thousands of others trading in the "Twitter-verse," your goal of patience will be thrown out the window. The more you watch other people trade, the more you will want to trade, the more your account will churn, and the less successful you will become. *In the world of trading, action is the enemy of success.*

Like "news," having hundreds of ideas thrown your way is highly addictive and only serves to make you less certain in the positions you already have. If you feel the need to actively participate on Twitter or in an online forum, my advice is to do so outside of market hours when you won't be able to make an immediate transaction. Personally, I try to watch the last half hour of the market day since this is typically the time when smart money enters or exits positions. I then try to perform a majority of my research in the evening. This practice enables me to process new ideas much more rationally.

## FROM PATIENCE TO "FAT PITCH" TRADING

Mastering patience and learning to appreciate periods of inactivity allows you to be exceptionally opportunistic. The best buying opportunities emerge when all other investors' emotions have been completely beaten to a pulp. Even if others are able to see the unbelievable opportunities in front of them, their emotions are so frayed by the carnage that they simply can't bear the thought of re-entering the market. It is precisely in these situations that the patient few on the sidelines are able to swoop in and make money hand over fist. We've seen patience in action dozens of times over the years when Warren Buffet steps in as buyer of last resort during a major crisis. Buffet has said, "I will tell you the secret of getting rich on Wall Street (pause)... Close the doors. You try to be greedy when others are fearful and you try to be very fearful when others are greedy."

Although it pays handsomely not to watch your positions throughout the day, you still must be alert for new opportunities that emerge from time to time. Through practicing "active inaction," your prior due diligence of the stocks on your watchlist allows you to be perfectly present when that proverbial fat pitch is briefly thrown in your direction. By knowing precisely what you are looking for, by knowing the qualities of the best stocks inside and out, and by waiting patiently, you will be able to swing away when conditions line up in your favor.

## ACHIEVING PEAK PERFORMANCE

In his best-selling book *Flow—The Psychology of Optimal Experience,* Mihaly Csikszentmihalyi described the concept of "Flow" as "the state in which people are so involved in an activity that nothing else seems to matter; the experience itself is so enjoyable that people will do it even at great cost." I'm certain you have experienced such a state from time to time in your academic or professional career. I achieve such a state quite often during my marathon Superstock research sessions. I become so laser-focused and totally involved in the due diligence process that I have absolutely no concept of time. In this state, an entire day can come and go in what seems like the blink of an eye.

In "Flow," you'll find that stress melts away, you work much more efficiently, and it becomes much easier to identify the few winners in the sea of deadbeat stocks. Additionally, the ability to achieve such a state during market hours helps decrease the likelihood of making emotionally-based trading errors. In short, achieving mental and physical peak performance can revolutionize your investing.

Rather than enter this desired state of peak performance purely at random, I follow a set of guidelines to help me achieve it more consistently:

## EXERCISE

They say that happiness, success, and wealth are attracted to those who are full of energy. In this pursuit, the very first thing I do every morning is to exercise for at least one hour. It could be running outdoors (never indoors) or lifting weights in the gym. Running outdoors is a necessity as I find that being surrounded by nature and breathing fresh air helps to stimulate creative thinking and clarify my thoughts. Exercising first thing in the morning gives me a significant energy boost throughout the entire day. After working out, I am able to think and communicate much more effectively. I also feel happier, healthier, and much more confident in my trading.

Additionally, running or any other sustained aerobic activity has a powerful effect on blood levels of dopamine, serotonin, epinephrine, and endorphins which together give you a more rational perspective on the market. This potent drug cocktail also serves to significantly lower stress which left unchecked can have seriously detrimental effect on your success. Upon firing up the computer in the morning, a clear mind allows you to deal with overnight portfolio developments much more rationally.

On those rare days when I sleep in and skip my morning exercise routine, my trading mindset suffers greatly. On those rare days, I've been known to make totally irrational spur-of—the-moment portfolio decisions which almost always have negative financial consequences. I've learned my lesson too many times to take daily exercise lightly. No matter what, I highly recommend that you take care of your physical self daily. You won't regret it.

## ENVIRONMENT

Like any other work situation, it pays to keep your work space neat and orderly. For whatever reason, having orderly surroundings tends to translate into an orderly and efficient mind. I simply clean up and organize my immediate surroundings before I start my day. This tends to free my mind from clutter and allows me to think more effectively.

To further reduce distractions, I ensure that the television is turned off, the Twitter feed is non-existent, all non-essential browsers are closed, and email is only checked a couple times per day.

I often find that working in the same environment day after day kills my spirit, and negatively affects my trading results. A stale environment can trigger boredom and stimulate daydreaming which make it nearly impossible to achieve a state of flow. To prevent this, I like to rotate my work environments. One day I'll work from home, the next day at a Starbucks, the next at the library, the next at Panera Bread, and so on. Rinse and repeat.

I find that I am exponentially more productive around new people in new environments. With the assistance of a pair of headphones and a cup of coffee, I can easily attain a state of flow in these environments. When I enter the zone, I tend to come up with ideas that never would have occurred to me otherwise.

## MUSIC

Listening to relaxing melodic music without vocals puts me in the perfect frame of mind for doing just about anything that requires a high degree of focus. Great music leads to increased creativity as well. Maybe it's just me, but for whatever reason I find vocals to be distracting. Listening to George Winston, Vivaldi, or Mozart keeps me focused, creative and alert; going strong all day long.

## ENERGY, FUEL, AND JUICE — MY STORY

*"The foundation of success in life is good health: that is the substratum of fortune; it is also the basis of happiness."*

P.T. Barnum

People believe that if they simply had more time, all of their problems would disappear. I would suggest that it is not time but extra energy that is what we are truly after. Whether in trading or in any other aspect of life, high energy is the essential factor of peak performance. By far the most important components of peak performance for me are nutrition and living a healthy lifestyle.

This is a subject very near and dear to my heart. I wrestled with whether or not to include this section in the book. I felt strongly that I should include it to demonstrate how modifying lifestyle can change everything.

I don't know about you, but I treat my Labrador Retriever like the princess that she is. She gets constant exercise, proper attention, and the best food. Likewise, if you have young children, I am sure that you give every consideration to what they watch, what they read, what they eat, and how much exercise they get. Do you give the same careful consideration to your own well being?

Throughout the majority of my life, I abused my body and generally disregarded it and treated it like crap. For me, ten beers, an entire large Domino's pepperoni pizza, an entire key lime pie—all in the course of an evening—no problem. And Thanksgiving? Watch out!

After eating a meal, I would be lethargic for literally hours afterward. From the age of 18, I generally went on a diet two or three times per year in order to shed my layer of beer. I found that during these dieting phases, despite severe caloric restriction and increased physical activity, my baseline energy level always surged through the roof. Once the diet ended, however, my energy level would plummet to previous levels. I would quickly put on body fat, lose muscle, and revert to my previous lethargic self.

Everything changed for me during a family trip to Southeast Asia several years ago. Prior to a flight to Bangkok, I purchased a book titled *The China Study: The Most Comprehensive Study of Nutrition Ever Conducted* written by T. Colin Campbell and Thomas M. Campbell II. To make a very long story extremely short, it turns out that China is the world's best laboratory for the effects of diet on energy and long-term health. Specifically, there are several provinces within China where per capita consumption of vegetables is high while consumption of meat is virtually non-existent. Meanwhile, in other provinces, the per capita consumption of meat is quite high and consumption of vegetables low.

Researchers found in study after study that the rate of diabetes, obesity, cancer, and heart disease was virtually non-existent in the geographic areas showing high consumption of vegetables combined with low meat consumption. In comparison, the rates of these diseases in every low-vegetable/high-meat consumption province throughout China and other parts of the world were several hundred to several *thousand* percent higher.

To me, the evidence was overwhelming. The people eating the veggies were not only living much longer, but they were far healthier and far more active until the day they died. I would surmise that they had far more nerve energy and were much happier as well. The evidence from several studies over several decades was too one-sided for me to ignore. Since finishing the book, outside of a rare slipup (I am still an occasional sucker for the P's—pizza, pepperoni, and pie) I became a vegetarian for life.

One of the fortunate byproducts of my new plant-based diet was a dramatic reduction in my consumption of sugar and all of its derivatives: fructose, sucrose, corn starch, corn syrup, flour, and so on. Once I switched to this plant-based, low sugar diet, my level of energy shot through the roof. In fact, there have been several studies demonstrating that rats fed a strict plant-based diet spend a majority of their days on the treadmill while their "traditional diet" friends spend their days scavenging for food in an effort to perpetuate the glycemic roller coaster.

These days, I automatically wake up before the crack of dawn and my body literally *NEEDS* to run. Without thinking, my body forces me to put on my shoes and run out the door. This was *NEVER, EVER* the case before I modified my diet several years ago.

As my new dietary lifestyle progressed, I became acutely aware of just how addicted I was to all forms of sugar; cakes, pies, juices, pasta, beer, bread, and *ANYTHING* in a package. Like any other potent addiction, my urge to consume sugar is so strong that once every few months, in moments of weakness, I find myself at its mercy. In these moments, all it takes is a piece of pie or a couple of beers for the relentless sugar cycle to begin anew. The cycle gains steam, and can knock me out for days at a time. My energy level retreats to prior levels, clear thinking disappears, and all motivation is extinguished.

During the occasional slipup, all I can think about all day long is what I will eat next. To say the least, the difference in energy level is quite dramatic. Zero sugar lifestyle = energy level 10. Reversion to "American diet"= energy level 2. The sugar epidemic is so prevalent in our culture that it is hidden in virtually everything we eat today. In the old days, I didn't think sugar and its derivatives had any effect on my energy level because over my entire life I had never gone a *single* day without it.

As our culture is so focused on the scale, I'll make it abundantly clear in terms of weight. At 6'2", my college weight was 205 pounds. My "normal weight" is 188 pounds. My diet weight was 175. Today, my 365 days per year plant-based weight is 164 or less. And the best thing about it is that due to the suppression of the sugar/insulin cycle, I very rarely get hungry. I simply eat because I know that I have to.

In a nutshell, I no longer eat anything processed (packaged), I only eat foods that spoil, I cut out sugar derivatives (fruit being the exception), I prepare 99% of my meals myself, and I go to the fruit and vegetable market twice per week. That's it. My energy goes through the roof. It's a foreign notion to most Americans, but this is how roughly three billion people on our planet eat every single day.

The point is that if you take the necessary disciplined effort to focus on diet and exercise, you can expect that your energy, your outlook, your focus, your motivation, and ultimately your investment success will surge to a whole new level. Not only that, but you will look better, feel better, be happier, be more optimistic, and your creativity will skyrocket. Mentally, you will think faster and clearer leading to better investment decisions. There is no downside.

It should go without saying that a healthy lifestyle goes well beyond investing. Our health and well-being trump all else.

# CHAPTER 6

## *Systems and Simplicity*

Now that we've discussed nutrition, exercise, environment and all of the other crazy things that you never thought you would see in an investment book, let's gradually make the transition into stocks, yes *STOCKS*. Let's start with my investment method: what it is and what it is not.

### A BRIEF HISTORY OF INVESTMENT SYSTEMS

In the most dramatic parabolic move in the history of the stock market, the NASDAQ surged from 1,355 to over 5,130 in under fourteen months during late 1998 into early 2000. During this period, Initial Public Offerings (IPOs) surged 100%, 200%, even 300% on their first day of trading. Firms adding a .com to their name suddenly leaped 50%. A stock split announcement sent a company's shares through the roof. It was simply a circus of epic proportions. Overnight, taxi drivers, shoe shiners, housewives, and hair stylists were experts on the market. In fact, a pool cleaner literally set the world record for two year portfolio return!

This fourteen month COMPLETELY vertical market move was so easy; too easy. We will most likely never see anything like it again in our lifetimes.

Most of today's well-known trading gurus developed and marketed their personalities, their trading records, and their trading "systems" based on their returns from this "once-in-a-lifetime" event. Almost to a person, these gurus admit that their returns from this period cannot be replicated in today's market environment.

Because a majority of individual investors are unwilling to put forth the "sweat equity" required to find a needle in a haystack, they often turn to these technical trading systems. The systems are promoted as processes that take "thinking" completely out of the equation. The promoters of these systems want you to believe that their complicated system is the best way to make money in the market. This is simply not true.

With such a system, all you have to do is sit on your couch in your spare time, run an automated scan, and blindly buy or sell whatever stocks adhere to the specified technical criteria. Even if such a system did make you loads of money, it sure doesn't sound too intellectually stimulating and fulfilling if you ask me.

Not only were many of these systems developed during an irrational market but many have been developed by savvy marketers with limited trading success. I have no doubt that many of these systems worked extraordinarily well in the late 90s, but then again, just about every trading methodology worked well back then.

The truth about the market is that it is truly a living, breathing beast with several personalities that evolve over time. People change, society changes, the market changes. Technical signals that worked well thirty years ago may not work nearly as well today. Furthermore, when a system is known to be successful, the investing public typically pile into it en masse which ultimately nullifies any edge it had in the first place.

Look, if there was a system out there that consistently lead to stratospheric multi-million dollar returns, it would be selling for tens of millions of dollars at a minimum. I certainly haven't seen any recently at that price point.

Fortunately, I do not have a "system" to market. I simply pound the table on taking a disciplined approach to investing while focusing exclusively on the very few variables that make a noticeable difference. The discretionary approach that I endorse has worked exceedingly well going back to the 1800s. In any period of history, high growth stocks that are significantly undervalued, undiscovered, with a contagious theme, a great chart, and ideally supported by insider buying, have proven to outperform the market by a wide margin. Blockbuster chart patterns combined with 5-star research will forever stand the test of time.

Sadly, such an investment style is too difficult for most to follow. My approach is based on the principles of hard work, focus, and determination. It is not an approach that will hold your hand.

As we sit well-entrenched in the information age, we have evolved into creatures of immediate gratification. We want everything and we want everything right this very moment. In addition to technical and fundamental metrics, my method focuses on sentiment and psychology. It requires the super-human ability to delay gratification. Such a method simply goes against our emotional tendencies. That is precisely why it works so well.

Systems can produce dozens of stock picks per day. Using my principals, you might be fortunate to discover 8 or 10 potential Superstocks per *YEAR*. Sure, you can certainly make money investing in Tier-2 Superstocks on a more regular basis, but the really big fish only come along once every so often. The big fish are the ones that can truly change your life.

There are investment styles and techniques to fit every personality. Who is to say that my approach is the best for you? There may be several other approaches that are much better suited to your particular needs. You may turn out to be the best day-trading "scalper" the world has ever seen. By all means, I urge you to seek out what works best for you.

According to psychologist Dr. Bob Rotella, "The key is to find what works best for you and this can take years to discover. There are many good approaches out there, but in reality there is only one trading approach that will best utilize your skills, talent and personality to create and sustain your profitable edge. One of the most common mistakes a trader can make is to try to embrace or copy a strategy of someone else. Like a fingerprint, your strategy and focus should be unique to yourself. Yes, learn as much as you possibly can from others who are successful, but still understand that in the end your priority is to develop your own strategy toward the markets and that path will be unique and unlike any other."

## FEATURE CREEP – KEEP IT SIMPLE, STUPID

After experimenting with several methods over the years, I have learned that the simplest strategies have worked the best. In terms of technical analysis, I believe without a shadow of a doubt that the more indicators you monitor, the less successful you become as an investor. I recommend that you wholeheartedly embrace the Pareto Principal and focus 100% of your efforts on the 20% of variables that make a difference. Discard the 80% of variables that have little to no impact on your investing.

The more time you spend on the marginally important information, the more the dreaded "analysis paralysis" will creep into your mind to sabotage your efforts. Successful trading does not require you to gather more and more evidence. It requires you to examine the basic essentials in an organized fashion and to disregard all else. They say that the key to success boils down to being yourself, but in a streamlined and organized way. I believe trading success is no different.

My advice to a new investor would be to find and develop his own simple "bread and butter" investment strategy and religiously stick to it while ignoring everything else. The longer you stick with it, the better your results will be and the more of an expert you will become. Just remember that increased output requires decreased input.

Many people far more intelligent and successful than me have stressed the importance of keeping your method as simple as possible. Who better to learn from on this topic than some of the greatest traders the world has ever known:

> *"The best strategies are often so simple that you should be able to explain how they work to those who aren't intimately involved in the markets."*
>
> Warren Buffet.

> *"You'll always find that the simplest of methods work the best."*
>
> Nicolas Darvas

> *"The power of a narrow focus is amazing. The key is to be a real pro at something. Know all you can about a style or tactic. Then you can build on that foundation. Traders give up too easily and jump around too much when things get difficult. How good do you think Kobe Bryant would be if while he was developing his skills growing up every time he had a really tough game he changed to a different sport or played a different position?"*
>
> Mark Minervini.

*"Charlie and I decided a long time ago that in an investment lifetime it's too hard to make hundreds of smart decisions...Therefore, we adopted a strategy that required our being smart- and not too smart at that- only a very few times. Indeed, we'll now settle for one good idea a year."*

Warren Buffet.

*"People have a tendency to believe that complicated ideas are better than simple ones. Many find it hard to comprehend that Richard Dennis could have made several hundred million dollars by using a handful of simple rules. It is natural to think that he must have had some secret. ...My theory is that this belief and the need for complication come from insecurity and the resulting need to find some reason to feel special in some way. Having a secret knowledge makes us feel special; possessing simple truths does not. Therefore, our egos drive us to believe that we possess some kind of special knowledge to prove to ourselves that we are somehow superior to others. Our egos don't want us to limit ourselves to commonly known truths. The ego wants secrets."*

Turtle great Curtis Faith

*"Feature creep, creeping featurism or featuritis is the ongoing expansion or addition of new features in a product, such as in computer software. Extra features go beyond the basic function of the product and so can result in over-complication rather than simple design. Viewed over a longer time period, extra or unnecessary features seem to creep into the system, beyond the initial goals. The most common cause of feature creep is the desire to provide the consumer with a more useful or desirable product, in order to increase sales or distribution. However, once the product reaches the point at which it does everything that it is designed to do, the manufacturer is left with the choice of adding unneeded functions, sometimes at the cost of efficiency."*

Wikipedia

*"Simplicity is the ultimate sophistication."*
Leonardo DaVinci

## IT'S ALL ABOUT THE CHARTS

*"Few people have absorbed the hard neuroscience research that reasons arrive afterwards."*

Charles Faulkner

I just *LOVE* charts. In a stock chart, where others see random lines, I see reliable patterns of possibility and potential. A stock chart is simply human emotion and psychology in graphic form. It is a picture-perfect representation of the anguish and ecstasy experienced by thousands of a stock's shareholders over a given period of time. But get this—if you are an expert in predicting future chart patterns, you are instantly smarter than anybody in that particular industry. You will be able to see industry and firm specific trends even before the CEO's. If you become a lifelong student of, and ultimately a master of human psychology as reflected in chart patterns, you are guaranteed fortunes.

By mastering stock patterns and the emotion embedded within them, you will be able to reliably predict how the masses will react. You might have noticed that during my trading hiatus over the past few years, I mentioned that I read books on psychology. I have found that once you have a firm grasp on the trading fundamentals, you must make a dramatic shift in your focus. You must then focus all of your energy on not only learning to master your own emotions but to develop an ability to *predict* the emotions and psychological reactions of others.

While the other 99% of investors spend hours of precious time gathering articles, reports, and press releases for every single stock of interest, you will get most of what you need to know within two seconds of glancing at the psychology embedded in a chart. As an example from my own experience, *WAY* before there were any *reasons* to invest in AAPL, while the stock sat at just $8, its chart screamed that game-changing developments were rapidly approaching. Later in the book, I will detail my chart thought process prior to entering AAPL at $8 in 2003.

Because charts paint the whole picture months or even years before the fundamental "story" becomes evident to Joe Six-Pack, you should search tirelessly for the most powerful chart patterns the market has to offer. And it is only *AFTER* you see a blockbuster chart pattern that you should begin to look for blockbuster fundamentals. Going about it any other way is downright suicidal to your success.

For me, this approach has me flipping through hundreds of charts daily in an effort to potentially find one or two whose chart pattern warrants further fundamental research. The singular moment of joy and ecstasy in finding that "needle in the haystack," or that "one-in-a-million stock," makes the days or weeks of combing through countless charts totally worthwhile. A chart pattern truly is a "picture worth a thousand words." (Please see the "Resources" section for charting programs and websites that I've used.)

While analyzing charts, I generally don't worry about GANN lines, Fibonacci levels,

Stochastics, and other pretentious technical indicators. Although I may use many technical and sentiment (very important at extremes) indicators when looking for market tops and bottoms, I find most technical indicators to be totally unnecessary a majority of the time.

Ordinarily, it is only *AFTER* a significant move in a stock that most of the indicators become important to me. The millions of people who I consider to be my competition are all intensely focused on the same technical indicators. I hate running with the crowd. We have learned that what everybody knows isn't worth knowing, right?

## NEVER BUY A COMPANY'S STORY

Never buy companies. Buy stocks. Better yet, buy prices. The world's most exciting company can have the world's worst stock. CSCO was pretty darn exciting in 2000. I spent four days at a Morgan Stanley "training bootcamp" in 2000. It was crazy—almost every young stockbroker I spoke with said that CSCO would dominate the world and it was the only stock to own for the next decade. Well...

That goes to show you just how powerful groupthink and "story" can be.

Conversely, you can have one of the slowest growing, least glamorous companies in the world with a stock that dances to the beat of its own drum and outperforms 99% of its peers. Take the example of the previously mentioned ArcelorMittal Steel. It is involved in literally the world's *most* boring business: steel. In 2003, it had *ZERO* growth. It had no "story." Yet, if you bought this unglamorous stock in 2003 when its *price* indicated a reversal, you would have been 3,500% richer four years later.

Many investors who have been in the markets for decades still can't grasp the concept of companies and their stocks being two totally separate entities. Although they may insist that they understand this concept, their returns indicate that they simply do not. On a subconscious level, 99% of investors will invest in a company they "like" rather than a stock that will make them money. The process of due diligence and the emotional connection to a particular company and its products provide most investors with emotional satisfaction that on a subconscious level outweighs potential financial gain. Fortunately for me, I left my emotions at a truck stop in Albuquerque some fifteen years ago.

The same approach applies to countries. The average investor puts hard-earned savings into a foreign market because they are spoon-fed a *story* about how the country's vast resources and/or billions of people will cause its market to surge for years on end. Take China for instance. When I visited China, some sixteen years ago, none of us knew anything at all about China. China had little to no *story* but it had a blockbuster chart pattern. The Shanghai market subsequently increased 1,200% over the next twelve years. On the other hand, in 2008, China had a better *story* than any other country... *EVER*. We all know what happened to its market going forward as its *story* continued to get even better.

Invest in a great chart first, and low and behold, a great *story* will appear well into the future out of nowhere. Or better yet, invest in a great chart with an *undiscovered story* and you'll be on the path to riches. For good or for bad, don't give a damn about companies or countries. Only care about winning prices and winning stocks.

# CHAPTER 7

# *The Elusive Superstock*

*"An object at rest tends to stay at rest and an object in motion tends to stay in motion with the same speed and in the same direction."*

Isaac Newton

We now transition into the event we've all been waiting for. A bona fide Superstock is like a NASA rocket. It takes a major thrust (volume) to get it out of Earth's atmosphere (the base) but once it reaches orbit, it doesn't require much energy to keep it moving in the desired direction. Because of unbelievable earnings or a never-before-seen theme or catalyst, Superstocks attract the market's very best traders.

Superstocks attract Superstar Traders. These stocks attract the smartest momentum (momo) traders in the world. You will see the same group of momo traders in the same stocks time and time again. These are traders who live and breathe these stocks to the exclusion of all others. Through strategic purchases, these traders like to use their large bankrolls to manipulate these stocks to nosebleed levels.

As Superstocks are most often "one-of-a-kind" stocks, they can act entirely independent of their sector or the market at large. During their multi-month moves, Superstocks tend to be the biggest percentage gainers on the major exchanges. In fact, many Superstocks end in parabolic runs that defy all traditional limitations. However, once their bubble pops and the big-money momo traders depart, these stocks can crash and burn in a relatively short period of time. An eventual 70% decline from their peak is not out of the ordinary for the best performers.

For this reason alone, NEVER, EVER delude yourself into thinking that you will sell a Superstock once it reaches long-term capital gain status. As you will see in the charts section, this strategy is doomed to failure. The only way to avoid paying short-term capital gains tax on a Superstock is to sell it when it returns to your buy point...and it eventually *WILL* return to your buy point. It will; just give it enough time. Every extreme action has an equal and opposite extreme reaction, and Superstocks are no exception to this rule.

## THE SUPER LAWS OF SUPERSTOCKS

How in the world do you discover these stocks? We will first examine the technical aspects of these stocks before they become big winners. I understand that many of the technical concepts I discuss will be difficult for novice investors to fully understand. Not to worry—the best way to understand these concepts is to analyze them in graphical form. That's why I have also included more charts and commentary for some of my biggest gainers in the all-important 12th chapter of this book.

In the remainder of this chapter we will discuss the identification of potential Superstocks. Specifically:

- The technical conditions to look for.
- The fundamental qualities to look for.

In the next chapter we will discuss how to trade Superstocks by:

- Determining a potential price target.
- Identifying a low-risk entry-point.
- Position sizing.
- Potential sell criteria.
- Super Laws Summary.

## THE 8 TECHNICAL SUPER LAWS

As mentioned earlier, before digging into a company's fundamentals I must first see a picture-perfect chart pattern. When analyzing chart patterns, I prefer to look at weekly charts. Throughout history, the market's biggest winners have adhered to weekly technical patterns much more consistently than daily patterns. For this reason, institutional investors tend to base their buy and sell decisions based entirely on weekly (and sometimes monthly) patterns. If the smart money is doing it, I'm not going to argue.

The first 5 technical indicators are absolute requirements for a Superstock at breakout. To keep it simple: at breakout, a killer Superstock will 1) be under $15, 2) break out of a strong base, 3) break out above its 30 week moving average, 4) show massive weekly volume, and 5) show a steep angle of attack. These are the "Top 5 must haves" that I will present first, followed by the "best of the rest" requirements of a Superstock.

But remember, rules are meant to be broken. Yes, you might occasionally see a $30 monster stock at initial breakout, but by far the biggest gainers are those that start their runs at much lower price points.

## *THE TOP 5 MUST-HAVES*

As promised, here are the "Top 5 Must-Have" requirements for a Superstock at breakout.

### 1 – STRONG BASE BREAKOUT

The critical component of a Superstock's future success is its chart pattern. The stocks that have the biggest gains are typically those that have the longest "bases." In other words, we're looking for a stock that has traded sideways in a narrow vertical range for an extended period of time. This boring trading activity tends to weed out the emotionally-charged short-term traders. The only shareholders left are the long-term fundamentally-biased shareholders who have no intention of selling their shares any time soon. I have found that the longer a stock sets up in a base, the larger the ultimate advance. Almost every one of my big winners exploded out of a long period of unexciting, low volume trading.

The beauty of a long base is that it adds a significant layer of protection. A great stock generally does not trade below the level of support that has been repeatedly tested in the past.

Stocks that have been basing for a year or more generally offer no clue signaling a break out to the upside. On the other hand, a stock that trades down from say $60 to $10 over the course of several months and then bases in a very tight range for eight weeks or more can show some telltale signs of an imminent breakout. In my experience, many such stocks are prime candidates for a low risk entry prior to a move higher. Most "breakout investors" would never consider buying a stock before it breaks out, but I find that a strong base limits downside to such an extent that risk/reward can be highly skewed in your favor.

The concept of a strong base is a necessity for successful trading. A strong base provides a stock with solid footing to stand on before climbing higher. Ultimately, we want to see a very long base of several months' duration to provide rocket fuel for the initial breakout. We then want to see shorter multi- week bases at higher levels to serve as steps as the stock climbs higher. The following is an example of a very powerful breakout from a strong base formed over many months. Dynamic Materials (BOOM) was one of my favorite holdings from 2005.

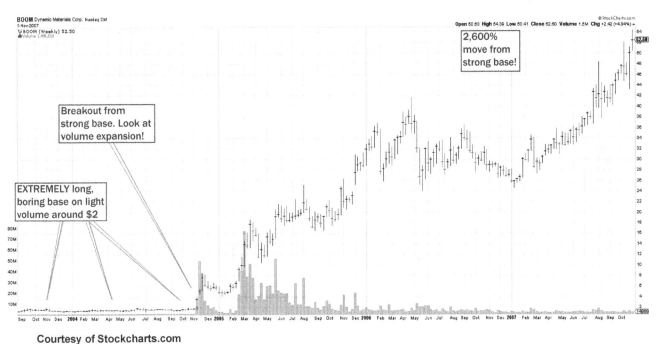

Courtesy of Stockcharts.com

## 2 – BREAKOUT ABOVE 30 WEEK MOVING AVERAGE

90% of history's biggest gainers broke out above (or stayed above) their 30 week moving averages during the first week of their high volume breakout. If a stock is breaking out of a strong multi-month base, chances are good that it is breaking out above its 30 wma. We want a powerful stock to ideally start its ascent in the vicinity of its 30 wma.

If a stock does not break out above its 30 wma on its initial weekly breakout, its declining 30 wma could prove to be resistance and ultimately could push the stock lower over time. The following chart is from one of my favorite holdings from 2004 and 2005: Forward Industries (FORD).

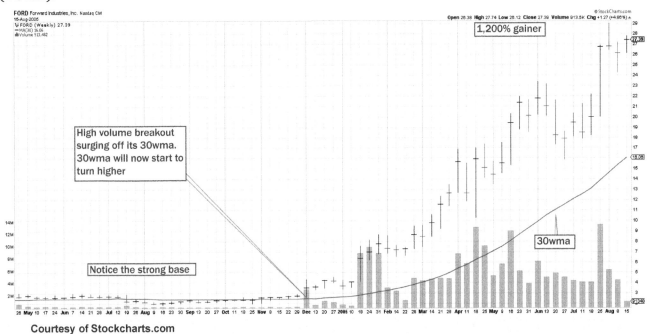

Courtesy of Stockcharts.com

## 3 – VOLUME EXPANSION

An essential feature of all Superstocks is an extreme volume (number of shares traded) expansion at the initial breakout. This surge in volume is best seen on a weekly chart. The best stocks exhibit lackluster volume for extended periods of time during their basing process. When great news hits, signaling dramatically improved present or future fundamentals, volume will typically expand 500% to 5,000% and will remain at elevated levels for months on end. This increase in volume is a direct reflection of a substantial increase in stock accumulation by deep-pocketed smart money institutional investors. It should be abundantly clear from the volume pattern that the investment community is showing much more interest in the stock.

Additionally, you want to see big "accumulation bars" before and/or during a stock's advance. Significantly more volume on up days indicates that institutional investors are accumulating shares in anticipation of higher prices.

Trio-Tech (TRT) was one of my favorites from 2006 and 2007. Check out its volume expansion upon breakout.

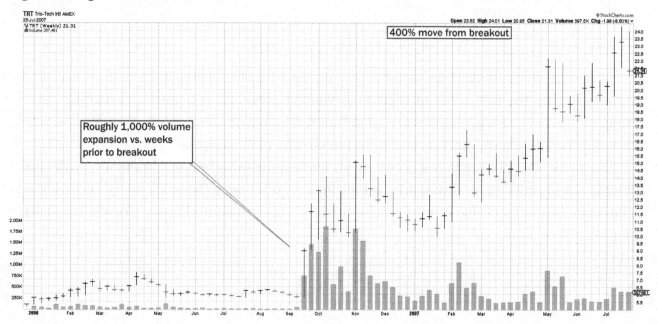

Courtesy of Stockcharts.com

# 4 – HIGH ANGLE OF ATTACK

If your focus stock has already broken out of its long-term base, you can estimate a possible future price target by drawing a line from the base (support) through the new trading zone. I have found that most of the biggest winners advance at roughly a 45 degree angle from their base over time. They generally keep this "angle of attack" for a few months. At some point, the angle may steepen and turn higher if the momentum crowd takes over.

To visualize a stock's present and future trend, you can construct or visualize a trading channel by drawing a line through the stock's recent lows and likewise by drawing a line through the stock's recent highs. The idea is that the stock will trend higher while trading within these channels.

The key, however, is to try to determine the anticipated percentage move in the stock. For instance, if you are looking at a $100 stock that is moving at a subtle 10 degree angle out of its base, it may hit $110 in a couple of months—a 10 percent return. On the other hand, a $4 stock breaking out of its base at a 45 degree angle would be trending to $6 or $7 within a couple of months; a much greater 50%-75% short-term return.

As the goal is to make the most money in the shortest period of time, we want to look for the stocks that are likely to experience the greatest percentage moves. As seen in the example of the $4 stock, we should seek lower priced stocks breaking out of a base at a high angle of attack.

FORD was an excellent example of a $4 stock with a steep/high angle of attack. BIG gains were to come..

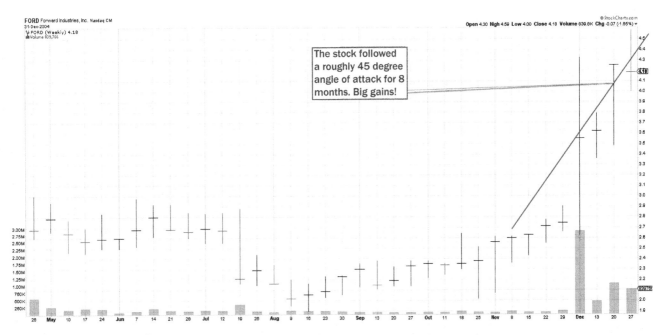

Courtesy of Stockcharts.com

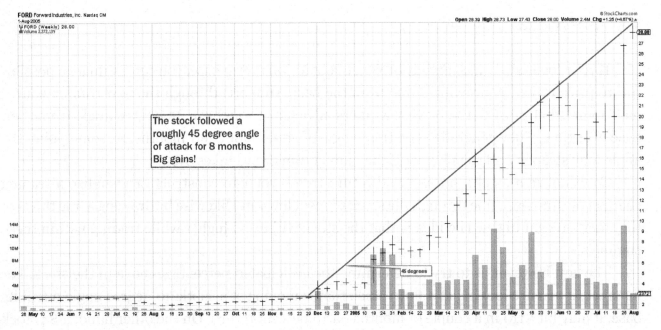

The stock followed a roughly 45 degree angle of attack for 8 months. Big gains!

Courtesy of Stockcharts.com

## 5 – UNDER $15

As a matter of arithmetic, the stocks with the largest percentage moves begin their moves from lower prices. When was the last time you saw a $500 stock go to $10,000 in a short period of time? It doesn't happen. On the other hand, I've seen plenty of $5 or $10 stocks go to $100. The absolute sweet spot for maximum percentage moves tends to be the $4-$10 area for an initial low risk entry.

On rare occasions you may encounter a potential Superstock under $5. The great thing about a lower priced stock is that it becomes "marginable" around $4 or $5 (depending on the particular broker). To put it simply, when a stock meets this margin threshold, a broker will allow shareholders to borrow 100%-300% or more of the stock's value to purchase additional shares. If your stock is non-marginable below $5 and *IS* marginable above $5, it may see a significant flow of funds as large shareholders add significantly to their positions.

As many institutions are only allowed to buy marginable stocks, they may start accumulating a significant stake in your stock once it breaches this key level. I've seen several fundamentally strong stocks linger at $3 or $4 for months, but once they breach the magic margin level, they can hit $5, $6, $7 or more within a matter of weeks.

In rare instances, I will consider a stock priced under $4, but I'm generally highly skeptical as the lowest priced stocks tend to have negative cash flow, shoddy accounting practices, or repeatedly dilute shareholders. So while I favor lower priced stocks, I generally dig a little deeper in my research of lower priced stocks.

## *THE BEST OF THE REST*

In addition to the Top 5 Superstock "Must Haves," it is also worth considering the "Best of the Rest" requirements detailed here.

## 6 – NICE CLEAN CHART

I like to look for a chart that is "orderly" in nature. I know this is somewhat of an abstract concept for most people, but bear with me for a second. Some companies (mostly small caps) have volatile stock charts whose prices spike up and down in violent fashion. For instance, over a few weeks' time, the price of a stock may shoot from $1 to $6, consolidate for a few sessions, then drop back to say $2. The next time the company issues a press release, the stock may shoot back up to $5. Given its extreme historical volatility, the stock might then again trade back down to $2.

Such stocks are totally unpredictable and don't warrant much attention from us. I much prefer patterns that are smooth and orderly with a sense of predictability. Sudden spikes based on improving fundamentals are fantastic as long as the stock forms a higher base after the breakout and ultimately moves higher in an orderly fashion.

For me, part of a "clean chart" is an "orderly decline." All stocks decline. I want to see a decline play out over several weeks. I never want to see a stock drop a large percentage (let's say 30%) in a single session. I absolutely love slow and steady declines because this kind of frustrating movement gives large shareholders sufficient time and volume to exit their positions. This orderly downward trading completely devastates the morale and sucks the patience out of the "dumb money" traders who will end up selling near the bottom.

A sudden dramatic decline, on the other hand, traps large shareholders who were not able to sell on the day of the drop. As the stock attempts to climb higher, these large shareholders sell to recoup a portion of their losses. Their selling overwhelms the stock and puts an end to any potential momentum. Here is an example from Westport Innovation's (WPRT) daily chart from 2012.

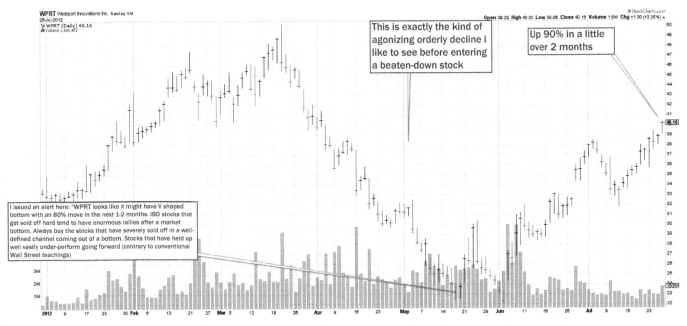

Courtesy of Stockcharts.com

## 7 – PRIOR MOMENTUM / PRIOR SUPER STOCK

Has the stock in question been a big momentum mover in the past? Lightning can definitely strike twice! As many momentum stocks can decline by 70% or more after their enormous runs, they often consolidate at lower levels to form another long term base. During this period of rest, momo traders have a habit of taking these stocks off their radar. After completing their base building period, former high-flying stocks can experience a dramatic rebirth.

Because the former momentum stock was widely known throughout the trading community in the past, its resurgence can happen in the blink of an eye as word spreads. Momo traders want to re-live the magic from the past, so they tend to jump back in all at once causing a dramatic burst in the share price. The moral of the story is to never take a former Superstock off your watchlist.

As an example, momentum darling Travelzoo (TZOO) ran from $10 to $107 within 6 months in 2004. Like a majority of other momentum stocks, it crashed hard, moving from $107 to under $30 in 3 months. For the next three and a half years, it formed a long term "cup and handle" base on very light volume. In 2010, momentum traders re-entered TZOO in a *BIG* way. Within a year, they pushed it from $15 to $104, just a few dollars short of its former high. This formed a massive multi-year double top. As a good stock should do, it crashed to the mid $20's within 4 months.

Courtesy of Stockcharts.com

## 8 – IS THE STOCK ACTING LIKE A SUPER STOCK? IS IT RESPECTING ITS "MAGIC LINE?"

Once a stock has broken out of its base and has been trading for several weeks, is it acting like a blockbuster stock should? Has the stock's average volume increased since it broke out of its base? The best performing stocks should trade down to key support levels from time to time. The "Mack Daddy" ultimate support level or "magic line" for a Superstock generally is near its "10 week simple moving average" (10 wma). This is a line representing the stock's average weekly price over the preceding 10 weeks.

Many investors are taught to strictly use "exponential" moving averages (ema) versus simple moving averages. Ema's place more weight on recent closing prices versus sma's that equally weight all closing prices in the series. I just find that sma's have worked better for me over the years, thus I use them throughout the book. Feel free to experiment with both sma's and ema's to see which works better for you.

As you will see in Chapter 12, most Superstocks hit their magic line or 10 week moving average at least once every 10 to 12 weeks. They either fall down to meet this line or they rest in a base and wait until the line catches up. Once they meet their magic line, a majority of Superstocks will start flying again. The best stocks will hit their magic line and make new highs 4-6 times before their run ends.

Occasionally, a winning stock's magic line of support can be quite a bit different from its 10 wma. It may end up being its 5 wma, 20 wma, 30 wma etc. But generally, the very best performers have magic lines of support near their 10 wma. The only way to discover a stock's magic line is to pull up the stock's weekly moving average and utilize the trial and error approach. Keep plugging in different daily or weekly moving averages until you find one that "fits"; until you find a line where the stock repeatedly bounces aggressively higher. Although a stock may trade below its magic line during any particular week, we want to see it close *above* the line by week's end.

As stocks have different personalities, it makes perfect sense that some would have different magic lines. The secret is to fit the moving average to the stock. This is a unique approach that is seldom used by traders. Most investors are taught to look for the standard moving averages like 10/20/50/200 *day* moving averages or 5/10/20/30 *week* moving averages. Because those are the levels that are taught in the textbooks, they are the only levels that most investors ever look at. But the secret is that if you can find a stock's magic line, you can make a small fortune by formulating your buying and selling criteria based on this secret level of support.

For shorter time frames, there are several moving averages that can provide support. The 5, 10, and 20 day moving averages are followed by most investors. For longer durations, the 50 and 200 day moving averages can work well. To learn more about these traditional moving averages, please see the resources section of the book.

Flotek Industries is an example of a former holding of mine that "acted well" throughout 2007 (next page).

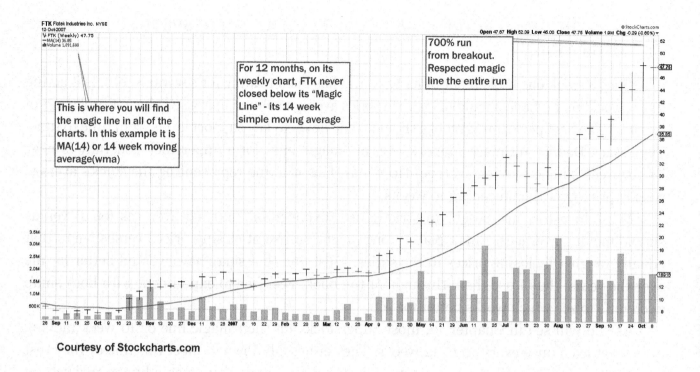

This is where you will find the magic line in all of the charts. In this example it is MA(14) or 14 week moving average(wma)

For 12 months, on its weekly chart, FTK never closed below its "Magic Line" - its 14 week simple moving average

700% run from breakout. Respected magic line the entire run

Courtesy of Stockcharts.com

## THE DIRTY DOZEN FUNDAMENTAL SUPER LAWS

The first 12 fundamental Super Laws that I will share with you are (in my opinion) the most important ingredients for a potential Superstock. My very best Superstocks met every single one of these dozen criteria. These ingredients provide the essential fuel to the fire. A stock doesn't have to meet every single one of the criteria described below, but the more Super Laws a particular stock has going for it, the higher the likelihood of success.

### 1 – EARNINGS WINNER

This is the #1 secret-ingredient for the ultimate monster stock. For world-class momentum, we are looking for a situation where a company has consistently reported quarterly revenue and earnings per share that have not deviated significantly from each other over the past few quarters. In a best case scenario we would like to see earnings trending *slightly* higher over the past few quarters. What we don't want is a company that has a "lumpy" track record where revenue and earnings jump up and down from quarter to quarter.

Once we have established that the company's results have been relatively consistent over time, we want to see revenue and/or earnings per share (more important than revenue) in the most recent quarter jump significantly higher than previous quarters. Many people say that revenue has to be up at least X% (e.g. 20%) or earnings need to be up at least X% (e.g. 30%) year over year. I simply haven't found there to be a hard and fast baseline number for revenue or earnings growth as it relates to stock performance. I have seen companies with 5% revenue growth outperform 99% of all other stocks. That being said, it is *MUCH* more important to see a jump in earnings versus a jump in revenue.

As is often the case, many investors will assume that a "monster quarter" is a one-time event. Because of this thinking, investors don't initially bid the stock up in line with its newly improved fundamentals. While a substantial temporary disconnect exists between the stock price and the improved fundamentals, the astute investor is presented with an excellent low risk/high reward window of opportunity for entry. You will see multiple examples of these short term windows of opportunity in the charts section.

For example, stock XYZ trades at $5 and the recent quarterly earnings per share progression goes something like this: $0.09, $0.11, $0.10, $0.12, $0.09, $0.11, $0.10. Then... BOOM! The company reports $0.25 EPS! If this new level of earnings is sustainable, this could easily be a $15-$30 stock sometime in the not too distant future.

## 2 – ARE EARNINGS SUSTAINABLE?

The most important question to answer is whether or not this new level of earnings is sustainable.

To help answer this question, we must ask: has the company recently started selling a new product or a new product line? Has the company embarked upon a sustainable cost cutting/ profitability initiative? Does the company have any new customers? Has the company recently discontinued an unprofitable division? Is there a new industry-wide catalyst affecting sales and profitability? Has the company recently merged with another company whose earnings are just starting to hit the bottom line?

Whatever the catalyst, your job is to poke around to find out if this catalyst will continue, or better yet, will increase in subsequent quarters. Buried somewhere in the quarterly earnings statement, management will often explicitly state that revenue and earnings will continue to grow over the next several quarters. If this is the case, your job becomes *much* easier.

If management has not issued guidance for future quarters, you must listen to recent conference calls and be alert to any clues regarding future revenue and profitability. To save time, rather than listen to the conference call, I try to find an earnings call transcript (Seekingalpha. com is a great place to look). I go directly to the question and answer session with analysts. You can occasionally find nuggets of great information from an off-the-cuff remark by a CEO or CFO in response to an analyst's question.

You should also read through the company's quarterly report (10q or 10k) filed with the SEC to see if management left any clues that were not alluded to during the conference call. Lastly, you should call the company to try to speak with a C-level executive in order to squeeze out any non-public information that he might provide.

Here are a few questions you may want to ask an executive: How is the company's backlog progressing? Is the increase in revenue unique to this company or is it industry wide? Is there any reason why margins would decline in the future? In the end, be blunt and ask whether or not the results are sustainable. You never know—you might get lucky and get a candid answer!

Trust me, you will be surprised by the amount of key information you can extract from a five minute conversation with an executive at a small company. Generally, it is a total waste of time to speak with an executive at a large company, because executives at large corporations have had years of practice in not revealing anything important. This fact alone is reason enough to focus exclusively on the smaller companies where information arbitrage is there for the taking.

## 3 – ANNUALIZED PE OF 10 OR LESS (UNDERVALUED = IMMENSE OPPORTUNITY)

I had the good fortune of entering many of my biggest winners when their price to earnings "run rate" (quarterly EPS x 4) was 10 or less. Would I consider purchasing a stock with a run rate greater than 10? Absolutely! But the idea is to put ourselves in situations of abundant potential reward with minimal risk.

Entering a growth stock at such a ridiculously low valuation not only limits your downside risk immensely, but also gives you tremendous confidence. Should your stock trade lower, you only have to remind yourself just how undervalued it is. In my experience, if a potential Superstock traded below a PE of 10, I would simply add to my position—no questions asked. As long as the stock held solidly above its base, I was confident that it was only a matter of time before it was discovered by the momentum community.

There is no question that the best performers are the ones where there is a huge disparity between the stock's value and its current price. If you can accurately calculate a stock's fair value and buy it at a 50%-80% discount, you are setting yourself up for massive success.

## 4 – SEQUENTIAL IMPROVEMENT

Along the same lines as sustainability, ideally you want a company whose revenue and earnings are increasing *EVERY* quarter. You want to find the stock after its first big breakout quarter, but there may also be significant upside in subsequent quarters.

As discussed, if investors are uncertain about the sustainability of the new level of earnings, they typically don't bid the stock up to a high multiple of current earnings. It is only after 2-3 quarters at this new level of earnings that the stock becomes fairly valued (which in turn sets the stage for the stock's decline). Investors may initially only bid the stock up to 10 times its new earnings run rate. The stock may be a high growth company being valued at roughly half the current market multiple. Such situations are rare.

After the second quarter of earnings growth, investors become more comfortable with the earnings trajectory and generally bid the stock up to a higher multiple of earnings. If the company posts yet higher earnings in quarter number 3, watch out. After a few quarters of increasing earnings, investors become very confident in the earnings sustainability and can drive a stock's annualized PE well above 30.

Let's assume that we have a $5 stock that has an initial breakout EPS of $0.25, and it subsequently reports $0.30 and $0.35 in the following 2 quarters. Due to momentum caused by the belief that results are now sustainable, within a few quarters, this "increasing multiple-effect" could propel the stock from $5 to $42 based on a 30 PE multiple. Not bad.

## 5 – EASY EARNINGS COMPARISONS

One of the worst things that can happen to a stock is for it to run into difficult year-over-year (yoy) revenue and earnings comparisons (comps). If a stock posts $0.25 EPS vs. $0.05 (up 500%!) a year earlier, the chances are good that it will perform very well. But what happens if the company posts $0.25 again the next quarter *but* earnings were $0.27 a year earlier? Its year-over-year earnings comparison would be negative. Assuming there are no one-time earnings adjustments involved in either period, the stock would not attract much attention.

We ideally want to hold stocks that are posting substantial year-over-year earnings growth. Before purchasing a stock, we need to look at the *next* quarter to see if it has easy upcoming comps versus the year earlier period. If we believe the company will post $0.36 earnings per share next quarter vs. $0.03 in the year earlier period, the stage is set for the stock to become a huge gainer. $0.36 vs. $0.03 is going to make one heck of an earnings report headline. Investors will see "Stock X reports 1,200% earnings growth." A blockbuster earnings headline like this will spread throughout the investment community in a flash.

## 6 – HIGH OPERATING LEVERAGE AND INCREASING MARGINS

If you conclude that a company's earnings are in fact sustainable, it is time to dig a little deeper into its income statement to get a feel for its operating leverage. Operating leverage is how much a company's net income will increase per dollar of additional revenue. Firms with high operating leverage tend to have a low level of variable costs relative to their fixed costs. As revenue starts to exceed fixed costs, you can see an explosion in net income and thus a significant expansion of gross margins and earnings per share.

Every so often, a company that has lost money for several years will all of a sudden experience rapid profit growth in spite of a much smaller growth in revenue. The company's surge in net income may be the result of its high operating leverage. This is exactly what we are looking for.

The best scenario, of course, is to find a company with the ultimate combination of soaring revenue and extremely low variable costs. Such a situation can be an absolute gold mine. These are the perfect situations where a 30% increase in revenue can trigger earnings per share to increase a ridiculous amount—perhaps 1,000%. If operating leverage is high and your research suggests that revenue should increase sequentially in coming quarters, earnings per share should literally explode. My friends; this situation is the Holy Grail of investing.

## 7 – INCREASING BACKLOG

Some companies will include a backlog figure in their earnings release. Backlog is the amount of future business a company currently has under contract but has not yet completed. This gives a rough estimate of how much revenue the company will earn in the coming quarters.

A public company will ordinarily quote a backlog figure that goes out a specified period of time. More often than not, a majority of the backlog will make it to the income statement within the next 2-4 quarters.

An increasing backlog figure gives the investor further confidence that the firm's financial performance will continue to surge in coming quarters. Backlog figures are extremely important to examine for companies that do not issue specific earnings guidance. This happens to be the case with most small cap companies. As the market is a forward-looking mechanism, investors tend to bid up the price of companies with increasing backlog well before the revenue hits the income statement.

## 8 – OPEN MARKET INSIDER BUYING

*"Insiders might sell their shares for any number of reasons, but they buy them for only one: they think the price will rise."*

Peter Lynch

I'm sure you've heard similar quotes by many different people. Because insiders are individuals with a deep knowledge of their company and the industry dynamics, we must take their stock transactions very seriously. But, as you will see, there's much more to insider buying than the filing alone. Yes, executives sell their shares for a variety of different reasons including estate planning, diversification, retirement, charity funding etc. However, in *MOST* cases, they buy shares for one reason and one reason only: they believe that the price of their stock will increase in the future. Their buying is sending a signal that there just might be a major fundamental catalyst on the horizon.

In reviewing my trading history, insider buying turned out to be a double whammy of sorts for Superstocks. Running the numbers backed up my long held belief that not only is insider buying an indicator of future fundamental success at the company level, but it also promotes significantly higher levels of investor confidence in the stock. This confidence ultimately translates into higher multiples on earnings resulting in much higher stock prices.

Our goal is to find open market purchases by multiple C-level executives or directors. I find that insider buying is most effective when the insider buying takes place either during a long base building period or just after the initial breakout. If a stock is climbing out of its base and insiders continue to wrestle for shares at higher prices in the open market, there's a good chance spectacular things are going to happen down the road. For instance, TRMM (one of my biggest winners) insiders were sending a *powerful* signal when they were buying at $0.25, then $0.50, then $0.75 etc...all the way up to $12! The stock eventually topped out at $27. For those of you who are mathematically inclined, that's a 10,800% return within 2 years. Makes me wonder how widely-held and "safe" Kodak stock performed during that period.

Due to stock option grants, executives already have a significant stake in their company. It is only when they go to the open market to purchase *ADDITIONAL* shares with their *OWN* money that you should start to take notice. We want to see that the size of the purchases are large in relation to the executive's salary. For example, a small insider purchase of $9,000 can be meaningful if the executive's salary is only $70,000. Such a buy can be important, especially if other insiders are following suit. Regardless of the purchase size, any time I see a small cap insider buy, I definitely take notice and begin further research.

Along the same lines, it is usually a very positive sign to see an institution or high net worth individual file a fresh 13d or 13g with the SEC. 13d/g's are legally required documents that indicate that an individual now holds 5% or more of a company's outstanding shares. In theory, whoever is purchasing such a large stake has information that the ordinary investor is not privy to.

Insider Buying Caveats:

- Token buys—occasionally, executives will make small purchases of their stock on the open market in an attempt to instill confidence in their stock. If the company is stable and the stock has been building a solid base, a token buy can be a subtle message to long term shareholders to hold on to their shares. For companies in turmoil, a token buy is probably not a reflection of a future fundamental shift within the company. The token buy may just be a means of "pumping" the share price. This practice is commonplace for firms whose stocks are trading beneath the NYSE or NASDAQ minimum price threshold. If a company's stock is to be delisted, insiders will do whatever it takes to manipulate their shares higher.

- Beware of open market purchases at prices significantly different from current market prices. These can be purchases from quite some time ago. I'm not sure how or why this happens, but it does. Take a look at the date and the price to make sure they line up.

- Beware of stock option buys that may at first appear to be open market buys. Look closely at the filing to determine exactly what kind of purchase it was. Some option purchases can be very misleading to novice investors.

- Beware of trust, family, and related party stock transfers. Many times, when an executive transfers stock to a related party, it may at first glance appear to be a buy or sell. If you examine the actual filing, it will usually state clearly whether or not it's a related-party transaction.

- Watch out for post-disaster buys. When a company announces bad news such as poor earnings, its stock may drop off a cliff. A few days later you may see insider purchases being filed with the SEC. Most often, such purchases are losing propositions in the intermediate term. Executives are definitely *NOT* traders. After a big drop, they might see "value" in their stock and are purchasing the shares for the very long term. It could also be that the situation within the company is so dire that the purchases are a public relations ploy. Don't fall for it.

- Stock buybacks. Amateur investors always get excited about corporate buybacks. Unfortunately, buybacks are rarely indicative of future outperformance. In fact, buybacks can signal precisely the opposite. The period of greatest corporate buyback activity in history took place during 2007 when it seemed like every single S&P 500 company announced a huge buyback. These buybacks coincided with a surge in private equity purchases of public companies. A year or so later, many of these stocks were down 80% or more. There must be a reason for it, but companies virtually never buy their stock at the bottom. Likewise, merger activity never happens at the bottom. Merger activity almost always happens at a major cycle top. Buybacks are not a reason to buy a stock.

- The last caveat is that there can be a significant gap in time between when an insider buys and the eventual move in the stock. Insiders often buy because of a catalyst that may not appear for several quarters. Because of this, it is best to be patient and wait on the sidelines until the stock's chart starts sending the appropriate buy signals.

- Although insider buying can give significant fuel to a Superstock, it is only in combination with other essential fundamentals does it prove to be a reliable indication of a future stock surge. I would never, ever buy a stock simply because it has insider buying alone. I go through every single insider buy filing each evening and I can tell you that 90% of these stocks do not significantly outperform the market. It is only in conjunction with the other essentials that the magic is unleashed.

## 9 – LOW FLOAT AND LOW MARKET CAP

The "float"—the number of company shares available to trade in the open market—is a key determinant in how easy it will be for momentum traders to manipulate the stock to higher levels. These are the shares in the public domain that are not held by company insiders. Since insiders must file with the SEC every time they buy or sell shares, their shares do not enter the market on a day to day basis.

If you find a $50 billion dollar company that you believe to be undervalued, it will take billions and billions of dollars over a significant period of time to slowly move that behemoth up to its target price. Think about MSFT. It takes billions of dollars in buying pressure to nudge the stock up just a couple of percent. On the other hand, if your $5 Superstock has a float of just 4 million shares, it may only take a million dollars or so in buying pressure to move it 20% higher.

When hedge funds and momentum-traders latch on to these low float stocks, they skillfully accumulate their positions at low prices without disturbing the market. Through additional buying pressure and thoughtfully placed "news leaks," they then take full advantage of the low float to manipulate these stocks higher to their price targets.

It is also vitally important to take a look at the average volume in relation to the float. If the float is 7 million shares while the average daily volume is 50,000 shares, chances are that the stock won't move very much until a surge in volume shows up. On the other hand, if the float is 4 million and the average daily volume is 800,000, the available float will be eaten up in no time. The volume-to-float ratio in this instance would no doubt lead to dramatic price swings; most often to the upside.

The best performing stocks generally have floats under 10 million shares. In my experience, the biggest movers had floats of 4 to 8 million. Additionally, most of my biggest gainers started their advances with market capitalizations under $100 million. There are plenty of exceptions, but it isn't too difficult for momentum traders to propel a $50 million market cap to $200-$300 million over the course of a few quarters.

## 10 – THE "IT FACTOR" – A "SUPER THEME"

Almost every Superstock has a unique theme to attract the attention of new investors. It could be either a sector-wide or company-specific theme. Like so many other things in life, stocks need an "It Factor" to stir up imagination, optimism, enthusiasm, and speculation. Be on the lookout for new industries and new innovative products. Look for a company that has new customers, a new partnership, a new invention, a new technique, or a new technology—especially a *disruptive technology* that may be set to shake up an entire industry. *NEW* is the magic word. Momentum traders *LOVE* new catalysts. New catalysts keep them stimulated and coming back for more. Investors always want to wager on a better imagined future.

The idea is to find such a stock before other investors stumble upon the future catalyst. If nobody is talking about it, you may just have discovered a gem. Since emotions are highly contagious, there's a good chance that a potential catalyst will go viral and infect the momentum trading community. Eventually the stock or sector theme will become popular in the mainstream. That will be your indication to sell and move on to the next big theme.

Examples of great sector themes over the years have included the internet/.com bubble of

1999, fiber optics in 2000, the September 11 security stocks in 2001, stem-cells in 2005, various biotech themes every few years, global positioning in 2007, Chinese stocks in 2008, potash in 2008, peak oil in 2008, shipping stocks in 2008, the "coal super-cycle" of 2009, Graphene and cloud computing in 2011, 3-D printing in 2012, and big data in 2012.

As you will see in the chart section, many of my biggest winners had an individual or sector "Super Theme" to attract and sustain momentum for huge advances. If a stock does not have a special theme, it may not become a Super Stock.

## 11 – CONSERVATIVE MANAGEMENT

Sustainable moves tend to happen to stocks whose management team and chief executive officer are modest in respect to their past statements and future projections. Unlike penny stocks, Superstock management teams never predict big things. They consistently under-promise and over-deliver and let their results speak for themselves. The stock market is all about exceeding expectations. If management of a small company boasts that they will soon be a multi-billion dollar company or get X% of a multi-billion dollar market, sell your shares and run for the hills. Over the years, in each of my biggest winners, management never predicted big things. Big things always came as a surprise to the investment community.

In 2006, the CEO of a large armored vehicle company boasted that his company would dominate the military armored vehicle market by selling millions and millions of units. He claimed that his stock would soar, making it a billion dollar company. Skeptical of his grand claim, I sold the stock immediately. The company soon entered a long term bear market. The company ultimately received NASDAQ delisting notices and was eventually acquired for a fraction of the CEO's billion dollar claim.

Likewise, Superstock management teams tend not to dilute their reputation by issuing many press releases. They issue no-nonsense press releases about their quarterly earnings or about significant developments that have a meaningful impact on the company's fundamentals. They certainly never issue "fluff" press releases like so many run-of-the-mill companies. Superstock management teams are no-nonsense players.

## 12 – SIMPLE AND IMPRESSIVE BLOCKBUSTER EARNING RELEASE HEADLINE

A Superstock should have a quarterly report that is both impressive and easy for the average investor to understand. As with investing methods: the simpler, the better. A simple headline such as "XYZ corp. announces revenue growth of 50% and earnings per share growth of 400%" really grabs the attention of Wall Street.

On some occasions, companies will release consolidated results for the previous 6, 9 or 12 months. A complicated consolidated report like this can be the kiss of death for a momentum stock. I've read through reports like this where it literally took me ten minutes to figure out what the company earned for the quarter. Most investors don't have the patience or the inclination to dig through reports with their calculator to figure out a firm's most recent earnings. Because of this, investors will turn their attention elsewhere.

The dirty little secret is that companies will often release a consolidated multi-quarter report to obscure lackluster recent earnings.

## FUNDAMENTAL SUPER LAWS 13 – 24: ADDITIONAL FIREPOWER

I have found that although the Super Laws found below are not essential to a stock's success they certainly add fuel to the fire should your stock possess them.

### 13 – NO LISTED OPTIONS

When a stock hits the big time and gains a mass following, it will attract coverage from investment banks and market makers. Eventually, it will be possible to buy call and put options on the stock due to its popularity. A majority of the time, the stocks that we are searching for have yet to be discovered and there are no listed options for them.

Once a stock *does* have listed options, a can of worms is opened. Manipulation runs rampant for such stocks due to strike prices, the degree of open interest in calls and puts, and expiration dates. This is another subject for another day but just remember that undiscovered gems rarely have listed options.

### 14 – LITTLE OR NO COMPETITION

The best performing stocks are those that have a unique product or business model with little or no competition. If investors want to invest in this small niche, there are few alternative venues in which to put their investment dollars. Without investment alternatives, a lot of investment funds tend to flow into these "lone wolf" stocks.

In 2005, the Motorola RAZR became the best selling cell phone in history. There were very few if any pure play stocks to piggyback on the success of the RAZR. Sure, one could buy Motorola, but the multi-billion dollar behemoth moved at a snail's pace. When investors discovered that Forward Industries (FORD) was producing "in-box" (included in the box with the phone at purchase) carrying cases for the RAZR, share volume exploded from a couple hundred thousand shares per week to over 12 million. The stock surged 3,000% in a little over 2 years. When earnings spiked and extreme operating leverage began to take hold, I hopped on the FORD train and sat tight as it surged over 700% in 6 months.

### 15 – LOW SHORT INTEREST

Superstocks almost always have a low short interest at breakout. As they surge higher, the short interest will increase as naive traders attempt to short "high prices." To me, a low short interest would be a short position that is less than 20% of a stock's total outstanding shares. I will tell you a secret that will absolutely blow your mind—great stocks have low short interest when they start their advance because there's simply no reason to bet against them! The company doesn't have any dirty laundry that the shorts are privy to. Many inexperienced traders think that the best stocks have a high short interest. Their theory is that shorts will be "forced" to cover all at once leading to a huge surge in the share price.

The shorts tend to be the "smart money" with sensitive industry or company-specific information that is kept at arm's length from other investors. It is certainly not in the short's best interest to share this information in a public forum as their goal is to catch longs by surprise when the bad news hits. High short interest stocks can have massive 1 or 2 day spikes followed by slow declines for months on end. Studies show that stocks with high short interest significantly underperform the general market.

The strongest stocks don't have shorts hanging around to manipulate the shares lower. The strongest stocks don't need the assistance of short covering. They will outperform all others by attracting new investor capital due to superior fundamentals.

## 16 – NO "HIGHLY LEVERAGED" FIRMS ALLOWED

Superstocks tend to have little or no long-term debt. The stocks that move at the slowest pace are the large cap stocks saddled with billions and billions of debt. Profitable companies with a clean balance sheet with little if any debt expense are the ones most likely to perform well over time.

Once a company (usually a more mature company) starts taking on more and more long-term debt, its stock performance tends to suffer as the company invests in new plant and equipment which leads to increased fixed costs and interest expense. Seek out nimble companies with low fixed expenses and low interest expense which together increase the likelihood of high operating leverage for explosive earnings potential.

## 17 – A GREAT TICKER!

Surprisingly, many of the biggest gainers have memorable ticker symbols. Logically, this doesn't make much sense but in reality this is often the case. The connected group of momentum traders is more likely to pass along a memorable ticker symbol than one that is not. In the age of social media, memorable tickers go viral. Stocks with great tickers like TASR (Taser guns), CROX (Croc's shoes), DDD (3-D printing), TZOO (Travelzoo), and BOOM (a simply awesome ticker for any company!) are all easy to remember and are much more likely to go viral than lame tickers like ACSEF or ELTK.

## 18 – NO COMMODITY PLAYS

There are always exceptions to every rule, but in general, I try to steer clear of commodity stocks. An investor ordinarily faces two types of risk: systemic (market) risk and idiosyncratic (company specific) risk. Because of these two risks, you are always at the mercy of overall stock market gyrations as well as at the mercy of company specific events. Commodity stocks, however, add a third layer of risk to the equation; they add *commodity risk.*

As an investor in a commodity stock, your stock can decline due to a decline in the stock market, due to a negative company development, or due to a decline in the underlying commodity. Since you want to control risk as much as possible, I rarely recommend investing in commodity stocks. There are simply too many variables that are out of your control.

## 19 – IBD 100

Pick up a copy of *Investor's Business Daily (IBD)* or log onto their website and look up your stock's *IBD* numbers. If its relative strength, earnings, and composite number are all in the upper 90s, chances are good that your stock will attract capital from momentum investors.

I've been very fortunate to discover several *IBD 100 (Investor's Business Daily Top 100)* stocks well before they joined the *IBD* party. Unfortunately, the *IBD 100* only includes NASDAQ stocks above $15 and NYSE stocks above $20. It is only after they reach these lofty price levels that *IBD* considers them to be "safe." If I discover a Superstock at $3 or $4, I'm already starting to formulate my exit strategy when *IBD* "discovers" it above $15 (usually *well* above $15).

If you did your research, you're already sitting on a potential 400% or 500% gain when *IBD* starts promoting the stock. There's certainly nothing to prevent a run from say $18 to $30, but the big money has already been made before the stock is "discovered" by the investment community. Should the stock be lucky enough to ride a 66% *IBD* surge, you would be up some 1,000% from your entry; leaving your competition in the dust.

In general, if a stock meets most of the Superstock requirements, there's a good chance that it will be included in the sought after *IBD 100* list. That is a gigantic plus for you and your stock.

## 20 – NO ANALYST COVERAGE

Look for a stock that has not yet been discovered by the investment banking community. A majority of Superstocks do not have analyst coverage when they begin their runs. When holding a stock that has no analyst coverage, you don't have to worry about an analyst capping your stock's advance by slapping a ridiculously low price target on it. You also don't have to worry about a random analyst downgrade causing your stock to drop 15% in a session.

Without analyst's price targets, investors often do not know how to value the company. This can create tremendous opportunity caused by information arbitrage. But what happens when an investment bank *DOES* decide to begin coverage of an undiscovered stock?

In the weeks prior to initiating coverage with a buy or neutral (never a sell) rating of a stock, a bank's trading department will begin accumulating shares. Their consistent buying pressure can send the shares higher heading into the announcement. When the analyst "buy" report is released, the stock can surge 10%, 20% or more in a session. It doesn't matter whether the recommendation is buy or hold. The shares will surge regardless as new capital flows into the name.

In addition to profiting from the stock run-up, the investment bank wants to earn investment banking fees from the company in the future. In return for promoting the stock, the bankers are hoping to get future fees from mergers and acquisitions, secondary stock offerings, private placements, or debt offerings. Oftentimes, a future stock offering has already been agreed to between the bank and the company. This exact scenario unfolded with two stocks that I owned: CVV and TRMM. After juicing the stocks with new buy recommendations, secondary offerings were announced shortly thereafter. In each case, the momentum came to a screeching halt.

## 21 – SUPER TRADERS ON BOARD

Some of the best sources of information for a small company are stock message boards like those found on *Yahoo! Finance* or *InvestorVillage*. The very best stocks tend to have orderly and less active message boards, which is a rarity these days. These message boards tend to be inhabited by a few experienced investors with informed opinions. On occasion you may even encounter hedge fund traders or industry insiders on the boards.

The very best boards are chock-full of actionable information provided by these intelligent investors who offer up their due diligence. If a hedge fund is on board, they will strategically feed the board information to goose the share price higher. These "boring" message boards lack the minute-by-minute hyper-posting of the message boards of less desirable stocks.

You might also notice that you continually see the same traders on the message boards of the very best stocks. I continually see the same couple of dozen momentum traders on Superstock message boards. They are the smart money; the best of the best momo traders. When you keep bumping into these players, you will know that you are doing something right.

Stay away from message boards whose posters express radically different viewpoints. Be wary of a board that has several posters calling for the stock to go much lower while their counterparts continuously claim the stock will go to infinity. A low volume, unemotional message board is a sign of intelligence, experience, and reflects the stock's undiscovered nature. By extension, avoid stocks whose message boards are filled entirely by political and social rants. Political debaters tend to migrate to message boards whose stocks offer nothing of promise to discuss.

## 22 – INSIDER OWNERSHIP

A management team that holds a large stake in its stock is preferable to a management team that does not have much "skin in the game." If management's fortunes and retirement funds are tied to its stock performance, they are incentivized to do whatever it takes to push the price of their stock higher over the long term. From an incentive standpoint, it is always a good sign if executives hold a 20% or 30% stake in their company. On the other hand, if several executives recently sold most of their stake in the company, don't even consider it for investment. Always remember that there are plenty of other fish.

## 23 – LONG TRADING HISTORY / BEWARE OF IPOs (IT'S PROBABLY OVERPRICED)

Has the stock in question come public within the past year? Out of dozens of efforts, I have only made serious money on recent initial public offerings (IPOs) on a couple of occasions. Historically, IPOs under-perform the general market by about 50% during their first year. That is quite an extraordinary figure. There are a few reasons for this. First, companies get a ton of cash from the offering and invest the new funds in assets that may initially be unproductive. These assets ordinarily have fixed costs that suppress net income.

Second, IPO's have "lock-up periods" after which time management is allowed to sell millions of shares into the open market. Investors tend to drive the share price lower in anticipation of the expiration of the lock-up period. Who would want to hold a stock before millions of shares are sold on the open market? Not me!

Third, traders tend to shy away from IPOs as the stocks don't yet have a proven trading track record. The stock has yet to develop its own predictable "trading personality" which most stocks develop over years of trading. Recent IPOs don't yet have long-term moving averages such as the 200 day moving average to trade against. Under normal circumstances, I like to see at least 12 months of trading history before I consider investing in a stock.

Lastly, IPOs are pumped and pumped by the sponsoring investment banks during the "road show" in the weeks leading into the IPO. Being in close contact with management, they have a pretty clear picture of what the earnings will be coming out of the gate. The IPO underwriters give the investment community their most optimistic take on these projections. The company is ultimately taken public at the highest valuation possible. For this reason, many people have another name for IPOs—"It's Probably Overpriced."

Contrary to the media's take on the Facebook IPO, it is the investment bank's duty to take any company public at the highest valuation possible. When you have a realtor sell your house, do you instruct him or her to sell it at a discount so the new buyer can experience a greater level of appreciation? Come on! If the company goes public at the highest valuation possible in combination with absurdly high expectations for the future, the risk is skewed heavily to the downside. Facebook was the dumb money IPO of the century. Every investor wanted a piece of it because they "love" the website ("buy what you know mentality"). Leave "IPO roulette" to investing newbies and day traders.

## 24 – POTENTIAL MOVE TO NASDAQ

On rare occasions you will uncover a stock on the NASDAQ bulletin board exchange that exhibits an outstanding chart backed by blockbuster fundamentals. Contrary to popular belief, there are actually quite a few legitimate profitable companies on the bulletin board exchange. If it is apparent that the earnings for a bulletin board company are legitimate and sustainable, it will eventually apply for listing on the NASDAQ exchange. Management will often hint at such a potential move in quarterly reports and conference calls.

During the application process, through the date of transfer, and into the weeks following NASDAQ listing, these stocks can experience massive gains. The anticipated increase in awareness for the stock attracts significant buying. I wouldn't invest in a stock simply because it was moving to a major exchange, but if I stumbled upon a growing bulletin board company with a 5 or 10 PE transitioning to the NASDAQ, I would certainly give it a thorough look over.

Several years ago, I ran across a bulletin board company named Rural/Metro (RURL); an emergency services provider that had recently made the transition to profitability. The company was growing its revenue, had little competition in its markets, and was trading at an absurd PE of 4. There was even some insider buying as well in addition to large 13d institutional filings.

As its chart pattern looked ridiculously bullish, I picked up a large stake around $1.50. Within a week or two of my purchase, the company announced the approval of its NASDAQ application. Over the next couple of months the stock tripled. RURL was definitely a big fat pitch.

## DIG A LITTLE DEEPER

After you have finished your initial due diligence, and a stock meets most if not all of the Superstock Super Laws, the next step is to take your research one final step further as you look for unforeseen variables that may come out of left field.

## BEWARE OF POTENTIAL SECONDARY OFFERING

Secondary stock offerings can absolutely kill a stock. Management will pursue a secondary offering for one of three reasons:

1. The company is bleeding cash and needs to sell more shares to raise cash to continue operations.

2. Management needs additional capital to expand operations.

3. Management believes the stock price is near a top and wants to take advantage of the euphoria.

By selling shares into an irrational run, a company can sell significantly fewer shares (less dilution) than they would otherwise. Regardless of immediate need, management teams often take advantage of overvaluation to give them a big cash cushion for the future.

Since our focus is on profitable companies, we don't have to worry too much about reason #1. Just make sure that the company's cash flow is strong enough to cover operating expenses going forward.

Reasons #2 and #3, however, are a major cause for concern for a high flyer. Stock momentum generally takes a breather well in advance of an announcement of a private placement or secondary offering. Why would momentum wane prior to a stock offering? Leading up to the placement, management is in close contact with the investment bank(s) to place the newly issued shares with the bank's customers. Word circulates within the banking community that a secondary offering is about to be announced, so those with knowledge of the offering start shorting shares of the company on the open market.

To make matters worse for shareholders, the individuals investing in the secondary offering partake in a little-known scheme called "shorting against the box." Most people assume that the investors purchasing shares in the secondary offering are bullish on the company and want to buy shares at a discount to the market price. This is seldom the case as these investors could really care less where the stock goes.

Let's assume stock XYZ is trading at $40 prior to the stock offering. Mr. Whale is contacted by the underwriter to participate in the upcoming offering at $34. Mr. Whale agrees to the deal and commits to purchase $1 million worth of XYZ at $34. Some time before the offering is announced, Mr. Whale "shorts against the box"—selling short $1 million dollars worth of XYZ around $40. Mr. Whale is now fully hedged and will make a profit no matter what happens to the stock.

As investment banks and stock offering participants accumulate their short positions days or weeks ahead of the offering, their action drives the share price down to say $37. On the day of the announcement, the share price drops near the price of the offering around $34.

Since the investors in the stock offering are long and short the stock in equal amounts at different prices, they are guaranteed roughly an 18% return when they ultimately unwind their positions. To make their deal much sweeter, there may also be warrants (similar to options which give the right to buy more shares at a certain price) attached to the shares. The offering investors may be required to hold on to their shares for 6 months or more, but in any scenario, they will make a large risk-free return.

After a secondary offering, momentum traders usually flee the stock while shorts tend to pile into the stock driving the price down even further. Management may spend the new cash on assets such as a new production line which can increase fixed costs. The increased share count and increased costs can depress earnings in the short run.

The moral of the story is to try to determine if your company has sufficient cash on hand for future operations and whether it might need cash to fund a potential expansion. For stocks that have already announced a stock offering, my rule of thumb is to wait at least 6 months before a potential purchase.

### BE A BEAR, EXPECT THE UNEXPECTED, AND DIG UP CONTRARIAN VIEWPOINTS

To fully understand potential pitfalls before you buy, you need to look at your stock from a bear's perspective.

I know that I recommend not reading mass-media, but in this case, read any recent bearish articles about your company to understand the bearish perspective. Go to the stock's message board and read the bearish posts. Ask the message board bulls what could possibly come out of left field to derail their rosy predictions. Read through the company's 10q filing and examine the "risks" section. Unlike a majority of investors, don't be afraid to uncover information that runs contrary to your position. This practice may keep you out of a bad stock.

The important thing to remember is to perform this contrarian research *BEFORE* you purchase the stock. Once you have entered your position, don't waste your time listening to the bears. This will only serve to knock you out of the stock at the worst possible time. Once you are a shareholder, stick to your bullish thesis and only sell due to one or more of the Super Laws of selling discussed later.

### WOW MOMENT!

If your research shows that your company is profitable, undervalued, growing like a weed, has insider buying, high operating leverage, a low float, no debt, and a great chart, you have probably arrived at a major *WOW Moment!* Now that you have found the stock, the real fun begins. What do you do with it? Should you go out and buy it immediately? Finding your stock means next-to-nothing. This is the case because the only two things that matter in this business are 1) when you buy the stock, and 2) when you sell it.

# CHAPTER 8

# *Stacking the Odds in Your Favor*

The worst thing an investor can do is to buy a stock and then watch in horror as it drops 20% from his purchase price. A majority of investors do not consider purchasing stocks *ONLY* when the likelihood of decline is extremely limited. The game is *100%* about low-risk entries in combination with high likelihood of price appreciation.

## *PRICE TARGET AND REWARD/RISK RATIO*

### 100%+ POTENTIAL AND HEAVILY SKEWED REWARD TO RISK RATIO = MONSTER

The key to successful investing is to stack the odds in your favor as much as possible. I like to calculate a back-of-the-envelope reward/risk ratio prior to entering a position. I choose to think of it as reward-to-risk ratio because we should focus most of our attention on the reward. In any case, I only take substantial positions in stocks that I believe have 100%+ potential. Once I determine that a stock can move 100%, 200%, or 300% or more, I then want to determine the downside.

If an $11 stock breaks out of a $10 supportive base, the potential downside would be only $1 or 9% because there's no reason to own the stock below its base of support. If the company just reported earnings-per-share of $0.35, based on a price/earnings multiple of 20, you determine that your target price is $28 ($0.35 x 4 quarters= $1.40 x 20PE = $28).

In this instance, the odds are stacked heavily in your favor: $17 upside and $1 downside—an almost 17 to 1 reward to risk ratio. On a percentage basis, you're looking at 255% upside and 9% downside. As the best momo stocks can trade up to 30 or 40 annualized PE's during their run, you could be looking at 510% potential upside versus 9% downside at the current EPS run rate.

Such a skewed ratio is extreme and quite rare in practice. When such little risk is present for such a comparatively large reward, you have to force yourself to get off the bench, take a swing at the fat pitch, and ride it as high as you possibly can.

With respect to the downside, *ALWAYS* determine in advance what you are willing to risk. Once this level is determined, you *must* have a pre-determined mental or physical stop-loss order in place with your broker to limit your losses.

At the other end of the investment spectrum, you have Joe Six-Pack trading exchange traded funds (ETFs) like SPY (S&P 500) or QQQ (NASDAQ 100). As we know all too well, the indexes move slowly over the long term. From day to day, who knows whether the major markets will trade higher or lower? I sure don't. Why would you want to risk hard earned capital if the risk/reward is virtually even? It's like going to a casino.

Do you have special knowledge that is not known by anybody else that supports much higher SPY prices? Do you have a SPY PE ratio of 5 that could easily increase 6-fold? Is there SPY insider buying? The answers are no, no, and no! Does it have a low float? Ha!

Given the possibility of an unforeseen market crash, you are virtually sentencing yourself to investment mediocrity should you invest in such run-of-the-mill vehicles. To be blunt, ETF investors are those who are too lazy to do their homework. I urge you to perform the work necessary to get the odds heavily stacked in your favor.

## ONLY SUCKERS "BACK OUT" CASH

When valuing a stock and determining its price target, I urge you not to take a firm's cash holdings into consideration. Yes, our company needs a healthy level of cash on hand to operate its business sufficiently. Yes, a healthy cash balance also helps us sleep better knowing that a secondary offering is much less likely. But the cash balance should not be taken into consideration when determining a price target. Our stock's potential price is entirely based on speculation about the *FUTURE*, not the cash accumulated in the *PAST*. As real estate is about location, location, location, successful investing is all about future, future, future. Speculation and speculative themes are future-based. Cash is a measure of the past.

The analyst community determines a price target based on a multiple of revenue, earnings, or cash flow, and adds the company's cash balance to the price target. These group-thinking Ivy League brainiacs see all of this cash and don't know what to do with it, so they just slap it onto the price target. In my experience, the higher a company's cash balance, the worse it performs relative to its peers.

I know that you may find this statement shocking, but having an extraordinarily large cash balance is a *NEGATIVE*. I know, I know...analysts say "AAPL's cash will help it become the world's first trillion dollar company." I'm not so sure about this current analyst groupthink. A large cash balance *usually* means that a company is in its mature stages and has few high-growth areas in which to invest its cash. Companies are punished over the long run for not re-investing their cash at high rates of return. In the past, I held companies such as Omnivision Technologies (OVTI) or MEMC Electronics (WFR) with *gigantic* cash balances almost equal to their market capitalizations. Their long term performance has been abysmal.

When momentum traders start pushing a Superstock to their desired price target, they pay absolutely zero attention to the firm's cash balance. Focusing exclusively on companies with a high cash balance leads you straight into "value-trap" hell.

A high level of cash is nice but it should not enter into our price target equation. Remember that it's all about the dream of *future earnings*.

## LOW-RISK WINDOWS OF OPPORTUNITY

A majority of fellow traders think that my entry points are absurd. Traders rarely follow me into trades because my entries make "no sense" to those who have been taught the standard curriculum. When I am buying at the bottom of a cup and handle pattern, they scoff and say that you are "supposed to" buy 30% higher as the stock breaks out of the handle. But what if I can see the cup and handle pattern developing before anybody else? When I buy several weeks into a low volume, tight weekly base, they tell me that I shouldn't buy until it breaks out. My low risk entries aren't always exciting or immediately profitable or gratifying, but they have worked wonders for my portfolio in the past. As you will see in the Charts chapter, low risk entries are much easier to identify on weekly charts.

The trading masses are taught in every book to buy a stock when everybody else is buying as it breaks out. It's the whole "safety in numbers" thing again. Here's the problem with that: turning points always happen when *everybody* is buying or *everybody* is selling. Unless it is a unique high reward post-earnings situation, a majority of the time, I want to buy in an uptrend when volume is at a standstill and *nobody* is buying. At these junctures, nobody is buying because nobody takes the time to visualize how the stock will react when investors return to the stock. And let me tell you...investors *always* return at some point.

Low risk windows of opportunity take place when everybody has given up, not when everybody is enthusiastic. I don't know about you, but my goal is to put myself in a situation where my account is appreciating at all times. I always try to put myself in a position where the likelihood of a big drop is extremely limited. My thinking is always "Why not wait to buy a stock until after the breakout traders sell the stock at a loss?"

Looking back through your investing history, wasn't it precisely the times when you and the others you followed sold a stock at a loss that the stock immediately turned around and surged higher without you on board? That's precisely how the market works year after year. A stock's only mission in life is to move higher with as few people on board as humanly possible.

One of three things may happen while waiting for a high-probability entry:

1. You will buy your stock significantly cheaper when short-term traders dump the stock.

2. If your stock consolidates, you will buy your stock sometime in the future at today's price. In this scenario, there is no wasted opportunity cost (your funds are hopefully earning interest elsewhere) or emotional anguish resulting from fluctuations during the waiting period.

3. In the worst case scenario, your stock will continue higher without you. If so, there will likely be another low risk entry point in the future (albeit at a higher price). If there is not another low-risk entry point, just remember that there are thousands of other stocks out there.

Choosing 1, 2, or 3 greatly reduces your odds of sitting on a short-term loss and getting shaken out of your position.

## WHEN DOES JOE SIX-PACK BUY HIS STOCKS?

After finishing their research, 99% of investors immediately place an order to buy the stock they have fallen in love with. Yes, almost everybody does this. And it is complete and utter lunacy. Remind yourself that you are no longer part of the 99% of investors; they are achieving average returns and going about everything the wrong way.

A male's perspective on dating traditionally has been that the only course of action is to aggressively pursue your potential partner until she succumbs to your advances. For better or for worse, some of the greatest relationships in my life were formed when I gave my future partner the right amount of time and space before *coming to me*. In the market, while everybody else is aggressively *chasing* the next hot stock, your goal should be to wait patiently on the sidelines until the very best setups *come to you*.

*If you love your stock, be willing to let it go. If it loves you, it will come back to you.*

Because of failed breakouts and post-earnings reversals, it is usually best to wait for a stock to consolidate or pull back during the days and/or weeks following an earnings announcement (there are of course exceptions for extreme valuation disconnects). There's nothing worse than buying a stock on its earnings day and subsequently watching it slowly trade 20% lower over the next few weeks. As the stock does what it is supposed to do, it will force us to sell at that 20% trough—just days before it rockets to new highs. We want to be the patient ones ready to snag the low hanging fruit when others are in panic mode.

## BECOME A STALKER OF HIGH QUALITY SUPERSTOCKS

> *"I just wait until there is money lying in the corner, and all I have to do is go over there and pick it up. I do nothing in the meantime."*
>
> Jim Rogers

Over a period of several months, you will most likely accumulate a list of stocks that you are interested in. It is very important to develop and occasionally monitor this list of exceptional stocks. Having a watchlist of stocks is absolutely essential to your success as it helps prevent you from focusing exclusively on one single stock. When you focus on one stock to the exclusion of all others, you are likely to fall in love with it and will be more apt to buy it at any price. What would happen if you immediately married the very first person you had a crush on in middle school? The odds of being happily married 50 years later are...slim to none. Having a steady stream of new ideas prevents you from doing something you'll later regret.

If you become an expert on a small number of outstanding stocks, you then have the luxury of waiting until one or two of them fall in your lap offering extremely advantageous entry points. Repeat this process over and over again and you will find yourself with a portfolio of the very best stocks in the market all bought at absurdly low temporary valuations.

## BE LIKE GEORGE CLOONEY, JACK NICHOLSON, AND COLIN FARRELL

Your favorite momentum stocks will often be quite extended to the upside, well above any support levels such as the "gold standard" of support—the 10 week moving average. You never want to chase a stock while succumbing to the "buy it at any price" mentality.

When it comes to stocks, I want you to become a dating aficionado and a confirmed bachelor (or bachelorette, for the women). From this day forward (if you're a man) you are now George Clooney, Jack Nicholson, and Colin Farrell rolled into one. Marriage is simply not an option. You only date supermodels and Superstocks. Never fall in love with a stock. From this day forward, *ONLY FALL IN LOVE WITH PRICES.*

Once you have several stocks on your radar, simply buy the ones whose prices fall down to low-risk support levels. Since the stock has already passed your strict criteria and has made your short list, unless something has fundamentally changed, don't think twice about buying it at a low price. Remember that you are George Clooney, so the stock *WILL* come to you. It will eventually trade down to your desired price. If not, there are plenty of other great stocks on your list that will. Never let emotions enter into the equation. Once you have done all of the leg work and have a select group of stocks on your radar, your job from that point is to monitor and buy *prices*. Nothing else should enter the equation.

Always be prepared and have a game plan in place while you wait. It is not at all unusual for a Superstock to take a huge dive in the middle of the trading session so as to take out all of the stop-loss orders. As most investors aren't watching their stock in the middle of the day, very few people are able to take advantage of these lightening quick "blue light" specials.

I've seen several stocks take 20% intraday dives and recover a substantial portion of that within a few minutes. These "no news" split-second opportunities are absolute gifts for the patient investor waiting for the price to come to them.

## BE MARK CUBAN

*"Make sure you don't buy at the wrong price or the wrong time."*
Warren Buffett

They say life is all about timing. The only thing that matters to your ultimate success is when you buy and when you sell *prices*. It does not matter what stocks you buy as long as you sell them at a higher price. There is one reason and one reason only to buy a Superstock; it offers you a vastly increased chance of selling it at a higher price. I repeat, we are not investing in stocks. We are investing in prices that we believe will significantly outperform other prices. Mastering the art of finding Superstocks may or may not change your life, but mastering the art of when to buy and when to sell *anything* will, without a doubt, change your life.

Take Mark Cuban, for instance. He formed Broadcast.com in 1995 and sold the company at the height of the .com frenzy in 1999 for some $6 billion. If he had sold his company in *ANY* other year throughout history, Cuban would be very lucky to be just another millionaire. Mark Cuban either mastered the art of the sale or got extremely lucky. For our purposes, it doesn't matter which one. The fact is that he pulled off the *ultimate* sale.

For all we know, if Cuban still owned it, Broadcast.com could be totally worthless today and he might be working at Dairy Queen for real. If you don't remember, in 2002 Cuban said he wouldn't hire referee Ed Rush to work at a Dairy Queen. Combining publicity with damage control, Cuban worked at a Dairy Queen for a day later that year.

Life is all about timing. Take full advantage of Superstocks to dramatically improve your results in buying and selling *PRICES*.

# CHAPTER 9

# *Low Risk Entry Super Laws*

*"In stocks, it's the only place where when things go on sale, people get unhappy. If I like a business, then it makes sense to buy more at 20 than at 30. If McDonald's reduces the price of hamburgers, I think it's great."*

Warren Buffett

The hallmark of every one of the best performing stocks throughout history is that they have extreme pullbacks. These pullbacks are absolutely necessary for the success of a healthy Superstock. The kiss of death for a Superstock is euphoria in the absence of occasional despair. Unabated optimism and euphoria marks tops. Large pullbacks and long base building periods are required to inject some healthy skepticism into these winners. Every one of the greatest bull markets in history climbed a wall of worry. Superstocks are no different.

I am living proof that you can shift the odds heavily in your favor if you not only find the very best stocks, but you buy them when nobody else is watching or when nobody else dare touch them. It all boils down to this: if you buy a great stock as it moves higher, it could go higher or lower. That's a 50/50 proposition if you ask me. But if you buy a great stock *in an uptrend* after it has pulled back, your odds greatly improve.

## THE 6 SUPER LAWS OF LOW RISK ENTRIES

While most investors are buying when buzz about their stock is hitting a crescendo, we want to be on the lookout for situations where the noise has died down and our strong stock presents limited downside.

### 1 – BUY THE "MAGIC LINE" HAND-OVER-FIST!

A majority of a Superstock's ultimate gains take place in the first few weeks after a brush with its "Magic Line" (again—near 10 week moving average in most cases). The magic line is the *ULTIMATE* low risk entry point. As you will see in the charts section, weekly setups should take precedence over any setups of shorter duration. This magic line is typically where smart money institutions set up camp to accumulate. As a breakout stock declines or rests in a multi-week base, the magic line is steadily rising from below.

As the stock price and its magic line slowly converge, multi-billion dollar institutional trading departments are busy behind the scenes buying as many shares as they possibly can without disturbing the share price. Once they finish accumulating their positions and/or the magic line meets the share price, they then set the fireworks in motion.

Once the conditions are primed, the billion dollar institutions make magic happen. They strategically buy large blocks of shares to move the stock higher, which attracts momentum traders to get the ball rolling. Their other course of action is to tell their contacts at the company whose stock is being accumulated that the time is ripe to release that press release they've been sitting on for the past several weeks. I've noticed that meaningful corporate news is usually timed to be released precisely when the technical conditions are ripe for a large surge in the stock price. It is often an investment bank or an institution(s) that advises the company precisely when to release the pent up news.

As the stock hits its magic line, an alternative course of action for an institution is to contact its sources in the mass media to spread positive rumors or positive "news" about the company. Furthermore, they can spread negative rumors about the firm's competitors implying that the competitors are losing market share. As you will begin to see over and over, great news always comes out about your stock right around the time that it meets its magic line. Trust me, it's no coincidence.

Here is an example of a current popular stock just to show you that the magic line *NEVER* goes out of style.

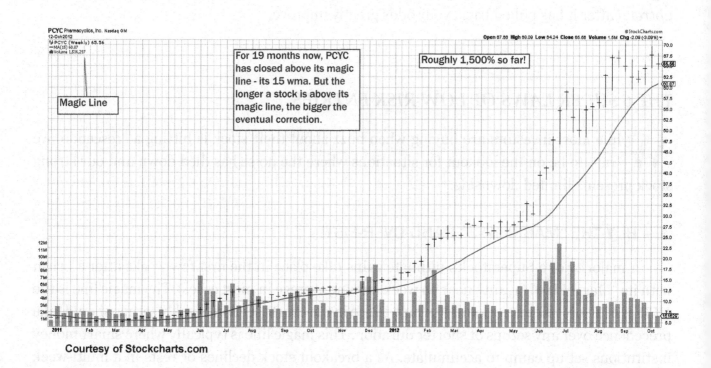

Courtesy of Stockcharts.com

## 2 – "BLT" – BUY LIGHT AND TIGHT

This has proven to be one of the best low risk indicators for me. At the tail end of a constructive multi-week base-building period, a Superstock will tend to move within a very *tight* band on relatively *light* weekly volume compared to prior weeks. After large weekly advances on accelerating volume, great stocks will rest or decline for several weeks in a row. It is only after volume declines dramatically that traders will forget about a stock. This is exactly what we want to see.

As a stock rests and garners strength for its next run, we want to see volume tail off in more or less a straight line. Ideally, we want to see volume decline to roughly 30%-50% of the peak volume seen during its biggest advancing weeks. On the chart, the weekly volume bars may form what is called a descending bullish wedge or descending bullish channel. When the volume pattern breaks higher above this wedge, the stock will usually surge higher.

The best low risk entry points are when the stock apparently goes absolutely nowhere for 1-3 weeks on very little volume when compared to prior weeks. We also want to see several weekly closes right around the same price *(tight* closes). This puts everybody to sleep and sends them in pursuit of greener pastures. Since volume moves price, when volume returns, it is usually off to the races for the stock. Furthermore, if we see a "BLT" setup taking place on a stock's magic line, it usually means that it is time to get out the big guns for a major advance. Remember that quiet trading usually means low risk entry.

Below is an example of a "BLT" setup from a stock that everybody and their botox "injectionista" owned in 2007.

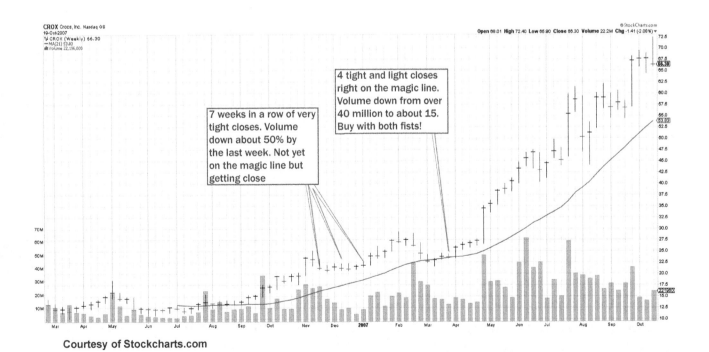

Courtesy of Stockcharts.com

## 3 – BUY EARLY IN A STOCK'S ADVANCE

We always want to buy a stock early in its advance just after its initial breakout from a long base. The average high quality momentum stock will have a 9-12 month advance out of its base. The large percentage returns go to those investors who enter during the stock's initial stages. For instance, I picked up Superstock VPHM just under $4 in 2005 during the first month of its 9 month assault towards $30. Had I waited another month, I would have had to enter 300% higher at $12. Getting in early is absolutely crucial. In this scenario, the return from an entry during the first month could have been over 800%. Investors getting in just one month later faced "only" a 100% return. That's a substantial difference.

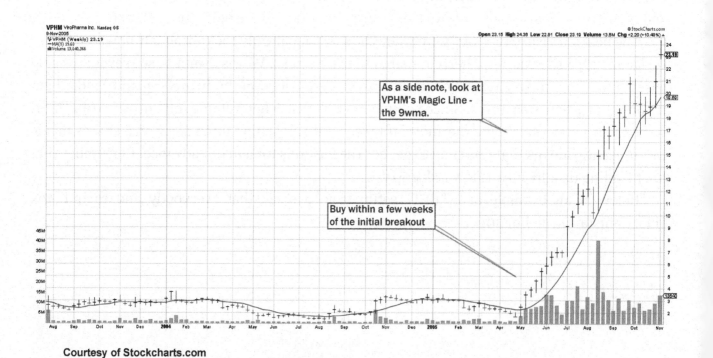

Courtesy of Stockcharts.com

## 4 – BUY THE "GAP"

After a substantial earnings surprise, most Superstocks will "gap" up and trade well above the previous day's close. Traders call this a "breakaway gap" or an "earnings gap." For example, let's assume that a $10 stock posts earnings of $0.40 per share for the quarter. The stock begins trading the following day at $14 and steadily trades higher throughout the session and closes at $16. In this scenario, "the gap" is the zone between $10 and $14- within which shares never traded.

As the stock's fundamentals have dramatically improved since the release of the earnings, this gap will be steadfastly defended under normal circumstances by the smart money any time the share price approaches this zone of support. The concept of a gap being a zone of support can be a difficult concept to understand. Because no shares traded within the gap, how can it be considered support? Rather than technical price support, it can better be described as fundamental support. I don't try to concern myself with trying to understand it logically. Just know that for our purposes, the gap should now be support.

In all honesty, if I saw a $14 Superstock report $0.40 for the quarter, I would probably violate my rules (some rules are meant to be broken, right?) and go ahead and buy it without waiting for a proper setup. However, in order to enter the position with the least amount of risk, we would love to see the stock re-test its breakout gap.

In an ideal scenario, after a surge over several days, we then want to see the stock completely demoralize the early longs as it trades down to its gap support around $14. This is precisely the point at which the early cheerleaders will dump their shares. Succumbing to their fear, they will assume that their investment thesis was all wrong. This is exactly where we want to be patiently waiting for our initial entry.

After a breakout, a test of the gap can happen on day 2, day 5, day 10, day 15...we never know. In fact, it may never happen. The stock may run higher without any meaningful pullbacks whatsoever. In those cases, we simply wait until another stock offers us a killer low-risk entry. It is often only after a successful re-test of a breakout gap that a stock's monster run truly begins. Here is an example from a stock that I owned in 2005—DXPE.

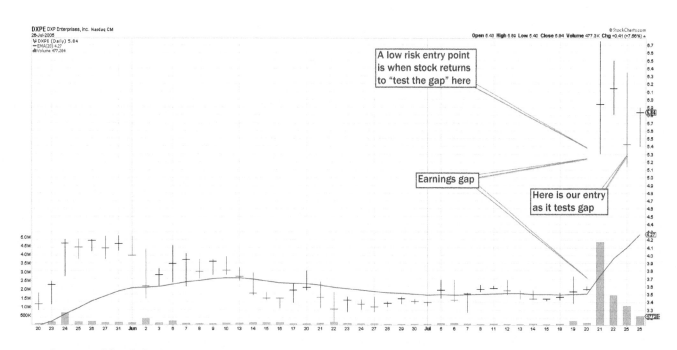

Courtesy of Stockcharts.com

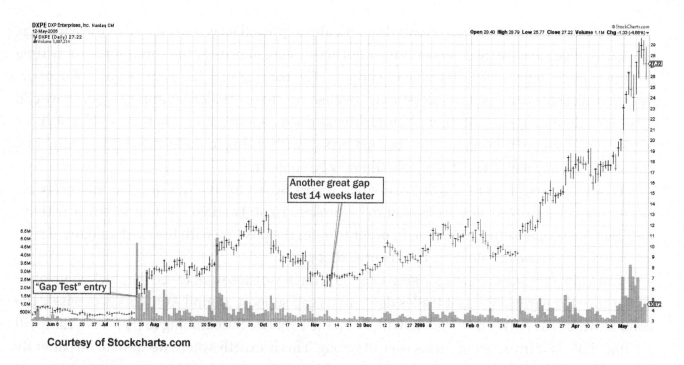

Courtesy of Stockcharts.com

## 5 – WAIT 2-3 WEEKS AFTER MONSTER EARNINGS

I have found that many of the biggest winners provide excellent low-risk entries 2-3 weeks after their breakout earnings announcement. After the initial earnings euphoria wears off, the dumb money tends to move on to the next "hot stock." As enthusiasm wanes, Superstocks tend to settle down for a couple of weeks while volume steadily declines

This cooling off period may be an outright decline to the gap or it could just be a healthy base-building period. We can't really predict how the stock will react after earnings. What we do know is that there is often a great low-risk entry 2-3 weeks after the breakout gap. If you're

Courtesy of Stockcharts.com

looking for a great low-risk entry, just give your stock some time to cool off and low and behold, a great entry may fall into your lap.

## 6 – BUY THE LOWER TRENDLINE

During the months following a breakout, great stocks will make higher highs and higher lows as they advance. They will trade within an upper and lower trendline or channel. As breakout traders are buying high risk "breakouts" at the upper trendline, you want to position yourself mentally for a possible low risk entry at the lower trendline. The dumb money will be buying hand over fist at the upper trendline as optimism reaches a pinnacle. At this point, they will think the stock is about to run away from them. Don't fall for it. This is the exact opposite of a low-risk entry.

You want to be the sheep herder who remains firmly entrenched at the lower trendline. You want to be one of only a few herders who see the trip to the lower trendline as a transitory gift. When the herd begins to panic, without thinking, be ready and willing to buy with open arms.

Of course, the more often a stock tests its lower trendline, the more likely it is to break below it. The best stocks will make infrequent trips to their lower trendlines. During their big runs, the best stocks might test their lower trendline four to six times before things head south. If a stock repeatedly tests its lower trendline in a short period of time, it may be nearing the end of its run.

Here is an example of a stock that I have never traded just to show you how violently a stock can bounce off its lower trendline.

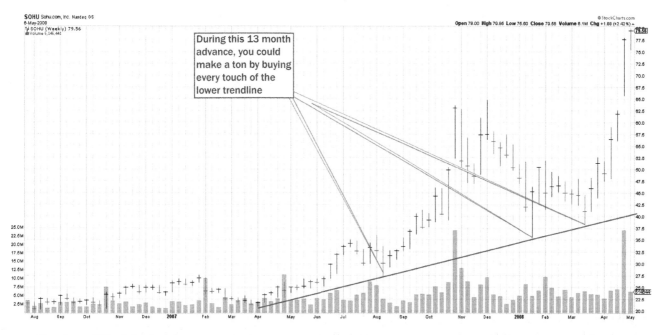

Courtesy of Stockcharts.com

## OTHER LOW RISK POTENTIAL ENTRIES

The following entry points often present themselves when selling has been exhausted. In strong stocks, we often see significant snapback rallies after one of the following low risk entries appear.

### BUY THE STINE "BCD" SETUP

A favorable risk/reward setup can occur when a stock in a multi-month uptrend declines and makes three lower lows within a short period of time (usually within 4 to 5 weeks). My rule of thumb is to look for a stock (or the market) to make three lower lows with the third low ideally even slightly below the trend of the first two. This is my "BCD (Buy,Cry,Die) setup" From a sentiment standpoint, "bottom picking" investors trying to time the stock's bottom BUY the first spike lower. At the second lower spike, these new investors CRY in anguish. At the third and final lower spike, they DIE and sell their shares in exasperation. The third spike lower is precisely where you want to be waiting with open arms. I've seen hundreds of stocks rocket out of such triple oversold conditions. Things in life tend to come in threes. Stock patterns are no different.

This example is a particularly memorable one from 2007. TNH was a very popular Superstock that was correcting in an orderly fashion culminating with a "BCD" buy signal on its daily chart.

Courtesy of Stockcharts.com

### BUY A LOWER BOLLINGER BAND RE-ENTRY

I don't want to get too bogged down into technical analysis, but for those so inclined: a sharp pullback *below* a stock's lower Bollinger Band followed by the first daily close *ABOVE* its lower Bollinger Band can be a great entry point. The Bollinger Band is essentially a measure of stock price deviation. When anything deviates substantially from its norm in a short period of time, it tends to snap back in short order.

Here are some examples from Mosaic Corporation's (MOS) daily chart from 2008:

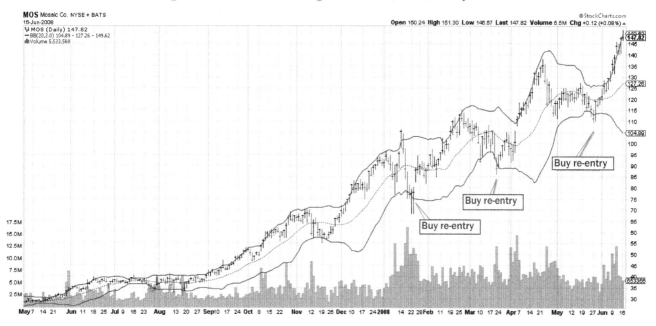

Courtesy of Stockcharts.com

## BUY THE DUMB FRIEND INDICATOR

Everybody, and I mean everybody, has a friend who is led entirely by his emotions. For our purposes, let's call him our "dumb friend." This friend is *ALWAYS* selling at the bottom and buying at the top. This is the same friend who devotes an hour each and every evening to watching *Mad Money*. Let's imagine that you are licking your chops as the price of your favorite stock has been falling day after day. You then get a call out of the blue from your friend who tells you that he just sold his entire position in this stock.

This could be your cue that the time is just about right to get in. Remember that your friend has been reading every article, reading every message board post, watching every tick, and has been consuming financial television "junk food" every day. He is an excellent barometer of the prevailing sentiment in your stock. Buying low sentiment is a great way to make a fortune.

## *OTHER LOWER RISK MOVING AVERAGES TO LOOK FOR*

Although we will be looking for the previously discussed "magic line" of a stock, there are a few standard moving-averages that may serve to provide low risk support.

## 10 DAY MOVING AVERAGE (10 DMA)

When a Superstock moves out of its current base to a new higher base, there's a good chance that it will bounce higher off its 10 dma along the way. If you feel that a stock is going much higher in a very short period of time, this is often a great place for an entry especially if it coincides with the lower trendline.

In 2012, PCLN was a great example of a 10 dma "hugger." It bounced aggressively higher every time it hit its 10 day moving average. Here is its daily chart (not weekly).

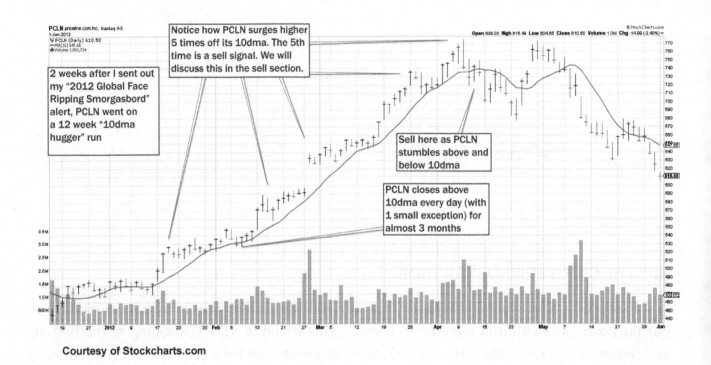

Courtesy of Stockcharts.com

## 20 DAY MOVING AVERAGE (20 DMA)

Once a stock's 10 dma stops working as support, the next moving average of interest is the 20 day moving average. A strong 20 dma trend can last a few months after a stock's initial breakout. Beyond that, a strong stock will typically trade below its 20 dma and wait for its 50 day moving average.

Goldfield Corp (GV) is an example of a 2012 earnings winner hugging its 20 dma. It got a little weak in May as global markets dove, but it ultimately continued to press higher. Notice the "staircase" as it steps up from $0.30 to $0.60, to $1.20 to $1.50. This is the most powerful pattern in existence. GV was a "penny stock" but it was a big time backlog/earnings winner. Here is its daily chart.

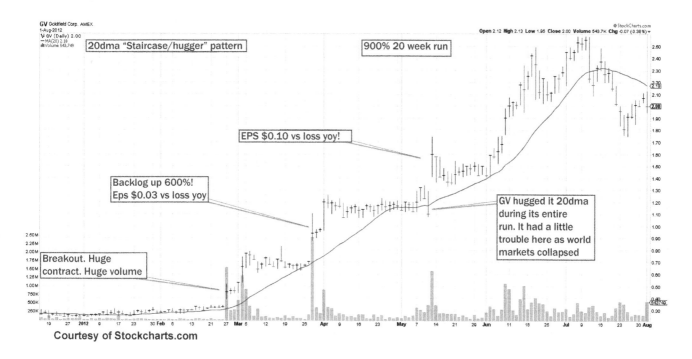

Courtesy of Stockcharts.com

## 50 DAY MOVING AVERAGE OR 10 WEEK MOVING AVERAGE RISING INTO A BASE

By far the safest moving average entry point is the 50 dma or 10 wma. After a month or two of advance, most of the strongest stocks simply run out of steam. Many will rest in a well-defined base until the 50 dma eventually catches up. If a stock has made a huge advance and trades well above these averages, there's a chance that the stock could fall substantially until it meets up with its rising 50 dma or 10 wma.

I prefer the 10 wma on the weekly chart vs. the 50 dma on the daily chart, but either one provides a great level of protection from a reward/risk perspective. One thing to note is that even though 10 weeks is 50 days of trading, the 10 wma and 50 dma are usually at slightly different prices. Buying either of these averages rising into a solid base is usually a recipe for a great low risk trade. You want to have the safety net of a base in combination with a strong moving average to greatly diminish downside risk.

Many traders will place their stop losses at the 50 dma. In order to have the fewest number of passengers on the train, it is the job of the market maker and the institutions to push the stock *below* the 50 dma to get traders to sell out of their positions. For this reason, it is common to see a strong stock trade 5-10% below its 50 dma for several days before it resumes its uptrend. If your stock trades below the 50 dma for more than a week or two, it very well could be a dud.

Remember this one rule: all momentum stocks visit their 50 day moving averages or 10 week moving averages within a few months of their breakout. If your stock trades 50% above its 50 dma several months after its initial breakout, it is likely that you will be able to buy it significantly cheaper sometime soon. Worst case, you'll be able to buy it again in the current vicinity when the 50 day catches up in a month or so.

BIDU is a stock that I've never been able to get myself to buy due to excessive risk from what I believe to be "overvaluation." The darn stock keeps proving me wrong, however. In 2009, its 10 wma rose into the stock's base a few times and triggered a surge in the share price.

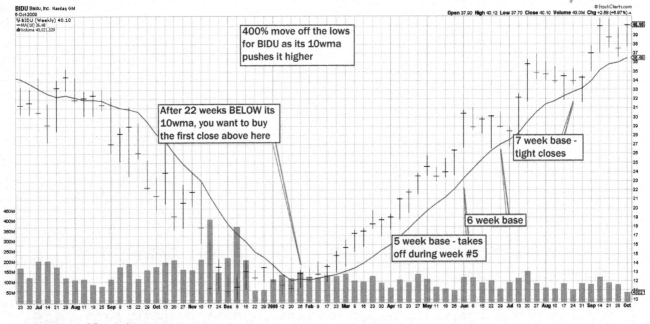

Courtesy of Stockcharts.com

## 200 DAY MOVING AVERAGE AND 20/30 WEEK MOVING AVERAGES

Most of the big long-term winners eventually visit their longer term moving averages such as the 200 day moving average, 20 week moving average or 30 week moving average. Investing in shorter term movers, we usually won't be looking for such situations, but if you find yourself in a long term play, a visit to these moving averages can be an excellent low risk place to enter or add to a position.

Courtesy of Stockcharts.com

"Potash" was a "Super-Theme" in 2007 and 2008. All of the potash "plays" performed spectacularly. My favorite was Potash Corp. Its 30 wma provided excellent support all the way up.

## POSITION SIZING

*"Wide diversification is a hedge against your lack of knowledge."*
William O'Neil

Position sizing and diversification are *ENTIRELY* dependent upon your risk profile and skill set. This is a topic that I can't give you much advice about. To determine your risk profile, you need to take into consideration your tolerance for risk, your age, your goals, your personality, your future financial obligations, and...the list goes on. You may have made the decision not to put more than 1% of your portfolio into a single stock. That is entirely up to you.

The fact of the matter is that most investors vastly overestimate their risk tolerance. A 40% drawdown? No problem, they say. Well, in reality, when this investor is faced with the common 20% account pullback, he instinctively liquidates his portfolio and swears that he will never again return to the stock market casino.

I have been an advocate of the Kelly Criterion in terms of determining my own position size. Developed in the 1950's, the Kelly formula determines your position size in proportion to the extent of your edge. Take 2 scenarios. In scenario 1, you are 70% sure that your stock will go up 20%. In scenario 2, you are 95% sure that your stock will go up 130%. The risk/reward ratio of scenario 2 would justify a larger position size. If you are 97% sure that your stock will increase 500%, your position size would be larger still.

There have been times when I have taken massive multi-million dollar positions in single stocks when I perceived that there was a massive disconnect between a stock's price and its value. In such times, I would have 90% or more of my net worth in one or two stocks that offered massive potential reward with very limited risk. The other 10% or so of my portfolio would be in a handful of stocks that didn't offer the same risk/reward characteristics. I do not recommend such a concentrated portfolio for most investors.

Ultimately, my portfolio concentration in any one particular stock is dependent on:

1) Whether or not there are other stocks available with similar risk/reward characteristics.

2) How much capital I have to play with: larger capital base=less individual exposure on a percentage basis.

3) The state of the market: where we are in the market cycle.

4) The extent of my edge: the probability and potential upside vs. probability and potential downside of the stock in question; risk/reward.

Warren Buffett has said that we should invest as if we will only own twenty stocks over the course of our entire lifetimes. Although a bit extreme, this has been the mantra I've tried to live by during my investment career. The fact of the matter is that if you are lucky enough to stumble upon five stocks with 200% upside, why would you consider taking money out of those five stocks to invest in something that you think might only have 15% upside?

To amass his fortune, there were seasons during Buffet's career when he held concentrated stakes in individual stocks. In fact, at one point, 40% of his Berkshire portfolio was invested in American Express. His position concentrations were even larger when his career began.

This is the way I see it: every day across the globe, millions of people start their own businesses. Not only do they put every penny of their savings into their business but they borrow a majority of the required capital from third parties. People don't think twice about doing such a thing.

The sad reality is that most new businesses fail. The risk/reward profile of such an endeavor is skewed heavily to the negative. On the other hand, a majority of stock market investors would never even think about allocating 50% of their capital to a hyper-growth public company that has a long-term track record of success led by an all-star management team (at a low risk entry of course). Most investors would never consider doing such a thing even if all of their due diligence points to a 700% return.

Buffet has said, "If it's your game, diversification doesn't make sense. It's crazy to put money into your twentieth choice rather than your first choice. The "Lebron James" analogy: if you have Lebron James on your team, don't take him out of the game just to make room for someone else. If you have a harem of forty women, you never really get to know any of them well."

Buffet continued, "Charlie (Munger) and I operated mostly with five positions. If I were running 50, 100, 200 million, I would have 80% in five positions, with 25% for the largest.....In 1951 I put the bulk of my net worth into GEICO... There were various times I would have gone up to 75%, even in the past few years. If it's your game and you really know your business, you can load up."

Buffet on leverage, "We've suffered quotational loss, 50% movements. That's why you should never borrow money. We don't want to get into situations where anyone can pull the rug out from under our feet."

Here's my advice if you feel like you want to concentrate your portfolio and perhaps use a little leverage. To keep your overall level of risk to a minimum, I suggest you do this: take a small portion of your overall portfolio (5%-10% for instance) and open up a separate margin account that you use only to invest in the rare "risky" Superstock. On the off-chance you uncover five or six game-breaking stocks, you may decide to utilize margin in this small account.

This way, you'll be able to see firsthand if you can significantly beat the market without taking on substantial overall portfolio risk. The formula for market success is massive trial and error along with dozens of small failures along the way. By isolating your "experimental account" in such a fashion, you can learn to beat the market without putting your entire life savings at risk.

In such an account, if you are so inclined, I would only recommend utilizing leverage on the rare occasion that you have several skewed risk/reward positions. I have used leverage in the past when the odds were not in my favor. The consequences were dire.

* I should clarify what I believe to be a margin account. I just recently saw a firm offering 10 to 1 leverage! Opening such an account is insanity. In this section, I am talking about your garden variety 2 to 1 (maximum) margin account.

## LET YOUR WINNERS RUN

*"For investors as a whole, returns decrease as motion increases."*
Warren Buffet

After screening for your stock, determining a price target, waiting for the proper buy point, determining your position size, and ultimately jumping into the shark-infested waters, it is imperative that you let your winning stocks run. I can't stress this point enough. Investing is never as easy as it sounds; since a majority of your stocks will most likely prove to be small losers, you must let your few winners really run wild.

After spending so much time flipping through charts, researching fundamentals, and then waiting, why in the world would you sell your stock a couple of days later for a 5% gain? It makes no sense whatsoever, but that's precisely what a majority of investors do. Due to their primal urge to be right at any cost, these investors are more than happy to forego any potential future gains. For most people, it's all about instant gratification isn't it? There is absolutely no way to win big over the long run if you don't let your best stocks appreciate significantly.

Buy your stock when everything lines up in your favor. Do *ALL* of your worrying *BEFORE* you make the buy decision and then let the stock do its thing. Don't even think about selling it until it triggers a sell signal.

## SWING AWAY IN THE SPRING

The market has many cycles and many personalities. There will be many months, if not years, when that perfect fat pitch never presents itself. During these long, brutally cold winters of life, many traders exit the market altogether and never return. Most traders try to fight the winter tooth and nail and end up brutalized and demoralized by the market's unrelenting vicious nature. They see their portfolio succumb to a death by a thousand cuts. But it is during these long winters that the very best traders step away to focus on improving their lives and their future trading.

But as sure as the tide goes out, the tide comes back in. As sure as the sun sets, the sun rises. As sure as somebody dies, someone else is born.

And just as it appears as if the eternal investment winter will never end, lo and behold a beautiful and blissful spring emerges out of nowhere. It is often during the early springs of the market cycle when truly extraordinary gains are as easy as taking candy from a baby. These are the very rare times in the market cycle when casually scrolling through charts for an hour can yield a dozen stocks that you are sure will rise several-fold.

The point is this: the thousands of hours of study, preparation, and hard work we put into investing are all for one reason. The patience and self-discipline we cultivate during the long falls and winters of the market cycle are eventually rewarded...in a *BIG* way. All of the sacrifice and every ounce of energy we put into this endeavor we call trading is for one reason:

*TO BE FULLY PREPARED FOR, FULLY AWARE OF, FULLY EMOTIONALLY STABLE FOR, AND TO BE COMPLETELY CONFIDENT IN TAKING FULL ADVANTAGE OF THE EARLY SPRINGTIMES THAT PRESENT THEMSELVES WHEN WE LEAST EXPECT.*

I would say that these springtime conditions are present less than 10 percent of the time. If you only invested during these brief windows of opportunity and did absolutely *NOTHING* the other 90% of the time, you would be a world-class investor.

The problem I continually see is that even when investors recognize the dawn of a new spring, they invest as they always have. They don't "seize the moment" so to speak. They don't fully realize how rare and "life-changing" these brief windows of opportunity can be. For example, Tony Loton (my editor) came off the sidelines and recognized an immense springtime opportunity in the spring (go figure) of 2009. He seized the brief window and swung much harder than he would have in any other market condition. For his efforts, he walked away with a 3,000% portfolio return.

So, when things don't seem to be going right and great stocks and great setups don't seem to be materializing like they used to, don't risk any capital. Try to be fully aware of the situation at hand and just step away until a better season comes along. During these times, remember the old adages—"Cash is King" and "Cash is a position."

Eventually, when things do take a turn for the better and you once again start seeing blockbuster "once-in-a-lifetime" opportunities, you must work harder than ever before and take confident swings at the fat pitches being thrown from every direction. These opportunities are never around for very long. Take every advantage of them.

## DON'T FOCUS ON THE GENERAL MARKET

Once everything sets up in your favor, don't spend time worrying about the general market. I have a friend who constantly speculated about market direction: "S&P 1250 before 1300," "S&P 1400, then 1300, then 1450 *before* the crash" or "the current market exactly parallels how it was in 1997...thus we are going 40% higher from here." And all of these statements would be in the course of one week!

I must note that these days my friend is focused much more on patience and individual stocks. Because of this, he has been knocking the ball out of the park.

The problem is that such beliefs about the overall market constantly shake us out of our best stocks. I know several investors who spend 90% of their time trying to *predict* the market, and 10% of their time trying to find winning stocks. That is not an exaggeration on my part. This has been, and continues to be, a recipe for failure.

The ratio needs to be more like *3%* market/*97%* winning stocks.

As I detail in Appendix A: "Major Market Inflection Points," there are those rare instances when the risk/reward ratio of the general market becomes heavily skewed against you. More often than not, it is precisely at these key junctures (usually a little before) that your Superstocks are flashing major sell signals as well. These are the outlying times when it may be advisable to exit your stock regardless of its individual technical conditions. But it bears repeating that the odds are quite high that your individual stocks will be singing the same tune, sending clear signals to head for the exits.

That being said, a vast majority of the time, I plead with you...do not spend time worrying about the general market. Let your Superstock do all the talking. Worrying about the general market will undoubtedly decrease your general level of happiness and will sabotage your ability to trade the very best stocks to the best of your abilities. If the market crashes, and your sell-point is triggered, so be it; At least you aren't wasting your life worrying about *potential* market scenarios.

## IGNORE DAILY ACCOUNT FLUCTUATIONS

Watching your account balance from day to day will absolutely drive you insane. Watching your digits move up and down day in and day out will cause you to exit a profitable position. I guarantee it. During my biggest run, I only looked at my account value when I believed that it had crossed another seven figure threshold. The rest of the time, I simply sat tight and enjoyed life.

# CHAPTER 10

## *The Super Laws of Selling— Mastering the Art of Selling High Risk*

*"Buy when most people (including experts) are actively pessimistic, and sell when they are actively optimistic."*

Benjamin Graham

*"Our research indicated that liquidations are vastly more important than initiations. If you initiate purely randomly, you do surprisingly well with a good liquidation criterion."*

William Eckhardt

Now that you know what to buy and when to buy it, let's move into a discussion about the most effective, yet most unpopular times to sell them.

I admit that this section is long. The topic of *selling* is boring. This section is definitely not politically correct. Nobody ever likes to talk about when to sell a stock. Books generally shy away from it. Studying selling is like pulling teeth. Selling is Wall Street's dirty little secret. Wall Street has groomed the dumb money to buy and hold forever.

But selling is *ABSOLUTELY ESSENTIAL* to success in the market. There is no way around it; where you sell a stock is 1,000 times more important than where you buy a stock. Think about it logically for a second...how could selling not be more important? If you master this one thing while not learning a single thing about what to buy or when to buy it, your returns would outperform 99% of your fellow investors. Seriously!

The average investor is notoriously bad at selling at the top. This is precisely why there are so few genuinely great short sellers in the market. For me, the art of the sale is much more difficult to master than the art of the buy. There is no surefire way to consistently get out at the very top. That's why it is so vitally important to sell as your stock is rising (at key junctures) even though at the time it feels like the most idiotic thing you could possibly do. Is it just me or doesn't it seem like everyone you know is always selling their positions at a stop-loss on the way down—after a big selloff—and more than likely at a loss?

The best times to exit are always at the sentiment extremes, when your ego least wants you to sell. These are the times when you are certain that, by selling, you will leave vast profits on the table. It goes against human nature, but the best time to get out is when everything looks great, everything is on track, there are no roadblocks ahead, there are a hundred reasons to buy and everybody universally agrees that there are absolutely no reasons to sell.

Imagine that your stock has moved 100% over several weeks without a meaningful pullback, you have made tens of thousands of dollars, you are patting yourself on the back, you find yourself surfing Priceline for an all-inclusive Tahiti package for you and your wife, and heck you are even considering writing a book! If this is the case, the alarm bells should be going off in your head. You may not find one surefire technical indicator signaling the top, but the series of events mentioned above are about the best possible indication that your fortunes are about to swiftly turn south. These are precisely the times when Murphy's Law kicks in.

I don't have to give you a million technical indicators for when to sell. After months of advance, when things are great and getting better, when the blockbuster earnings you anticipated months ago are now public, when *Investor's Business Daily* is prominently featuring your stock and when everybody is talking about your stock...*SELL!* It's as simple as that.

But to help you out a little, I have listed several liquidation criteria in this section that will hopefully allow you to exit your position with most of your gains intact. Always remember that when a Superstock's run ends, it ends in dramatic fashion. We are not talking about a run-of-the-mill 10% pullback. For the best performers, we are talking about a full-blown 50-70% shellacking that wipes everybody out. In the time it took these stocks to make their entire bull runs, it will take less than a third of that time for many of these stocks to entirely erase their gains.

When the music ends, you must be willing to sell at a moment's notice. As they say: sell first, and ask questions later. Sell when you can, not when you have to.

In the real world, I am notoriously bad about giving advice about selling. I am always getting out way too early. For this reason, I rarely tell somebody exactly when to sell. If I do, they will get mad at me for missing out on 40% of the move. The exact top is quite difficult to pinpoint in practice. But what I can give you here are some solid general guidelines for exiting when risk/reward is no longer favorable and when a low risk buy point is light years away. Since our goal is to *always* be in highly favorable risk/reward scenarios, we want to exit when a majority of the easy gains have been taken.

We first tackle technical sell signals. I have found that they are vastly more important than fundamental sell criteria. The simple truth is that the technicals will tell you to get out *well before* the fundamental reasons present themselves.

## THE 16 SUPER LAWS OF SELLING TECHNICAL RISK

*"Don't worry about where the prices are going. Worry about what you are going to do when they get there."*
Richard Dennis


*"Exit is the most important aspect of trading—very few study it."*
Bernard Baruch


Ordinarily, no one single technical sell indicator can reliably get you out at the exact top of a stock's advance. But when you start seeing a few of the following sell indicators triggering at the same time, you are best advised to sell first and ask questions later.

Assuming a stock's fundamentals are still intact, selling a risky price certainly shouldn't prevent us from buying the stock back at a later date when the next low risk buy point presents itself.


### 1 – SELL TIME AND LARGE DEVIATION FROM 10 WEEK MOVING AVERAGE OR MAGIC LINE

On your stock's initial breakout from its base, it really doesn't matter too much how far it trades above key support levels. If a stock doubles out of a strong long term base on its earnings announcement, it will likely be 100% above key short- and long-term moving averages. This would not be an automatic sell signal as this is just the first week of the stock's advance. Alternatively, if your chosen stock trades 60% or more *above* its magic line (possibly 10 wma or 50 dma) anytime after the first six weeks of its initial breakout, it may be time to take some chips off the table and wait until support catches up.

The biggest gainers ALWAYS visit their magic lines several times during their advances. If your stock is 100% above its magic line, one of two things is bound to happen: 1) Your stock is going to completely fall apart, or 2) It will wait patiently for a couple of months until things settle down and the magic line plays catch up. In either case, there are better places for your cash.

In my research, I have found that after surging off their magic lines, the strongest stocks hit an intermediate term peak no later than 7 to 10 weeks later. So, if your stock hits its 10 wma support and surges higher for 7-10 weeks without testing its magic line, it could be a great place to exit.

Jones Soda offered four major clear-cut weekly sell signals in April of 2007.

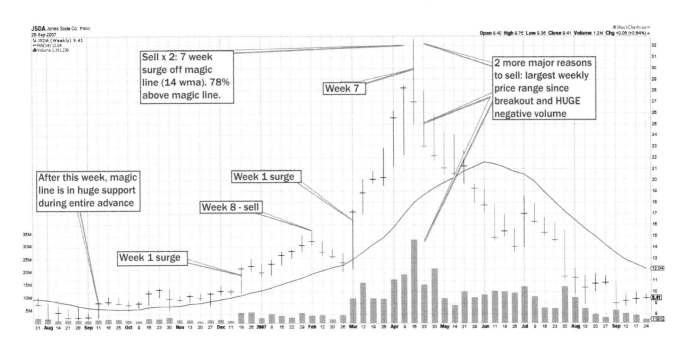

Courtesy of Stockcharts.com

## 2 – SELL AFTER A 9 TO 15 MONTH ADVANCE FROM BREAKOUT

Many of the biggest winners start collapsing between 9 and 15 months after their initial breakout. This is a pretty broad window. The point is to be extremely cautious when holding a winning stock beyond the 9 month mark. I don't know why, but there's something about 9 months. 9 months, 3 seasons, 3 earnings reports, 3 trimesters, 1 newborn baby. As you will see in Chapter 12, many of my big winners collapsed exactly on cue at 9 months. In light of this, if I'm sitting on a big gain at the 9 month mark, I'm out. Here is Graham Corp. (GHM) from a few years ago.

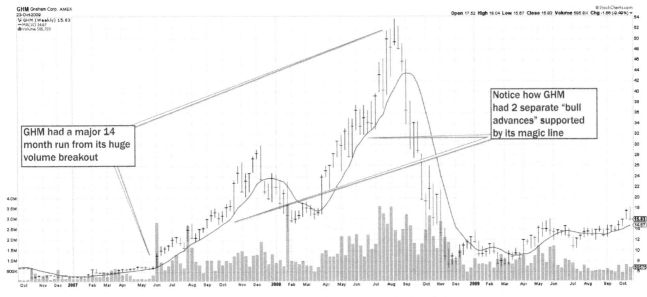

Courtesy of Stockcharts.com

## 3 – SELL A FLATTENING OR DECLINING MAGIC LINE AFTER A LONG ADVANCE

The strongest stocks have magic lines that steadily climb for the first six months or so of an advance. During this time, the magic line may flatten out for a few weeks, but you don't want to see it decline. Beyond the first six months of an advance, if a stock's magic line flattens out for an extended period of time or if God forbid, it starts to decline after a long period of highly volatile trading, it is time to move on to the next winning stock.

Notice that I have not said to automatically sell when your stock breaches its magic line. I bring this up because the traditional rule of thumb on Wall Street is to sell when your stock falls below this key level (again usually 50 dma and/or 10 wma). Since so many investors are

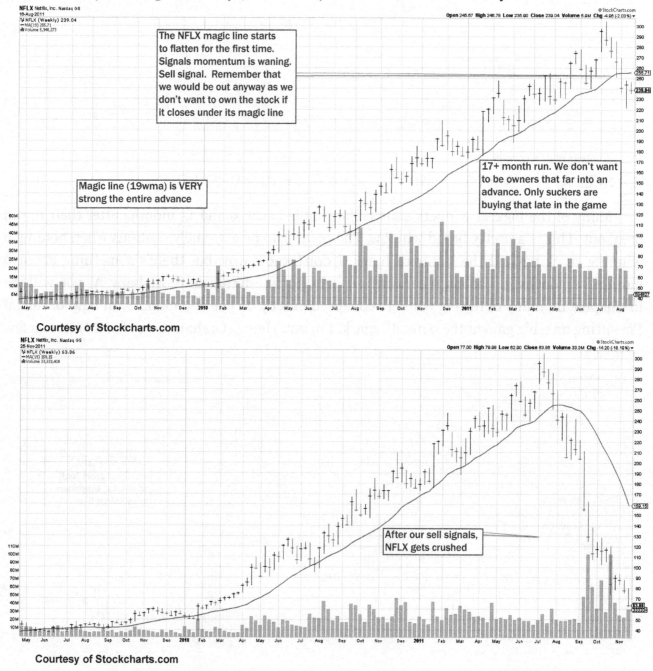

Courtesy of Stockcharts.com

programmed to do so, it is almost automatic these days to see a strong stock trade below its magic line for a brief period of time intra-week to "shake out the loose hands" before continuing on its advance higher.

There are just too many false signals to make it a hard and fast sell rule. The key thing to watch is where the stock closes at the end of the week. Let's assume that a magic line has been excellent support for a stock's weekly closing price for several months. If your stock closes *below* the magic line at the end of the week for the first time, I would most likely sell and only re-enter if and when it rises back above the line. Above is an example from the Netflix (NFLX) run of 2010-2011.

## 4 – SELL 4 SURGES OFF THE "MAGIC LINE"

The strongest stocks will surge off their magic line only a handful of times during their advance. I have found that many stocks turn down after their fourth or fifth surge off the magic line. At the tail end, a fading stock will no longer make a strong move off its magic line, but instead, it will trade erratically above and below its line for several weeks in a row. This is classic topping action. In any case, if your stock has trended higher for several months and has advanced significantly off its magic line on four or five occasions, the risk is on. Viropharma (VPHM) had four distinctive surges off its magic line before the party started to peter out.

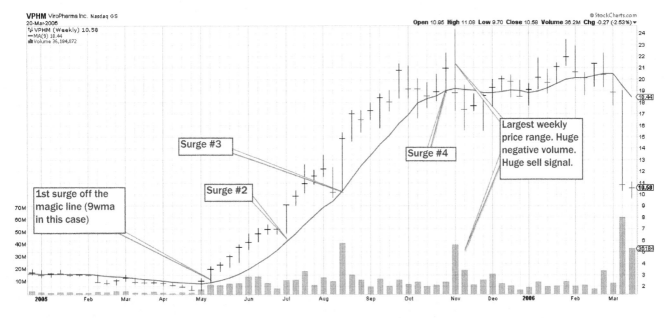

Courtesy of Stockcharts.com

## 5 – SELL A PARABOLIC RUN

At the end of a longer term bull advance, individual stocks and markets tend to have large buying climaxes that mark the end of their run in very dramatic fashion. A good rule of thumb is: the longer the bull trend, the larger the vertical "climax move." Did I mention that these parabolas end in dramatic fashion? The funny thing about parabolic chart patterns is that there is so much noise, so much enthusiasm, so much buying pressure, so much bearish capitulation, and so much certainty from the bulls ("this time is different" blah, blah, blah) that it is extremely difficult to determine the precise tops of such advances.

Assuming you bought a parabolic stock at a much lower level; consider yourself very lucky if you get caught up in such a euphoric frenzy. Chances are good that you are sitting on a *TON* of profit. The toughest part of such a move is determining when to sell. As you will see in Chapter 12, once these moves end, they collapse in the blink of an eye. They can decline 30% or more in the days after the top is reached.

The final day and the final week of this type of move most often display the largest trading range with the highest volume of the entire longer-term advance. Whenever caught in such a move in the past, I never quite knew when to sell. I often got burned due to my lack of experience and lack of sell rules.

These days, I would most certainly sell a stock that is trading well above its upper trendline, if:

1. the stock had a huge daily price move (not necessarily huge percentage move) that was much larger than previous price moves,

2. it was well above its 5 day moving average, and

3. if I missed 1 and 2, I would sell once the stock broke below its 5 day moving average.

Since the ultimate consequences are so dire, I certainly wouldn't hold it against you if you sold on any old up day after the stock's trend turned vertical. Some textbook parabolic moves in the shipping, currency, commodity, and global markets were Dry Ships (DRYS) in 2007, the Swiss Franc in August, 2011, Silver in April, 2011, and the NASDAQ in 2000.

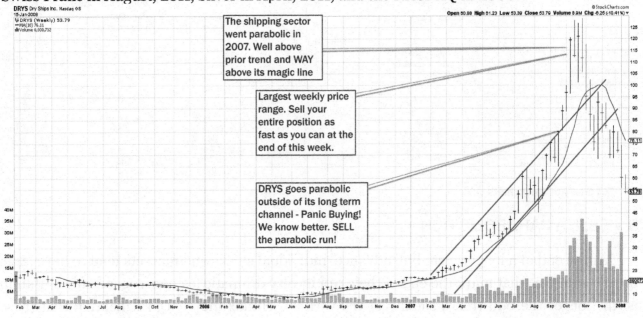

Courtesy of Stockcharts.com

Courtesy of Stockcharts.com

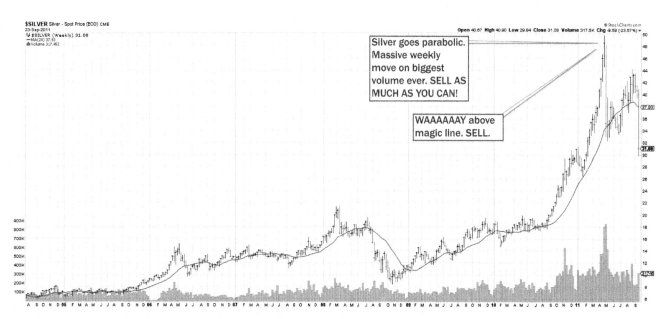

Courtesy of Stockcharts.com

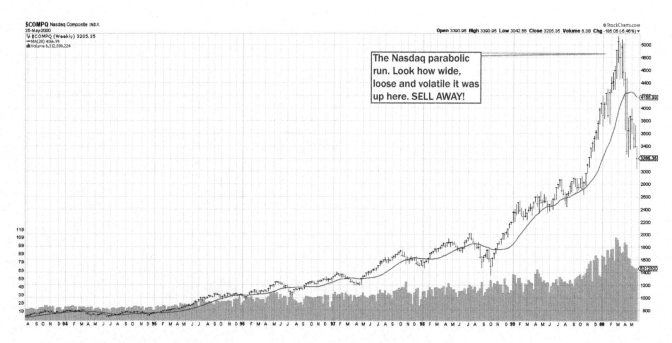

Courtesy of Stockcharts.com

## 6 – SELL LARGE PRICE RANGES

Let's say that your stock has traded 80% higher over the past three weeks. As it has trended higher, its daily range (difference between daily high and low) is $0.50 on average. During the stock's advance, the largest daily range was $1. All of a sudden, your stock moves up $2.25 in one day—which happens to be four and a half times its average daily range.

After an extended trend, this is often a sign of short- or intermediate-term buying capitulation. Buyers who missed the advance are all piling into the stock all at once fearing they will miss the move. On such a buying climax, volume is almost always well above average. After such price action, there may not be anybody left to buy.

The average range on the weekly chart is even more important. As we now know, weekly charts are much more important than daily charts in determining long term turning points. An extreme price range on a weekly bar coinciding with large volume while well into a stock's advance is often an indicator of longer-term buying capitulation.

When a stock deviates so violently in the span of one week, the entire investment community now knows about it. Remember that we want to buy when shareholders are bored and nobody is talking about our stock. On the other hand, we want to be selling when everybody is excited about our stock being in the limelight.

Here's an example of a gigantic weekly price range from a stock I owned in 2006: Titanium Metals (TIE).

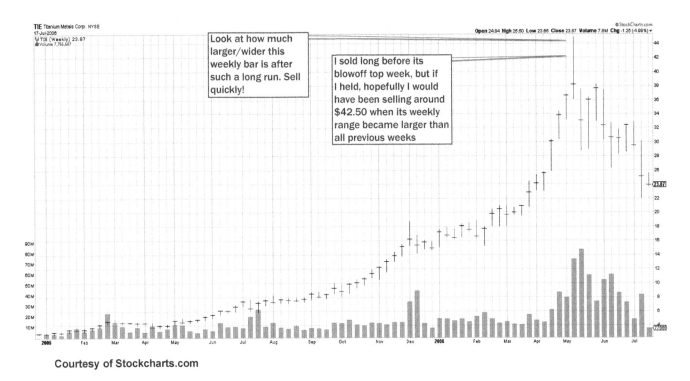

Courtesy of Stockcharts.com

## 7 – SELL A FALLING KNIFE BELOW THE LOWER CHANNEL

If your stock suddenly falls a large percentage and cuts below its lower upward trending channel, sell immediately and ask questions later. Trend reversals can be swift and steep. There is often no fundamental reason for such a steep decline. If your stock violates its long-term upward channel, get out of Dodge!

Here is an example from a rapidly growing Superstock from 2012: Westport Innovations (WPRT).

Courtesy of Stockcharts.com

## 8 – SELL VOLATILITY WHEN A STOCK IS EXTENDED

As our stocks advance, we want to see them form boring low volume bases in very tight price ranges. If our stock is well above its key moving averages, and volatility and volume begin to increase, you must take notice. Especially watch for an extended stock whose average daily trading range expands on heavy volume while its closing prices remain in a tight range. I like to refer to such behavior as the "shake-out before a reversal." With such price action, longs and shorts get thrown around and usually get totally confused by the stock's erratic behavior. This type of action is routinely seen at tops and bottoms.

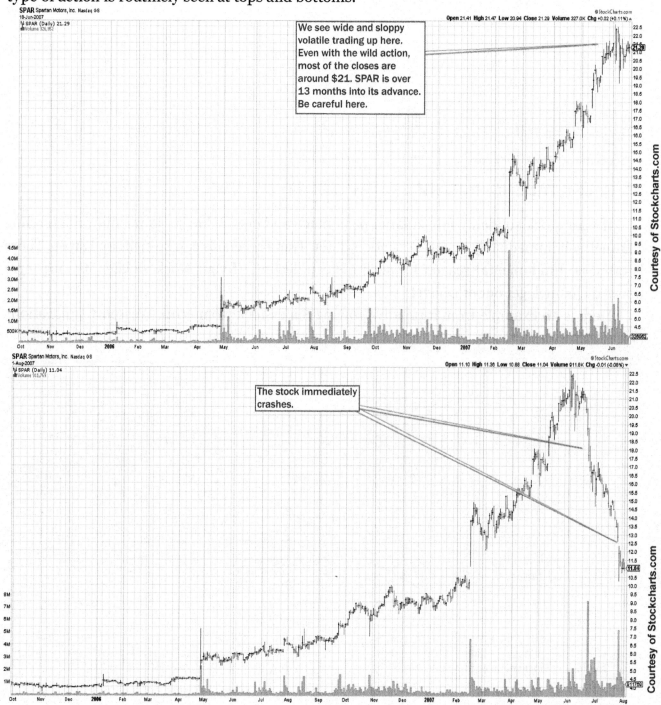

We see wide and sloppy volatile trading up here. Even with the wild action, most of the closes are around $21. SPAR is over 13 months into its advance. Be careful here.

The stock immediately crashes.

Above is an example of wide and sloppy trading indicating a potential reversal. An old holding of mine—Spartan Motors (SPAR).

Below is another example from an old favorite of mine—Bolt Technology (BOLT).

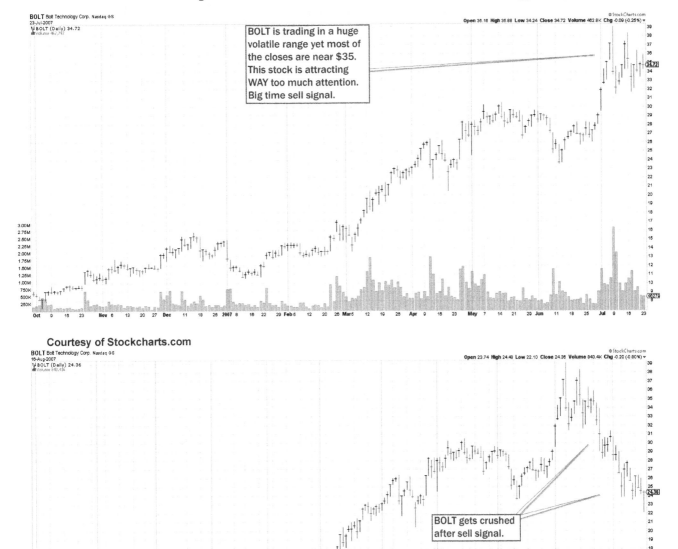

Courtesy of Stockcharts.com

Courtesy of Stockcharts.com

## 9 – SELL A WEEKLY EXHAUSTION GAP

If your stock has been trending higher for several months and *gaps* up to a new weekly high, this might be your signal to exit. This is a classic sign of buyers trying to get in at any price.

Gaps are great when they come off solid bases, but gaps well into up-trends are the kiss of death. This is an excellent example of a weekly gap at an extremely stretched overbought condition *WELL* into a stock's advance. Sell as fast as humanly possible.

This is an ugly weekly gap from one of my top 3 biggest portfolio gainers of all time. Viropharma (VPHM).

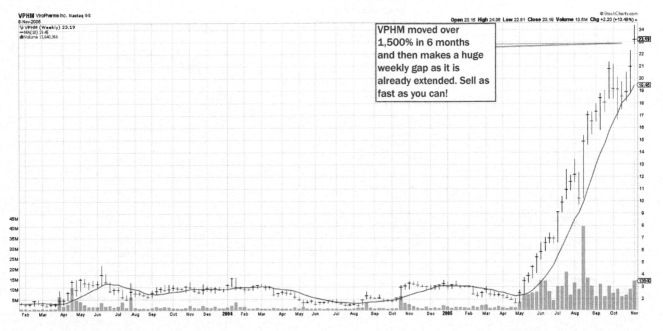

VPHM moved over 1,500% in 6 months and then makes a huge weekly gap as it is already extended. Sell as fast as you can!

Courtesy Stockcharts.com

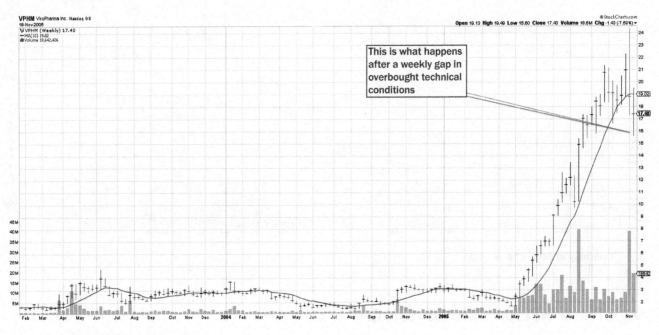

This is what happens after a weekly gap in overbought technical conditions

Courtesy of Stockcharts.com

## 10 – SELL AT YOUR STOP LOSS

Some people have a strict 5% stop loss for when to exit a trade no questions asked. For others, it may be 8% or 10%. Personally, I don't have a "standard" stop loss. Different stocks have different patterns, so in my book the stop-loss threshold is entirely dependent on volume, price, and volatility going into the trade. For more information on stop orders, you may want to check out my editor's book: *Stop Orders: A Practical Guide to Using Stop Orders for Traders and Investors* by Tony Loton. Whatever your individual stop-loss threshold may be, make sure you have determined it before you place the trade, and stick to it no matter what if things go south.

## 11 – SELL $25-$30

After breaking out of a strong base, it seems that momentum traders have no qualms whatsoever about bidding a hot stock up to the $25-$30 area. Beyond $30, the smart money tends to sell high prices as the risk reward ratio is no longer in their favor. After a large move to this level, the high percentage gains are no longer there for the taking.

The exact tops of most of my biggest winners—ALDA, INCX (LOCM), DXPE, FORD, AIRM, and JSDA—were all within $29-$31. The tops of TRT, TRCR, SPAR, VPHM, and TRMM ($27) were all right at $25. In most instances, $25 or $30 proved to be a lifetime top or multi-year top. Many of these stocks rang this significant price level and immediately crashed. I think it's safe to say that if you purchase a stock at $4, regardless of your ultimate price target, it is probably a sensible idea to dump it if it trades anywhere close to $25. I wouldn't get greedy trying to sell at $30.

## 12 – SELL A MISTAKE

If you made a mistake (there will be many) and your stock is not acting right and is going in the wrong direction, simply sell and move on.

## 13 – SELL 3 HIGHER HIGHS

Exactly the opposite of buying the third lower low, as described previously in my "B,C,D" setup. In combination with other sell signals, if your stock spikes to 3 or more new highs (preferably with the third high above the trend of the first 2) within four or five weeks, it could be a sign of buyers' exhaustion. After each spike, we want to see the stock immediately sell off. Like all other indicators discussed, it always depends on the stage of the advance and whether or not other indicators are in confirmation. Here's an example from a stock that I watched from a distance in 2011—Green Mountain Coffee (GMCR).

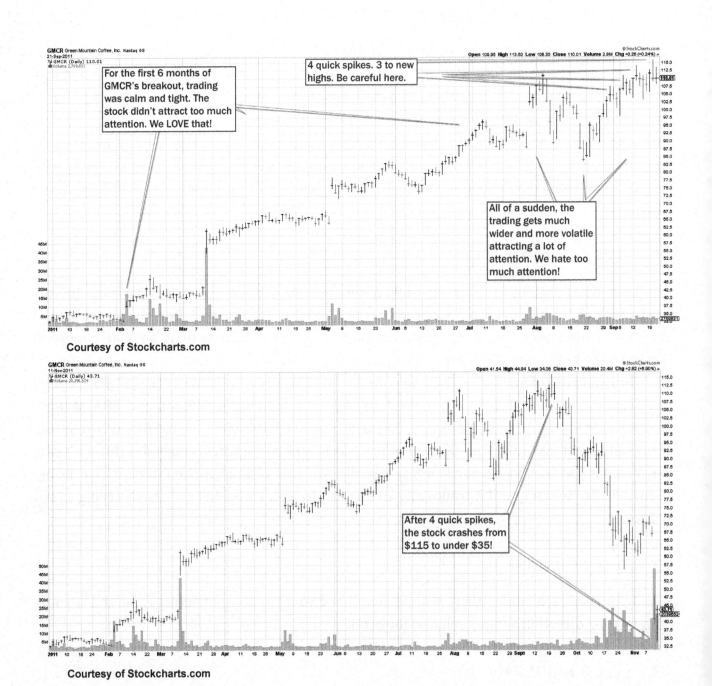

Courtesy of Stockcharts.com

## 14 – SELL IF PEERS ARE WEAKENING

If your stock is part of a broader group of stocks, always watch the leaders in that group for any signs of weakness. Assume for a second that your stock has moved 50% in the prior month and appears to be "resting" before another advance higher. You look at the other leading stocks in the group and you notice that they appear to be selling off one by one. Be extremely cautious in such a scenario. Your stock could be next in line to be taken out and shot down. Remember that your stock is part of an extended family that tend to move in tandem.

## 15 – SELL ON BREACH OF THE UPPER TREND LINE

After a lengthy advance, some stocks will advance up to their upper trendline, and instead of bouncing lower as they have in the past, they may trade above it for the first time. This is a tricky scenario because it can either mark the end of the advance or mark the beginning of a large parabolic move higher. Much of it depends on how overbought the stock is when it hits the upper trendline.

My rule of thumb is to closely watch a stock trading above its trendline for any signs of weakness. Since you don't want to miss out on the possibility of a big parabolic advance, I would look to sell on any close back below the upper trendline. Check out this trend break from W.R. Grace & Co. in 2011 (above). Traders were buying this "breakout" hand over fist. Not me.

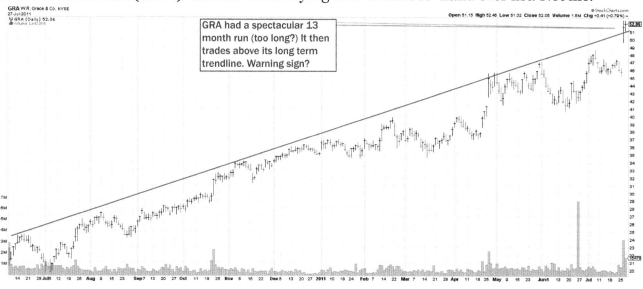

GRA had a spectacular 13 month run (too long?) It then trades above its long term trendline. Warning sign?

Courtesy of Stockcharts.com

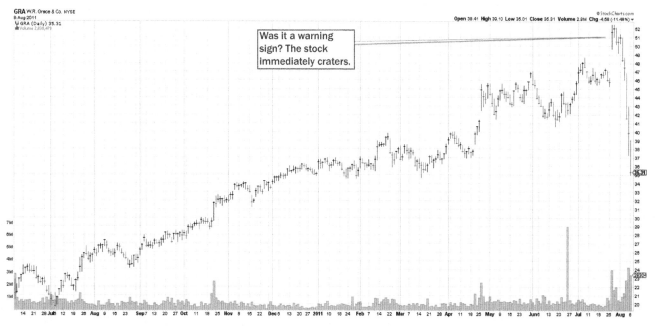

Was it a warning sign? The stock immediately craters.

Courtesy of Stockcharts.com

## 16 – SELL UPPER BOLLINGER BAND

This one is the exact opposite of the lower Bollinger Band buy signal. After a stock trades outside of its upper Bollinger Band, wait for the first close back within the band for a sell signal.

MCP was a powerful momentum stock in 2010 and 2011 being propelled by the extraordinary "Rare Earth Mineral" theme. Unfortunately, I missed out on this bad boy during my Asian travels.

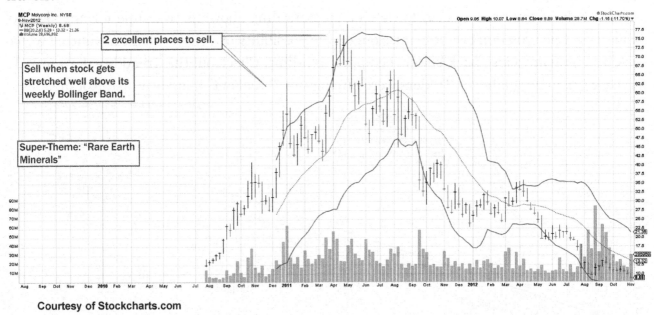

Courtesy of Stockcharts.com

# THE TOP 5 SUPERLAWS OF SELLING FUNDAMENTAL RISK

In general, if your stock meets any of the following fundamental conditions, it is best to sell and move on to the next big winner.

## 1 – SELL AT YOUR PRICE TARGET OR WHEN THE RISK / REWARD IS NO LONGER FAVORABLE

As our stocks continue their ascent into the heavens, we become brainwashed into thinking that they can continue their climb indefinitely, reaching heights previously thought impossible. Nonsense. Let's assume that all of your due diligence indicates that the fair value of your $8 stock is $34. If you let this stock run until it reaches your $34 price target, then—unless something changed *dramatically*—sell it and never look back. At that price level, the risk is simply too great for the potential reward. Take a break and look for the next round of skewed risk/reward scenarios that always present themselves. Let your winners run *until* risk/reward becomes unfavorable.

## 2 – SELL SECONDARY OFFERINGS / PRIVATE PLACEMENTS WITHOUT HESITATION

If your stock announces a secondary offering or a private placement, run for the hills as fast as you possibly can. Management's job is to issue a stock offering at the highest price possible. At the offering price, the executives (the *REALLY* smart money) don't see the stock heading much higher going forward. I don't give a hoot what the stock offering proceeds will be used for; whether it be "Massive expansion!" or "Increased market presence!"

Whatever the bullish BS argument presented by management, simply sell your shares and move on. Swimming against the tide of a much larger float, increased expenses, and a much larger short interest, the odds are significantly stacked against you. All of that aside, the only thing that truly matters is the fact that stock offerings scare away the momentum players and their billions in firepower. Without the smart money on your side, there's little reason to own a stock for at least six months after the offering.

Many stocks I've held or followed closely over the years have announced secondary offerings. OVEN, PEIX, MITK, MNGGF, NDAQ, TRMM, CVV, OMRI, and WPRT immediately come to mind. Not one of them performed well in the six months following the offering.

## 3 – SELL THE END OF A SEQUENTIAL EARNINGS RAMP

The instant your company announces earnings that are meaningfully *BELOW* the previous quarter, SELL. Momentum investors can absolutely destroy a stock whose earnings momentum is coming to an end. As is always the case, there are exceptions to this rule. If a company simultaneously announces rapidly increasing backlog or says that the earnings lull is temporary or seasonal and likely to ramp higher in the coming quarters, it may be a good idea to hold onto the shares.

## 4 – SELL ANY STOCK SPLIT

This one is a bit counterintuitive. Most investors just *LOVE* stock splits. New investors can now buy at lower prices and the shares will soar! Well, yes and no. As you will recall, a primary component of a Superstock is the fact that it has a low float. The momo players swarm to low-float plays because they can easily manipulate the price higher.

When a stock makes a significant advance to much higher prices and there are now two or even three times as many shares in the float, it becomes significantly more difficult for momentum money to move the stock. The result is that the smart money tends to leave, taking the momentum with them.

On the other hand, if your company needs to reverse-split its shares to get its share price *higher,* the company is probably in dire shape and you have absolutely no business being in such a stock. Reverse splits are the kiss of death.

## 5 – SELL MASSIVE INSIDER SELLING

After a major stock advance, it is routine to see a moderate increase in insider selling. What you need to be watchful of is if one or more insiders sell a majority of their stake in the company. This usually does not bode too well for the future.

In 2005, the CEO of Forward Industries (FORD—one of my favorite holdings) sold a majority of his long-term holdings as the stock advanced some 1,500%. The official reason for the selling was that he was in his 60s and he was simply nearing retirement. In hindsight, he made some pretty darn good trades. Within a year, the stock declined some 95%. Yes, 95%.

## *SECOND TIER SELL SIGNALS*

The following are not necessarily "automatic" immediate sell signals, but if you see them, you should carefully consider the potential remaining upside in your stock.

## 6 – SELL HEADLINES

As long as your stock is healthy and running higher, you want to keep its story a well-guarded secret. You want it to seem as if only you and a handful of others have ever heard of your stealth stock. If all of a sudden your stock is featured in the national media like *Fortune* or *Forbes,* it is *immediately* a crowded trade. Seeing your stock featured in a major publication after a long advance is about the clearest sell signal you can get.

In 2011, CVD Equipment Corp. (CVV) was on a major roll. Its product, graphene, was being hyped to be the next big thing in all sorts of applications. Investors were eating the story (Super Theme!) up. Even as the stock climbed 700% in one year, it seemed as if nobody knew about the stock. CVV had a very conservative management team that did not hype the company in any way. Press releases were very rare.

CVV's picture-perfect one year bull-run culminated with an 80% two-week climb into September of 2011. In the first week of September, Bloomberg released a major story about the company, its technology, as well as the dozens of applications for this little-known substance called graphene. Overnight, the message board was flooded with new investors. All of a sudden, everybody was an expert on graphene.

The stock topped at an all-time high within one or two days of the article. It then traded down from $19.50 to $12 within 2 weeks! Talk about a massive sell indicator.

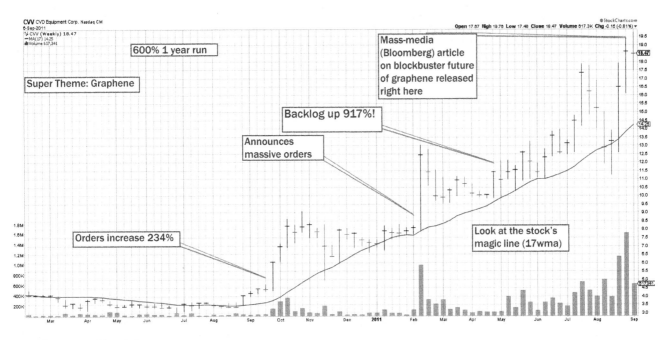

Courtesy of Stockcharts.com

# 7 – SELL MESSAGE BOARD EUPHORIA

> *"It's a basic fact of life that many things 'everybody knows' turn out to be wrong."*
>
> Jim Rogers

A repeated theme of this book is to base buy and sell decisions on sentiment, whether it be represented in the chart pattern or otherwise. A stock's message board is an excellent representation of the overall sentiment of a stock's shareholder base. If a message board's tone transitions from a quiet, informed, intelligent nature to one of utter pandemonium and speculation, start questioning the potential upside remaining in your position. Yes, I understand that the biggest moves, the parabolic moves, are made during periods of intense message board euphoria, but such instances are exceptions rather than the rule. If *"everybody"* thinks your stock is going to $100, the situation warrants your careful consideration.

## 8 – SELL EXPANSION

This is 100% counter-intuitive, but here goes. When a company decides to increase capacity, it takes interest-bearing cash from its balance sheet and buys new buildings and equipment. As we know, the market is a forward-looking mechanism that has a laser focus on margins. A company running at 100% of capacity should have pretty good margins based on economies of scale.

When a company adds a significant level of new capacity, much of the new capacity sits idle for many months, many quarters, or even years. The old cash is no longer earning interest and the new capacity requires increased expenses...thus margins tend to suffer.

Several of my past stocks announced capacity expansion—Spartan Motors (SPAR), Xyratex (XRTX), Fuwei Films (FFHL), Keytronic (KTCC), and CVD Equipment (CVV)—come to mind. Expansion stopped each stock's progress dead in its tracks. The best stocks have capacity utilization rates that are steadily climbing from quarter to quarter. Not vice versa.

## 9 – SELL IF YOU BECOME A GENIUS

This rule is very simple. Sentiment trumps all else. We all have those seasons in our life when everything seems to be going our way. You look in the mirror and you seem to be *MUCH* better looking than you were just last week. Every guy or girl you walk by appears to be checking you out. Every one of your stocks is heading higher. Every stock you've recommended to friends has made a huge move. It just seems like everything you touch instantly turns to gold. Confidence seeps from every pore.

When all of this happens in a short period of time, your head becomes a weapon of mass delusion! I can't tell you how many times this has happened to me. These are precisely the moments when things can and do turn on a dime.

It is your responsibility to hone your Emotional Quotient (EQ) and be able to take a step back and recognize your heightened emotional states. When your emotional state reaches such altitudes, it is probably a great time to take some chips off the table and re-invest when things settle down.

## 10 – SELL CONFUSING EARNINGS REPORTS

As discussed previously, some earnings reports are downright tough to figure out. Rather than a typical quarterly report covering 3 months, management may focus exclusively on the previous 6, 9, or 12 month time frames. Other times, management might include "one-time" charges or "one-time gains" which can make it more difficult to figure out the true earnings per share. These "one-timers" can arise from sales of investment securities, write-offs from layoffs, factory closings, obsolete inventory etc. The best stocks tend not to have too many one-time losses as they typically are not firing employees or closing factories.

A strong company might report one-time gains that temporarily boost earnings. This is not an automatic sell signal, but my rule of thumb is to carefully consider this type of news because management may be attempting to artificially inflate earnings in the short run. The other major consideration is that future earnings won't be as impressive as they will be compared to this artificially inflated figure.

If the earnings report is confusing and requires a great deal of time to decipher, chances are that other traders will find it confusing as well and will invest their funds elsewhere. If the report seems fishy, walk away.

## 11 – SELL TAX LOSS REVERSALS

If a company loses money for an extended period of time, the resulting tax losses become assets on the balance sheet called "tax-loss carry-forwards." Let's say that a company loses $50 million over three years. Eventually, when the company starts to generate a profit, it won't pay taxes on its first $50 million in profits. During this period, the company will deduct little if any income tax expense on the income statement due to the tax loss carry-forwards.

In the short run, this accounting treatment artificially inflates earnings per share and can lead many investors into thinking that the company is more profitable than it actually is. Once a company determines that it will be profitable on an "ongoing basis" (this may happen many quarters after turning profitable), it will reverse its tax-loss carry-forwards in one large lump sum. The end result is a large one-time gain on the income statement that triggers an enormous earnings-per-share figure.

As you know, I am not a fan of one-time gains. They screw up sequential earnings progression and make future period comparisons difficult. The worst part of this accounting declaration is the fact that the company starts deducting tax expenses in future periods. The result is a future reduction in earnings-per-share. As investors look to the future, they will sell knowing that the big inflated earnings are now in the past.

## 12 – SELL PRE-EARNINGS EUPHORIA

I am a big believer in selling "earnings pumps." Positive earnings SURPRISES create huge buying thrusts. Conversely, if a stock has been trending higher into earnings, and everybody on board has wildly optimistic earnings projections, once the news is out, the hangover sets in and the stock can sell off considerably. The last thing I want to see is a wildly optimistic message board community heading into earnings—it spells trouble ahead.

## 13 – SELL THE FLUFF!

Be mindful of a change in a company's character as it relates to reporting "news." A conservative company that goes from one or two press releases per quarter to one or two per *week* is a big red flag in my book. Any company that starts issuing press releases boasting about a *POTENTIAL* new customer or a *POTENTIAL* billion dollar market opportunity should be cause for concern.

An increase in public relations "fluff" means that the company no longer has anything of significance to report. Management may be attempting to boost the price and share volume prior to insider sales or an equity offering.

A solid company will never announce *POTENTIAL* customer contracts. Solid companies will never even announce *signed* contracts unless the new customer will account for a meaningful percentage of revenue. A solid company may hint at a new customer in the quarterly report or during the quarterly conference call, but it will seldom discuss customers by name.

## 14 – BUY THE RUMOR AND SELL THE NEWS

If you buy a stock because the company will release some wildly innovative product in four months, and the stock trends higher during those four months into the release date, by all means lock in your gains on the day of the release if not a few days earlier. Like we previously discussed, the market is entirely a forward-looking mechanism. It is all about future, future, future. Once the future arrives, your edge vanishes. Sell the news my friends.

## 15 – SELL STOCK ADVERTISEMENTS

This is an extremely rare occurrence, but once every so often you will see a company push their stock more than they push their products. A company should never advertise their stock. If you have a solid company, your stock will take care of itself—period. Management's success in marketing its products is the ultimate driver for the share price.

Every couple of years a company like LJ International (JADE) or Spongetech (SPNG) will come around and advertise its stock all over the place. Several years ago, I remember JADE advertising its stock on CNBC. Spongetech advertised its ticker symbol just about everywhere including on banners in baseball parks all over the major leagues. Although I can't confirm this, I was told recently that they advertised their shares on CNBC as well. If I could only tell you what I know about Spongetech! It was a total joke from the very first day it opened its doors. A close friend of mine had an insider's view of the massive fraud. I couldn't believe that the SEC let the fraud go on and on and on for so long. The stock was ultimately delisted and the SEC eventually did bring charges against them for a littany of bogus activity.

## 16 – SELL "STRATEGIC ALTERNATIVES"

Your intensive research should never put you in a stock that would ever consider such an announcement, but many companies issue press releases stating that they have hired an investment bank to assist them in "Strategic Alternatives." This is a fancy way of saying that they are putting themselves up for sale and the investment bank is actively seeking a sale to the highest bidder. The company's rationale is often that it is "undervalued."

I must first say that upon hearing such news, investors go nuts. "What great news!," "This stock is worth three times its current price, and GE will certainly buy us for what we are truly worth!." Yadda, yadda, yadda. The message board hype can go on for quite some time. I have seen dozens of these "strategic alternative" announcements over the years.

Surprisingly, if my memory serves me correct, not a single one of these firms was ever bought out. If anything, such an announcement marks the beginning of a death spiral for the company. About the only "strategic alternative" ever developed by the Investment Bank is a secondary offering or a "strategic bankruptcy." Bottom line—run as fast as you can if you see such a ridiculous announcement from a company.

## *HOW DO YOU GET OUT?*

Once your stock has flashed several sell signals, how do you get out? Get out FAST.

# CHAPTER 11

# The "Lazy Man's Guide" to Superstocks

Now that we have covered pretty much everything there is to know about the elusive Superstock, in the spirit of Pareto's 80/20 law of simplicity, I will give you the Super Laws that you should focus most of your time mastering. Think of this as *Cliffs Notes* for Superstocks.

## THE COMPOSITION OF A SUPERSTOCK

The composition of a Superstock is as follows:

- *BLOCKBUSTER* sustainable earnings release with high operating leverage + easy upcoming "comps."

- *HUGE* weekly volume thrust out of a strong base sending the stock above 30 wma at a high angle of attack.

- Price under $15 with annualized PE run rate of 10 or less.

- Low float and conservative management team.

- MEGA BONUS: insider buying, and a *SUPER THEME*.

The odds of success are enhanced further if the stock has little competition, low debt, low short interest, a good ticker, no analyst coverage, high insider ownership, and momentum traders on board.

## WHEN TO BUY – HIGH REWARD/LOWEST RISK ENTRY

The ideal time to buy a Superstock is:

- 2-3 weeks after initial earnings breakout. Wait for a gap test and/or low volume narrow price range.

- Buy lower trendline, especially coinciding with low volume and low price range.

- Buy AGGRESSIVELY at the magic line, ideally on the lowest recent weekly volume in a very tight weekly price range.

## WHEN TO SELL

The chart takes precedence over pretty much everything else. Regardless of fundamental developments, the chart will tell you loud and clear when it is time to sell. All of the below are major sell signals after a long stock advance:

- 7-10 weeks after a magic line thrust.

- 9 months into an advance.

- Parabolic surges.

- Weekly gaps at new highs.

- A weekly close below the magic line.

- Largest weekly price range after a longer-term advance.

- After the fourth or fifth surge off the magic line after a long advance.

- Wide weekly price ranges and high volume volatile trading above and below magic line (especially if flattening or declining).

Also watch other stocks in the sector and watch for a breach of the upper trendline and/or upper Bollinger Band.

A high risk chart pattern in combination with any of the following is a clear indication to exit your position: stock offering, end of sequential earnings ramp, stock split, massive insider selling, headlines in the media, message board euphoria, company expansion, confusing earnings reports, "fluff" press releases, stock advertisements, or "strategic alternatives."

# CHAPTER 12

# *Eleven Charts That Changed My Life and May Change Yours*

*"To believe in the things you can see and touch is no belief at all; but to believe in the unseen is a triumph and a blessing."*

Abraham Lincoln

This may well be the most important chapter in the book. If you want to make serious money in the market, you need to study these charts. In this chapter I lay out:

- The type of blockbuster earnings report you must look for.

- The type of powerful earnings to look for.

- Target price calculations.

- Low risk buy points.

- High risk sell points.

- The Super Laws I saw before I entered.

...and much more.

This is the whole book rolled up into one dense chapter. There is a wealth of information presented in each chart. I encourage you to take as much time as you need to understand each one. Some of the charts may appear overwhelming at first, but I've tried to keep them as simple as possible. Rather than include Bollinger Bands, trendlines, RSI and the like, I focused primarily on the three things that matter most: *VOLUME, PRICE,* and the *"MAGIC LINE"**.

*\*Yet again, the "magic line" tends to be near the 10 week moving average (10 wma) in most instances.*

In many of the examples, I have included the company's earnings release that triggered the stock's breakout. I've italicized key words in the reports to show you what initially caught my attention. These "blockbuster" earnings releases will help you get an idea of exactly what to look for in terms of revenue and earnings growth. I have also included key CEO commentary when applicable.

I try to go into extra detail in the first couple of examples, to paint a more thorough picture of my method. In these first examples, I have included my old investment emails sent to fellow traders. I hope these give you a little more insight into what I saw before the stocks made their big moves. These emails are original and were written years ago in my younger days. They were meant as informal communications between other traders and me. I present them verbatim and purposefully unedited, so please accept my apologies for any mistakes or informalities.

The stocks in this section are many of my biggest winners from my 14,972% run. Some of my other big winners were ANTP, INPH, MIND, TRLG, TRT, and IDSA. Unfortunately, several of my other big winners such as RURL, PARL, CADA, TGIS, IPSU, MUSA, TRCR, CKCM, LDSH, and PWEI have been bought out. It appears as if stock charts no longer exist for these companies.

As a side note, most if not all of the stocks just mentioned had significant insider buying. Insider buying is seemingly a powerful indicator of a future buyout, and it proves that it's difficult to go wrong when following the insiders.

## 1 – DYNAMIC MATERIALS CORP. (BOOM)

### DYNAMIC MATERIALS REPORTS
### THIRD QUARTER 2004 FINANCIAL RESULTS

(Boulder, CO - November 11, 2004) Dynamic Materials Corporation, (Nasdaq: BOOM), "DMC," today reported third quarter income from continuing operations of $1,135,275, or $.22 per diluted share, versus income from continuing operations of $358,568, or $.07 per diluted share, for the third quarter of 2003. DMC's third quarter 2004 sales were $12,070,114, a 24% increase from third quarter 2003 sales of $9,724,125.

Management Comments:

In commenting upon the Company's third quarter 2004 results, Yvon Cariou, DMC's President and CEO, stated, "The business fundamentals and near-term outlook for our Explosive Metalworking Group remain very good and, with a *record backlog* as of September 30, 2004, the Group *expects further improvement* in sales and operating results during the fourth quarter of 2004 and to get off to a strong start in 2005." Cariou continued, "AMK's sales and operating income are also expected to *show improvement* in the fourth quarter. Based upon our understanding of AMK's customer's 2005 production plans for its new product and an expected increase in demand for commercial and military aircraft engines, prospects for *measurable improvement* in 2005 sales and operating results at AMK appear to be quite good,"

Upon entry, BOOM had all of the makings of a Superstock:

TECHNICALS:

- Very long base before breakout.

- Huge volume expansion on breakout.

- Great angle of attack.

- Under $15.

- Breakout above 30 week moving average.

FUNDAMENTALS:

- Recent insider buying.

- Earnings winner with increasing backlog.

- I modeled sustainable sequential earnings increases going forward.

- Annualized PE of 10 upon entry.

- Very easy upcoming earnings comparisons (comps).

- Enormous operating leverage.

- A great earnings headline.

- A low float of 5 million shares.

- A super theme of *"EXPLOSION* bonded metal" (which nobody knew anything about).

- Very conservative management issuing very few PRs.

Furthermore, it had no options, no competition in this odd niche, little debt, low short interest, a *GREAT* ticker symbol, outstanding *IBD* numbers, no analyst coverage, and super traders on board. This stock had all of the essential ingredients to become a Superstock.

Note: BOOM has since split its shares 2 for 1.

*All prices and earnings per share should be adjusted in half to reflect stock split.

Here is what I saw word-for-word just prior to entering my position:

**January 13, 2005**

Email 1/13/2005:

"Now this one is interesting. Dropped from $17.50 to $8.65 or 50%. EPS of $0.22 last quarter. Earnings have gone from a loss to $.04, $0.11, $0.22 last 4 quarters. *Backlog* has gone from $11.7 million to $17.3, $21.1, $25.6 last 4 quarters. *Buried in their 10Q* is a $5 million order that will ship in the 4th quarter. After running through their numbers, *I get earnings of .27 to .35 next quarter* resulting in a *stock price of $12 to $28* depending on whether or not the momentum crowd returns. The *momentum traders* jumped on BOOM taking it from $3.75 to $17.50 in a few days when last quarter's numbers were published. Because of the *ticker symbol* and the *huge earnings growth,* I believe they (traders) will return in a big way if the earnings are impressive. *I spoke to the CFO* at length this morning and things appear to be going very well. I was concerned about their *capacity,* thinking that their earnings would be limited by their capacity. No problem. They have plenty of excess capacity. After a 300% run-up, I was concerned about substantial stock options being "in the money." Current *share count* is still at *5.2 million* which is pretty much unchanged from last quarter. Their earnings date is usually the second week in March. He stated that they will be moving that up. This is a sure sign to me that they want the numbers to hit the street as soon as possible. Usually a very bullish sign. *CEO just filed* today that he picked up *a few thousand more shares.* Lastly, they are about to hire an external investor relations firm. They are also considering holding their *first conference call* next quarter. This generally happens when a company issues impressive numbers.

(According to the)CEO-"The business fundamentals and near-term outlook for our Explosive Metalworking Group remain very good and, with a record backlog as of September 30, 2004, the Group *expects further improvement in sales and operating results* during the fourth quarter of 2004 and to get off to a strong start in 2005." Cariou continued, "AMK's sales and operating income are also expected to show improvement in the fourth quarter.

Based upon our understanding of AMK's customer's 2005 production plans for its new product and an expected increase in demand for commercial and military aircraft engines, prospects for measurable improvement in 2005 sales and operating results at AMK appear to be quite good."

The company's line of business is explosion bonded clad metal plates and other metal fabrications for the petrochemical, chemical processing, power generation, commercial aircraft, defense and a variety of other industries. They are currently #1 in the world in their market. All of the sectors they serve are extremely strong currently. Merrill Lynch published a report last week stating that the chemical/petrochemical industries will achieve a level in 2005-2006 not seen since 1988. (And) Of course, commercial aircraft and defense are gaining traction almost daily. My *only concern* right now is *their tax loss carryforward.* I believe this will be around for the next 1 to 2 quarters."

\*BOOM went on to blow away my estimates ($0.27-$0.35) as it released $0.41 EPS the following quarter and became a bona-fide Superstock.

## WHAT I SAW PRIOR TO ENTRY

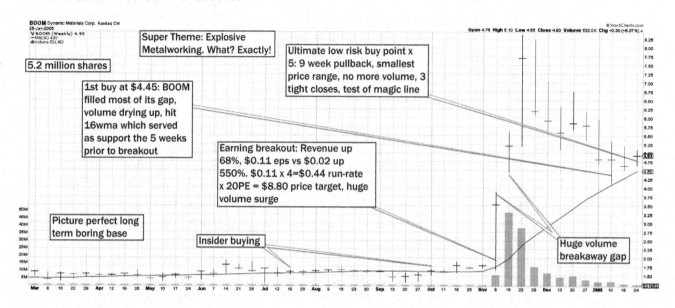

Courtesy of Stockcharts.com

## POTENTIAL BUY POINTS

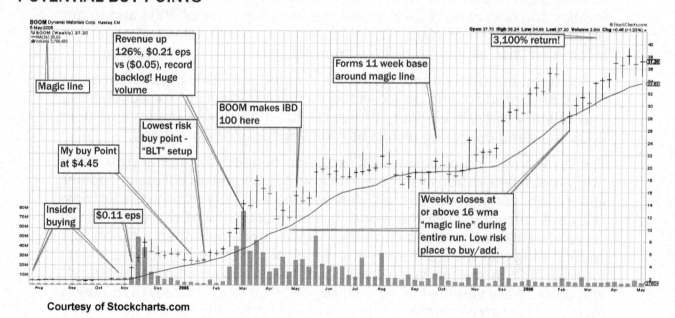

Courtesy of Stockcharts.com

## POTENTIAL SELL POINTs

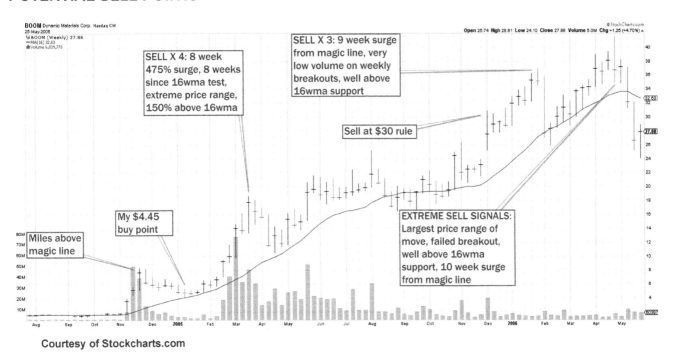

SELL X 4: 8 week 475% surge, 8 weeks since 16wma test, extreme price range, 150% above 16wma

SELL X 3: 9 week surge from magic line, very low volume on weekly breakouts, well above 16wma support

Sell at $30 rule

My $4.45 buy point

Miles above magic line

EXTREME SELL SIGNALS: Largest price range of move, failed breakout, well above 16wma support, 10 week surge from magic line

Courtesy of Stockcharts.com

## 2 – VIROPHARMA (VPHM)

### Reports First Quarter 2005 Financial Results And Increases 2005 Vancocin Pulvules Net Sales Guidance

Exton, PA, May 3, 2005

VIROPHARMAINCORPORATED(Nasdaq: VPHM) reported today its financial results for the first quarter ended March 31, 2005.

### *Quarter ended March 31, 2005*

For the quarter ended March 31, 2005, the Company reported net income of $17.4 million compared to a net loss of $16.6 million for the same period in 2004. Net income per share for the quarter ended March 31, 2005 was $0.64 per share, basic, and $0.36 per share, diluted, compared to a net loss of $0.63 per share, basic and diluted, for the same period in 2004.

159

"During the first quarter of 2005, we experienced progress in all areas of our business, particularly as it relates to Vancocin® Pulvules®," commented Michel de Rosen, ViroPharma's chief executive officer. "Among other things, we completed our integration of Vancocin into our business; we began our efforts in medical education for Vancocin; and we saw significant data presented by industry leaders on the increasing prevalence and severity of the disease treated by Vancocin. Perhaps most importantly, Vancocin had one of its strongest quarters in its history, yielding over $21 million in net sales."

*(Net sales were $27 million vs. $1.7 million the prior year!)*

## VPHM'S SUPER LAWS

TECHNICALS:

- Volume expansion at breakout.
- High angle of attack.
- Under $15.
- 30 WMA Breakout (closed at 30 wma week 1, surged above in week 2)

FUNDAMENTALS:

- Insider buying as stock advanced!
- Earnings winner.
- Annualized PE under 10.
- Sustainable earnings (new drug).
- Very easy comps going forward.
- High operating leverage.
- Super theme- drug to combat C-Difficil epidemic rampant in hospitals.
- Conservative management.

*Note: It had a high number of shares outstanding (51 million), a modest level of debt, and no "textbook" base.

## MY ARCHIVED THOUGHTS ON VPHM

### 5/26/05

"Bought a bunch of this one (VPHM) today. Sick insider buying along w/ a perfect chart. Posters are calling for $15 by EOY. Last earnings release was phenomenal. Biotech that is actually cash flow positive! Meaning no dilution... In at 3.94"

### 6/4/05

"VPHM appears to be the perfect biotech- highly profitable, accelerating earnings, super low PE, blockbuster potential drugs in the pipeline, insider buying, and a gigantic partner that may have a blockbuster on its hands which VPHM will see approximately 10% of the revenues (a guesstimate). Hmmmm...."

### 6/15/05

"I'm running some preliminary #'s and I'm getting a potential share price of around $30. Any developments in their pipeline would jack that up substantially. I'll continue working on it."

### 6/17/05

"I feel very strongly that the risk/reward in VPHM is very much in the long's favor here. I've been collecting data and modeling '06 revenue and EPS projections for most of the day. This one could be a big, big winner. As I posted on the breakouts board,today's close of 6.38 could prove to be an excellent buy point considering that the last insider bought at 6.60, the 9 dma is at 6.22, and the chart pullback looks excellent to me here. Will add on any dips into the red tomorrow."

### 6/20/05

"I have been going over 10 Q's, conference calls, presentations, and message board chatter all day. Some of my '06 revenue/EPS projections, and company developments are staggering to me. This one could easily be one of the biggest gainers into '06. Could leave FORD in the dust. Remember that last insider purchase was at 6.60, just bounced off 9 dma, nice consolidation, and May's Vancocin sales may be "leaked" on Monday. Usually come out on a Monday 2 weeks into the month. A sneak peak of my report has '06 EPS above $1, a biotech PE in 25-30 range, and possible approval of the "common cold" cure (VPHM would see N. American royalties) could throw all traditional valuation methods out the window."

### 8/8/05

"From a technical standpoint, VPHM has experienced strong support at the 20 day moving average which now sits at 11.50. The stock traded down to

11.68 today. Ideal buypoint would be 11.50 area if it trades down to that area.Increasing Vancocin sales and/or 10% price increase could alter EPS quite dramatically.The consensus is EPS for next 12 months of 1.00-1.20. Lazard raised price target to 16 or 17 last week (not sure exactly) w/ EPS projection of .84 or so. VPHM is a biotech co., so risks are higher than other co.'s- (possible) secondary for new drugs and/or pipeline setbacks."

## WHAT I SAW PRIOR TO ENTRY

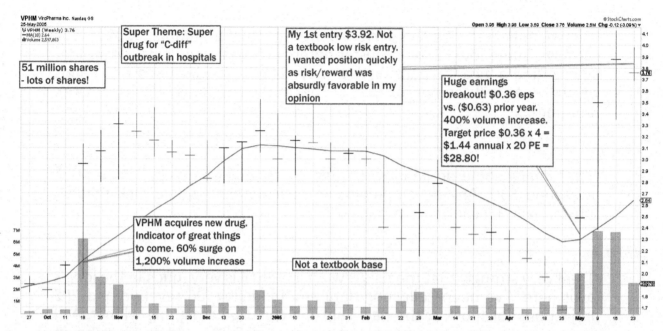

Courtesy of Stockcharts.com

## POTENTIAL BUY POINTS

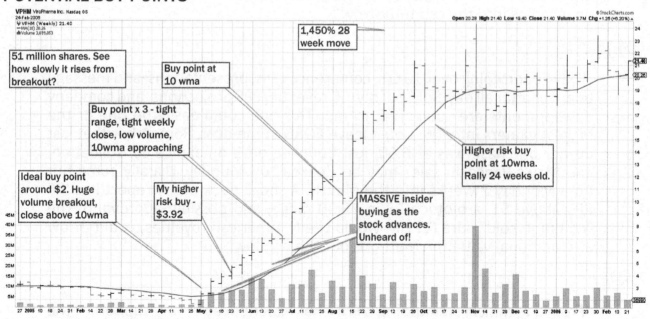

Courtesy of Stockcharts.com

## POTENTIAL SELL POINTS

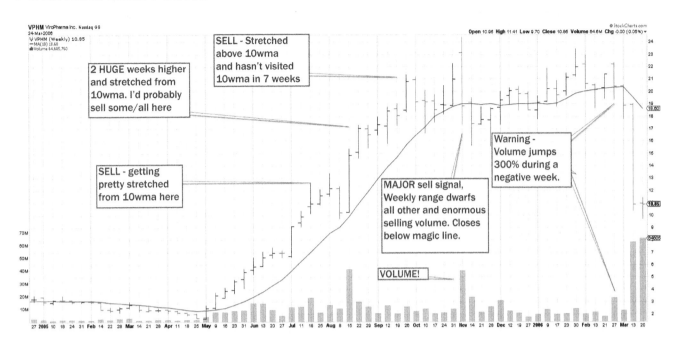

2 HUGE weeks higher and stretched from 10wma. I'd probably sell some/all here

SELL - Stretched above 10wma and hasn't visited 10wma in 7 weeks

SELL - getting pretty stretched from 10wma here

MAJOR sell signal, Weekly range dwarfs all other and enormous selling volume. Closes below magic line.

Warning - Volume jumps 300% during a negative week.

VOLUME!

Courtesy of Stockcharts.com

# 3 – FORWARD INDUSTRIES

### FORWARD INDUSTRIES REPORTS FIRST QUARTER RESULTS: EPS OF $.21 VS. $.03 AS NET SALES INCREASE 98% TO $8.9 MILLION

### CELL PHONE PRODUCT SALES INCREASE SHARPLY

Pompano Beach, FL, January 20, 2005 -Forward Industries, Inc. (NASDAQ:FORD), a designer and distributor of custom carrying case solutions, today announced results for its first quarter ended December 31, 2004.

**First Quarter 2005 Financial Highlights**- Compared to first quarter 2004 results:

*Total net sales increased $4.4 million or 98% to $8.9 million.*

Cell phone product sales increased $3.5 million or 166% to $5.6 million, driven by sales of "in-box" cases for new launches of Motorola and Nokia phones.

Net income increased more than *six-fold* to a record $1.37 million or $.21 per diluted share, from $192,000 or $.03 per diluted share.

Jerome E. Ball, Chairman and Chief Executive Officer of Forward, commented...

"Because of our relatively fixed cost structure and robust sales growth, our operating expenses, as a percentage of sales, declined to 16.3% from 28.9% in the prior year period. This contributed to setting an all-time quarterly net income record for Forward." (Note—*Extreme operating leverage!*)

..."We are *very optimistic about our overall prospects* for the year and we look forward to reporting our performance."

TECHNICALS:

- Long Base prior to breakout.

- Large volume expansion at breakout.

- High angle of attack.

- Under $15.

- Surge above 30 wma at breakout.


FUNDAMENTALS:

- Insider Buying.

- Earnings winner – EPS up 700% yoy ($0.21 vs. $0.03).

- Annualized PE under 10.

- Sustainable and sequential earnings (at least for next few quarters).

- Very easy future comps.

- Great earnings headline

- Extremely high operating leverage.

- Low float.

- Super-Theme- Carrying cases for hottest selling phone in history (Motorola RAZR).

*FORD also had conservative management, no competition for RAZR carrying cases, little debt, a good ticker symbol, great *IBD* numbers, no analyst coverage, and high insider ownership.

## NOTES PRIOR TO ENTRY

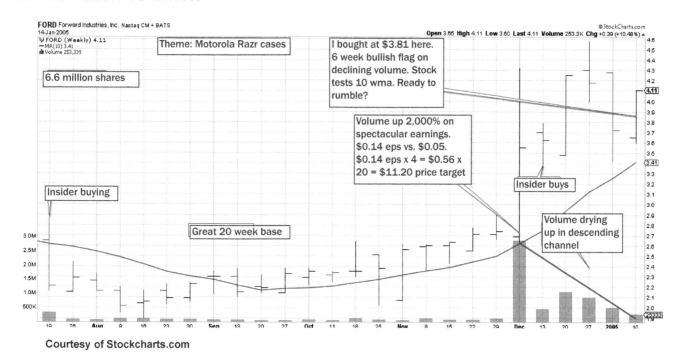

Theme: Motorola Razr cases

6.6 million shares

I bought at $3.81 here. 6 week bullish flag on declining volume. Stock tests 10 wma. Ready to rumble?

Volume up 2,000% on spectacular earnings. $0.14 eps vs. $0.05. $0.14 eps x 4 = $0.56 x 20 = $11.20 price target

Insider buying

Insider buys

Great 20 week base

Volume drying up in descending channel

Courtesy of Stockcharts.com

## POTENTIAL BUY POINTS

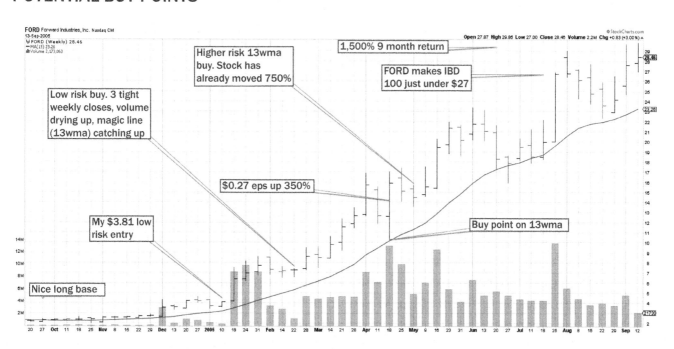

Higher risk 13wma buy. Stock has already moved 750%

1,500% 9 month return

FORD makes IBD 100 just under $27

Low risk buy. 3 tight weekly closes, volume drying up, magic line (13wma) catching up

$0.27 eps up 350%

My $3.81 low risk entry

Buy point on 13wma

Nice long base

Courtesy of Stockcharts.com

165

## POTENTIAL SELL POINTS

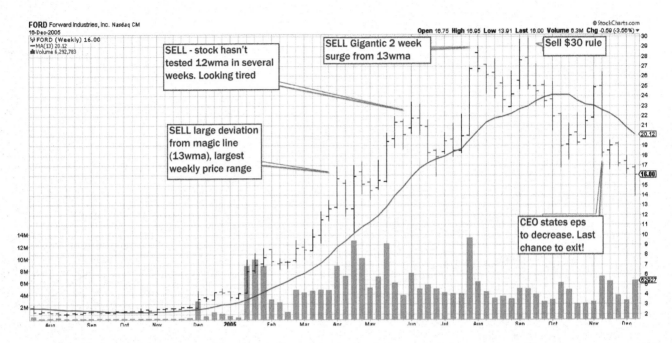

Courtesy of Stockcharts.com

## *4 – DXP ENTERPRISES (DXPE)*

### DXP ENTERPRISES ANNOUNCES SECOND QUARTER RESULTS
### NET INCOME INCREASES 107%
### EARNINGS PER SHARE DOUBLES

**Houston, TX, -- July 20, 2005- DXP Enterprises, Inc. (NASDAQ: DXPE)** today announced a *107% increase in net income* to $1,477,000 for the second quarter ending June 30, 2005, with diluted earnings per share of $.26 compared to net income of $714,000 and diluted earnings per share of $.13 for the second quarter of 2004. Sales increased 8.1% to $45.5 million from $42.1 million for the second quarter of 2004. Gross profit increased 21.7% from the second quarter of 2004.....David R. Little, Chairman and Chief Executive Officer said, "In the second quarter we continued to see solid broad-based sales growth with *higher margins.* Increased MRO sales in 2005 replaced several large, lower margin sales recorded in 2004. We continue to be enthusiastic *about the current level of business opportunities and our ability to increase sales and profitability.*

*Share split

TECHNICALS:

- Long base prior to breakout.

- 2,000% volume expansion at breakout.

- High angle of attack.

- Breakout above 30 week moving average.

- Under $15.

FUNDAMENTALS:

- Insider buying.

- Earnings winner (EPS up 100%).

- Annualized PE of 10.

- Sustainable earnings.

- Easy comps going forward.

- Low float.

- Great easy to understand earnings headline.

- Conservative management.

*Also had low debt, good *IBD* numbers, and no analyst coverage.

DXPE had a minor theme: "pumping solutions for energy industry." Oil services were seeing renewed interest at the time.

## NOTES PRIOR TO ENTRY

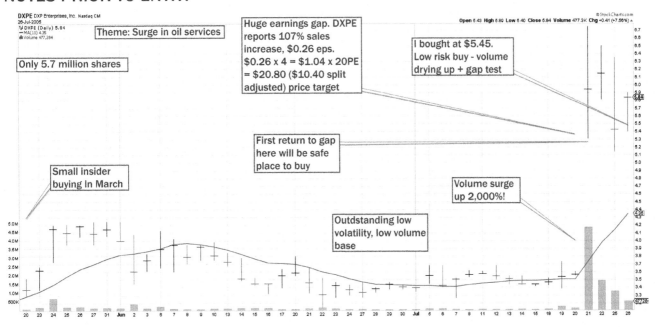

Courtesy of Stockcharts.com

# POTENTIAL BUY POINTS

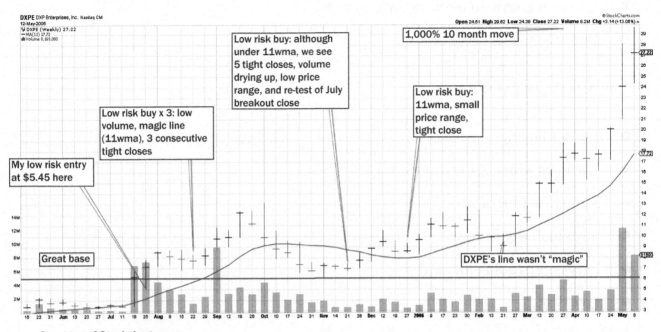

Courtesy of Stockcharts.com

# POTENTIAL SELL POINTS

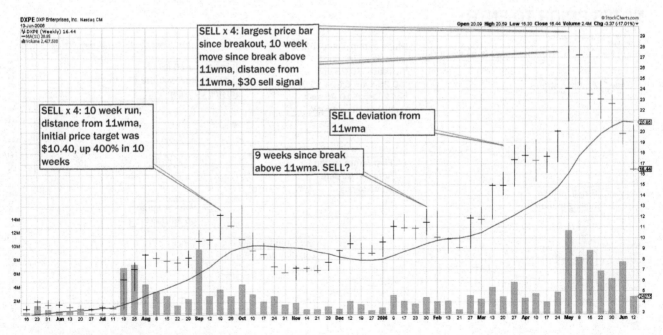

Courtesy of Stockcharts.com

## 5 – AIR METHODS CORPORATION (AIRM)

### AIR METHODS REPORTS 3Q 2005 RESULTS
**Company Earns $0.50 of Basic EPS, Revenue Increases 31% to $90.5 Million**

DENVER, CO., November 9, 2005—Air Methods Corporation (NASDAQ: AIRM) reported results for the quarter ended September 30, 2005. *Revenue increased 31%* to $90.5 million from $68.9 million in the year-ago quarter. For the nine-month period, revenue increased 20% to $246.7 million, up from $204.8 million in the prior-year nine-month period.

For the quarter, *net income increased over 2.7 times* to $5.5 million ($0.50 per basic and $0.47 per diluted share) as compared with prior-year quarter net income of $1.5 million ($0.13 per basic and diluted share).

Aaron Todd, Chief Executive Officer, stated "We also have continued to benefit from *reduced interest expense* attributed to the refinancing of our subordinated debt during the second quarter. We will continue to see this benefit over the next three quarters, as well.....We are also happy to report that our *fourth quarter has begun with healthy flight volume* in October."

TECHNICALS:

- 9 week base before entry.

- 450% volume expansion at breakout.

- Decent angle of attack.

- Under $15.

- Above 30 week moving average.

FUNDAMENTALS:

- Insider buying.

- Huge earnings winner.

- Annualized PE under 10.

- Sustainable earnings.

- Easy future comps.

- High operating leverage.

- Moderately low float.

- Conservative management.

- AIRM also had little competition, little debt, good *IBD* numbers, and no options.

- *Note—not the best theme: emergency flight transport.

## NOTES PRIOR TO ENTRY

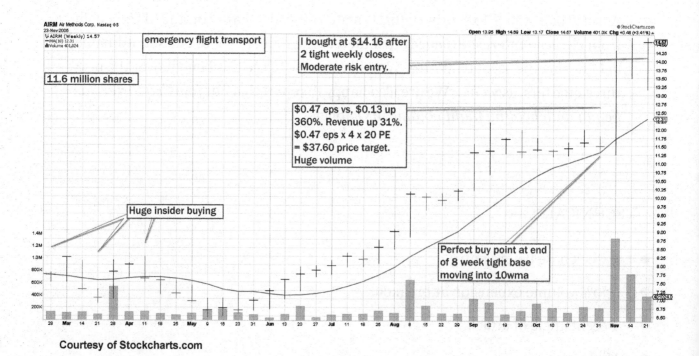

Courtesy of Stockcharts.com

# POTENTIAL BUY POINTS

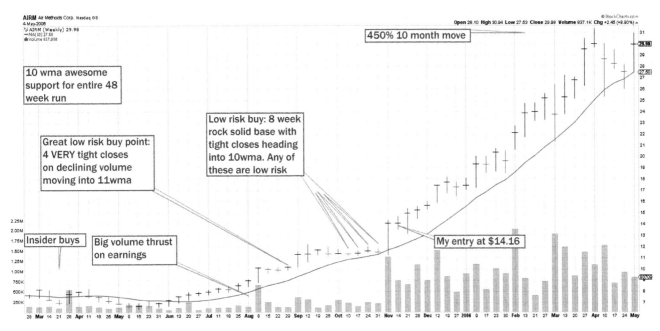

Courtesy of Stockcharts.com

# POTENTIAL SELL POINTS

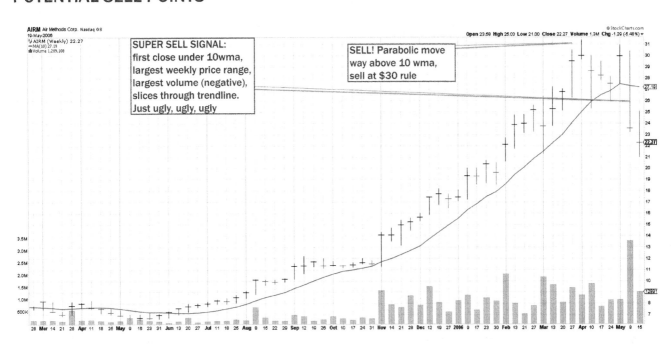

Courtesy of Stockcharts.com

## 6 – EMPIRE RESOURCES (ERSO)

- **EMPIRE RESOURCES ANNOUNCES THIRD QUARTER OPERATING RESULTS**

- FORT LEE, NJ, November 10, 2005—Empire Resources, Inc. (AMEX:ERS), a distributor of value added, semi-finished aluminum products, today announced net income for the three and nine months ended September 30, 2005 of $2,388,000 and $7,134,000 as compared to $1,415,000 and $3,614,000 for the same periods in 2004. Net income for the three and nine months ended September 30, 2005 *increased to $0.24* and $0.72 per share on a fully diluted basis, as *compared to $0.14* and $0.36 per share on a fully diluted basis for the same period in 2004.

- Net sales for the three and nine months were $90,777,000 and $260,237,000 as compared to $53,809,000 and $159,599,000 for the same periods in 2004. *Net sales increased 69%* for the three month period and 63% for the nine month period as compared to the prior year.

TECHNICALS:

- 2,000% volume surge on initial breakout in May, 2005.
- Long base at initial breakout.
- High angle of attack.
- Under $15
- Above 30 week moving average.

FUNDAMENTALS:

- Earnings winner.
- Annualized PE under 10.
- Sustainable earnings.
- Easy comps.
- Low float.
- Conservative management.

*Note: Not a good earnings headline. No Wow factor. Aluminum not a good theme.

## NOTES PRIOR TO ENTRY

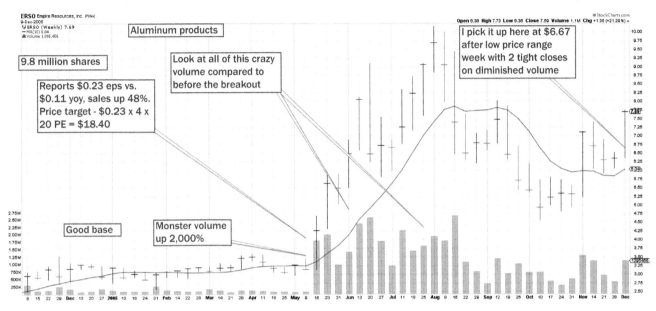

Aluminum products

9.8 million shares

Reports $0.23 eps vs. $0.11 yoy, sales up 48%. Price target - $0.23 x 4 x 20 PE = $18.40

Look at all of this crazy volume compared to before the breakout

I pick it up here at $6.67 after low price range week with 2 tight closes on diminished volume

Good base

Monster volume up 2,000%

Courtesy of Stockcharts.com

## POTENTIAL BUY POINTS

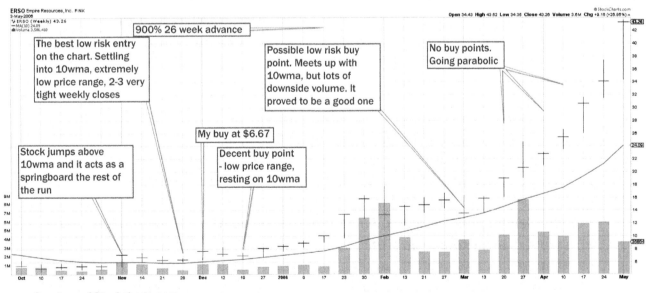

900% 26 week advance

The best low risk entry on the chart. Settling into 10wma, extremely low price range, 2-3 very tight weekly closes

Possible low risk buy point. Meets up with 10wma, but lots of downside volume. It proved to be a good one

No buy points. Going parabolic

My buy at $6.67

Stock jumps above 10wma and it acts as a springboard the rest of the run

Decent buy point - low price range, resting on 10wma

Courtesy of Stockcharts.com

173

## POTENTIAL SELL POINTS

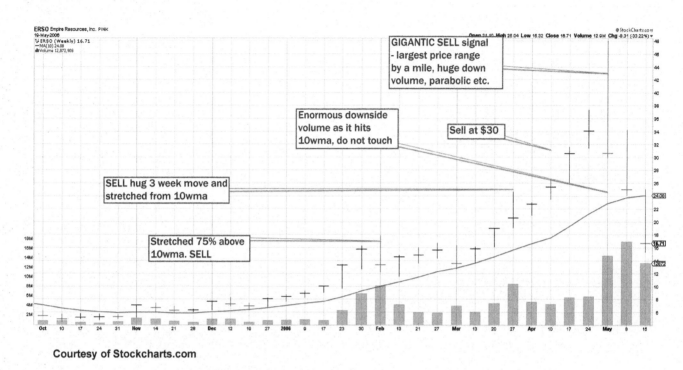

Courtesy of Stockcharts.com

## 7 – ALDILA CORPORATION (ALDA)

### ALDILA REPORTS SIGNIFICANTLY IMPROVED FIRST QUARTER 2004 FINANCIAL RESULTS

Poway, CA., April28, 2004—ALDILA, INC. (NASDAQ:NMS:ALDA) announced today net sales of $15.3 million and net income of $2.3 million ($0.46 per share) for the three months ended March31, 2004. In the comparable 2003 first quarter, the Company had net sales of $10.2 million and a net loss of $169,000 (a $0.03 per share loss).

"We are extremely pleased with the strong results achieved in our first quarter 2004. Driven by the overwhelming acceptance of our flagship NV™wood shaft line by the golfing world, *our sales increased by 51%* versus the first quarter last year. Our net income of $2.3 million or $0.46 per share represents the best quarter the Company has had in the last 8 years. Unit sales climbed by 11% and *average selling price increased by 37%* quarter on quarter...*Gross margin* in the 2004 first quarter *rose to 40% on a 252% increase in gross profit* to $6.1 million as compared to 17% and $1.7 million in the first quarter of 2003..."The success of the NV™wood shaft line has opened the door to a *multitude of new accounts* which broadens our already large customer base," Mr. Mathewson continued."

TECHNICALS:

- Nice base before breakout.

- Huge volume expansion on breakout.

- Great angle of attack.

- Under $15.

- Breakout above 30 week moving average.


FUNDAMENTALS:

- Recent insider buying.

- Earnings winner. $0.46 eps vs. loss.

- Annualized PE of 10 upon entry.

- Easy upcoming earnings comparisons (comps).

- Enormous operating leverage.

- A great earnings headline.

- A low float of 5 million shares.

- A super theme of next generation golf shaft used by PGA pros.

- Very conservative management issuing very few pr's.


## NOTES PRIOR TO ENTRY

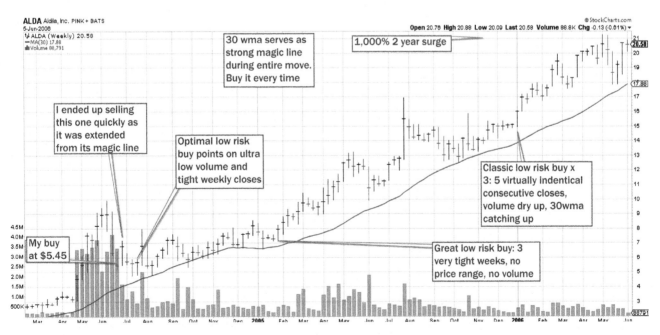

Courtesy of Stockcharts.com

## POTENTIAL BUY POINTS

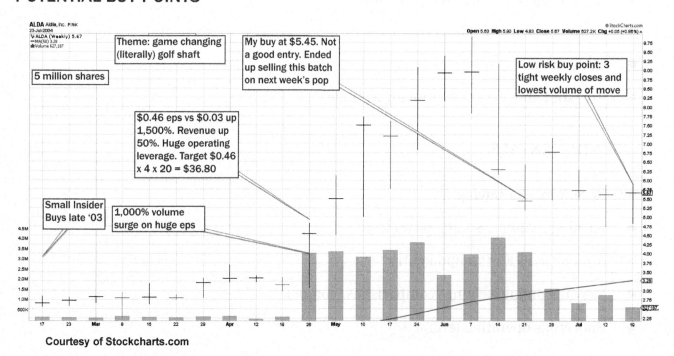

Courtesy of Stockcharts.com

## POTENTIAL SELL POINTS

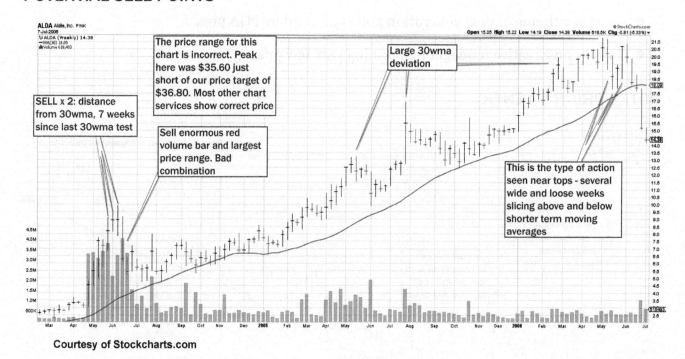

Courtesy of Stockcharts.com

## 8 – FREIGHTCAR AMERICA (RAIL)

### FreightCar America, Inc. reports quarterly pro forma earnings per share of $0.90 and net earnings per share of $0.76 as backlog reaches 15,867 units.

Chicago, IL, July 27, 2005—FreightCar America, Inc. (NASDAQ: RAIL) today reported financial results for the three months ended June 30, 2005. For the second quarter of 2005, sales were $230.7 million and net income attributable to common stockholders was $9.1 million, or $0.76 per diluted share. In comparison, for the second quarter of 2004, the Company had sales of $94.9 million and a net loss attributable to common stockholders of $4.3 million, or $0.63 per diluted share...*pro forma earnings per share was $0.90* on a fully diluted basis for the three months ended June 30, 2005, *compared to a pro forma loss per share of $0.11* on a fully diluted basis for the same period in 2004.

"We believe business conditions in the North American coal railcar sector remained strong in the second quarter, and the Company retained its market share of new orders. The Company's orders for all types of new railcars totaled 5,104 units in the second quarter, a *60% increase over the order activity in the second quarter of 2004.* In addition, the total backlog of unfilled orders reached 15,867 units at June 30, 2005, *nearly double the backlog* on June 30, 2004. We *will continue to ramp up production* output to deliver the increased backlog as scheduled and committed to our customers."

TECHNICALS:

- Breakout of strong base above 30 wma.

- Weekly volume expansion of 600%.

- High angle of attack.

  *Note: not under $30. But EPS of $0.90!

FUNDAMENTALS:

- Huge earnings winner.

- Annualized PE under 10 (PE of 8 at entry).

- Sustainable earnings- backlog growth, CEO commentary.

- Easy comps going forward.

- Increasing backlog.

- Conservative management.

*Notes—Share count just above ideal range. 12.7 million shares outstanding. Iffy theme—rising demand for new railcars due to improving economy and replacement cycle of old cars.

## NOTES PRIOR TO ENTRY

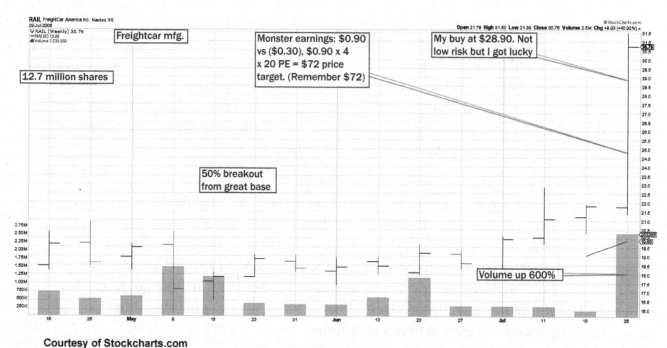

Freightcar mfg.

12.7 million shares

Monster earnings: $0.90 vs ($0.30), $0.90 x 4 x 20 PE = $72 price target. (Remember $72)

My buy at $28.90. Not low risk but I got lucky

50% breakout from great base

Volume up 600%

Courtesy of Stockcharts.com

## POTENTIAL BUY POINTS

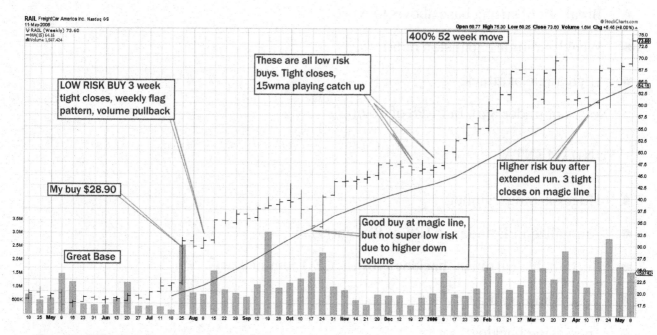

400% 52 week move

LOW RISK BUY 3 week tight closes, weekly flag pattern, volume pullback

These are all low risk buys. Tight closes, 15wma playing catch up

My buy $28.90

Higher risk buy after extended run. 3 tight closes on magic line

Great Base

Good buy at magic line, but not super low risk due to higher down volume

Courtesy of Stockcharts.com

# POTENTIAL SELL POINTS

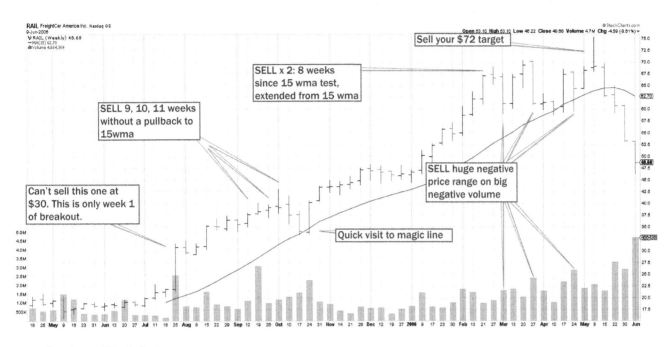

Courtesy of Stockcharts.com

.....AND RULES ARE MEANT TO BE BROKEN FROM TIME TO TIME.

## 9 – LOCAL CORPORATION (LOCM)

*Ticker symbol was INCX in 2004
*SUPER THEME + EXTREMELY LOW FLOAT = MONSTER*

LOCM came public on October 18, 2004. It had no earnings or trading history to speak of, so I can't comment on the fundamental or technical Super Laws as they relate to LOCM. However, it had one enormous fundamental factor going for it. INCX had a spectacular Super Theme that had never before been seen..."local search." It was also touted as "Baby Google." No search engine had local search at the time, not even Google. Investors were blown away by the possibilities. Its moves were so explosive that I was forced to trade it much more actively than I would otherwise. Since there was no recent earnings release or any other fundamental or technical factors I can point to, I will share my thoughts from my emails from that period. They mostly discuss the stock's super theme.

## THE SHORT-TERM TRADING OF "BABY GOOGLE"

### 11/01/04

"Traded INCX twice for huge short term trades thus far. Any opinions on it? My feeling is that it will either bounce big off the 10.73 gap or the 9 dma which is currently about $10. Volume is staggering.

179

Started establishing another position under $11 this afternoon.Just did a search for gyros and chicken wings in my zip code and was amazed by the results. Never even thought that half the places had wings. I'm not saying that the technology will translate into revenues, but it is groundbreaking. My hunch is that with its large investor following in such a short period of time, along with the "baby google," and "local search" buzz, it could prove to be a big gainer."

## 11/8/04

"I don't know where I first heard about INCX, but I watched it like a hawk after I heard about it. I didn't buy it. When the message board was activated around day 5 and I saw about 30 posts within about an hour of activation that night, I knew it would be an absolute monster. I bought all I could the next morning at 8.30-8.40. I sold just under 12, bought back in again at 11.80 and sold at 13.10. For the grand finale, after seeing textbook outstanding consolidation, I put all the chips (including Ameritrade's matching funds) in at 11.11-11.39 and sold it all between 16.10 and 16.90. I will wait to re-enter until after it fills the gaping hole and consolidates for a few days until the 9dma catches up. I rarely get emotional about stocks, but about 3 or 4 times per year, I will trust my gut and make a huge wager. After about 30 hours of research, I figured it was a gamble worthtaking."

## POTENTIAL SHORT TERM BUY POINTS

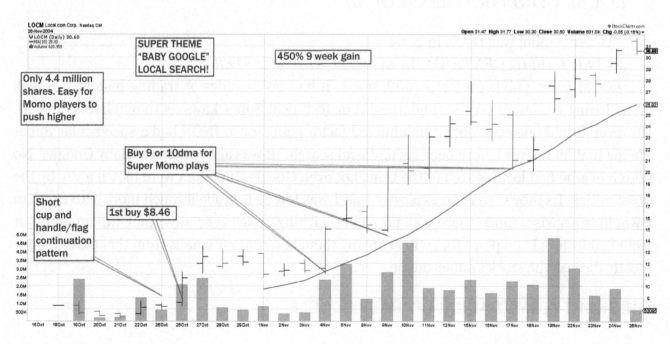

Courtesy of Stockcharts.com

## POTENTIAL SHORT TERM SELL POINTS

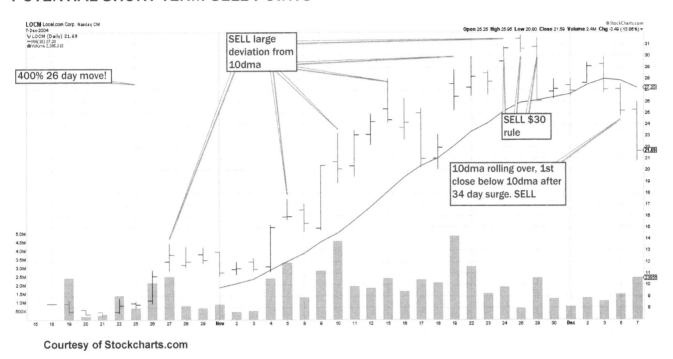

SELL large deviation from 10dma

400% 26 day move!

SELL $30 rule

10dma rolling over, 1st close below 10dma after 34 day surge. SELL

Courtesy of Stockcharts.com

## 10 – APPLE COMPUTER (AAPL)

This example is 100% about the predictive value of a chart. I picked up AAPL in 2003 for 2 reasons and 2 reasons only: a SUPER DUPER theme and a mind-boggling breakout chart on obscene volume.

TECHNICALS:

● Breakout of 5 month base.

● 500% volume surge.

● Nice angle of attack.

● Breakout above 30 wma.

FUNDAMENTALS:

● Massive game-changing theme: "I-tunes" release.

## NOTES PRIOR TO ENTRY

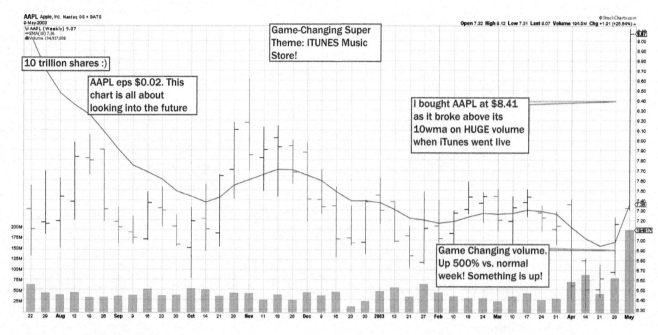

Courtesy of Stockcharts.com

## YOU KNOW THE STORY...

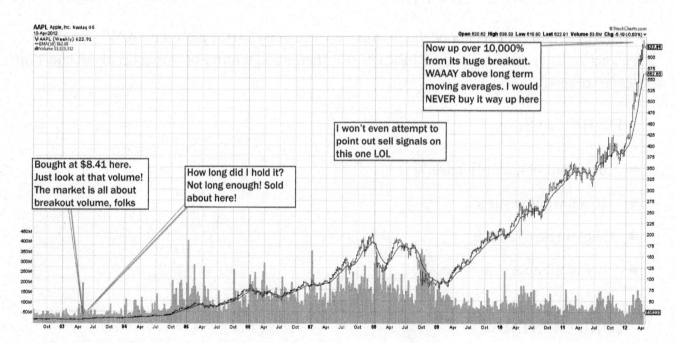

Courtesy of Stockcharts.com

## 11 - *HONORABLE MENTION: TRMM*

TRM Corporation– ATM Machines

## THE 10,800% 18 MONTH ADVANCE

Initially, I wasn't going to include TRMM because it was acquired by another company. Its chart no longer exists in any chart service database. I decided to include it because TRMM was the company that started it all. This stock got the ball rolling and helped me make several hundred thousand dollars. I was finally able to locate a chart, but I apologize in advance—it was the only chart I could find of TRMM anywhere.

### TRMM REPORTS SUBSTANTIALLY IMPROVED RESULTS

8/06/2003-TRM Corporation (NASDAQ: TRMM) today reported net income for the quarter ended June 30, 2003 of $1.15 million ($.16 per share, or $.11 per share after preferred dividends) compared to a net loss of $404,000 (($.06) per share, or ($.11) per share after preferred dividends) for the same period in 2002. For the six-month period ending June 30, 2003, the Company reported net income of $1.90 million ($.27 per share, or $.16 per share after preferred dividends) as compared to a net loss of $741,000 (($.10) per share, or ($.21) after preferred dividends) for the same period of 2002.Net sales grew to $20.22 million, representing an increase of $2.53 million (or 14.3%) when compared to the second quarter of 2002.

TECHNICALS:

- Rare "staircase" base-on-base pattern.

- Large volume expansion on its breakout.

- Steep angle of attack.

FUNDAMENTALS:

- The best series of Insider Buys I've ever seen. They kept buying as the stock crept up from $0.25 to $6!

- Unreal earnings winner. Sequential earnings progression was ($0.54), $0.11, $0.16, $0.20, $0.26, $0.31

- PE under 10- Annualized PE of about 6 when I entered.

- Very easy comps.

- Theme—Signed contract to sell and service ATM's for world's largest ATM manufacturer – Triton corp.

- High operating leverage.

- Low share count: 7 million shares.

Unfortunately, I can't dig up any old TRMM email alerts upon entering the position as this goes back before I regularly sent them out.

TRMM started its run at $0.25 and ended at $27 in about a year and a half. A return of some 10,800%. Unfortunately I didn't discover it until it was just under $4.

After hitting $27, the stock collapsed within a matter of days. Again, notice the $25-$30 topping price level. I held during the entire run and ended up going down with the ship.

Notice the "staircase pattern" evolving into a parabolic move in the stock price (white line) below.

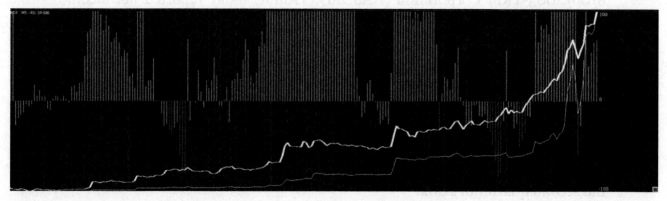

TC2000® chart courtesy of WordenBrothers, Inc.

# CHAPTER 13

# *Superstock Resources*

Like most serious investors, I have read many of the popular trading and investing books over the years. I have certainly read every one of the classics like *Reminiscences of a Stock Operator* by Edwin Lefevre, *How I Made $2,000,000 in the Stock Market* by Nicolas Darvas, or *The Intelligent Investor* by Benjamin Graham. Many of the books that I have read were outstanding and highly entertaining. To aid your pursuit of financial freedom, can I recommend them to you?

*NO.*

My job here is to help you make money...*PERIOD.* I want you to focus on the very few things that will make you serious money. I want you to leave the rest behind. By focusing *EXCLUSIVELY* on the things that truly make a difference, you will open yourself up to the distinct possibility of becoming a true expert. If all of your time is consumed by reading dozens of books, you may become good at several different methods, but you will never become *GREAT* at one. Sure, if you are heading to the Hamptons for the weekend and want an entertaining book to be read during the brief moments between Cosmopolitans, by all means, pick up a copy of *Reminiscences of a Stock Operator.*

But until then, my recommendation is to forget all of the noise. Like the Boston Celtics of the 1980s, you need to become a master of the fundamentals.

In that spirit, in the sea of financial knowledge, I can truly recommend these few resources:

*Note: I have no affiliation whatsoever with any of the following entities.

### 1) *HOW TO MAKE MONEY IN STOCKS* by William O'Neil

This book should not just be the number 1 resource on this list, but it should be numbers 1,2,3,4,5, and 6. It really is that essential to making serious money in the market. I recommend the latest edition (currently 2009) because it has updated charts from recent years. O'Neil's method has consistently found the market's biggest winners going back decades. Although the book is some 400 pages, it really does boil it down to the basics. If you can master his method, you will be ahead of 99.9% of other investors.

No, I don't agree with all of his "rules." In fact, there are quite a few that I disagree with. For instance, I don't believe a firm's revenues or earnings *NEED* to be up X% year over year. I definitely don't believe that a stock should be over $15 or $20 at entry (NO WAY-this absolutely *destroys* performance). I don't agree with a strict 8% stop loss or only buying pivots near 52 week highs. And I don't agree with making an investment decision based on a stock's more obscure metrics such as return on equity.

Have I ever had a subscription to *Investors Business Daily* (O'Neil's newspaper)? Never. In fact, I think I may have only purchased the newspaper five or six times over the years just to see if one of my stocks made the *IBD 100* list. Have I ever subscribed to their website. Yes. I signed up for a one or two week trial several years ago. That's it. Am I affiliated with them in any way. No. This cowboy is not affiliated with anybody.

Overall, the book gives you exactly what you need to know to *MAKE MONEY* in the market. It doesn't give you abstract theory. The book is written by somebody whose returns simply outperform the market year over year. The method taught makes sense and makes money. It is as simple as that. Most other books are entertainment in my eyes. You can borrow it at your public library for *FREE!* Or, you can pick it up used on Amazon.com for a few dollars. Buy it, read it, and study it...forever.

2) *TRADING IN THE ZONE* by Mark Douglas.

As I have said repeatedly throughout the book, mastering the market is 100% about mastering your emotions and developing a disciplined approach to investing. Douglas' book is by far the best book ever written on psychology and proper mindset as it relates to trading. You can pick up ten different books on the psychology of trading but all you really need is one. My advice is to master the fundamentals of this book and never look back. This book is essential. Neither of the above-mentioned books will produce outstanding results in isolation. You must study them both to become truly successful. Check them out from your library or much better yet, buy them used and keep them forever.

3) WORDEN.COM

Once you begin to accumulate a collection of winning stocks and sectors, you will need a way to monitor them. Rather than keeping a written list of stocks and manually typing them into a charting website, you can save a ton of time by subscribing to a chart service like Worden's "TC 2000." You enter all of the stocks that you monitor (could be hundreds or thousands) and you can scroll through them one by one by the press of your spacebar. What may take ten or twenty seconds to do manually on other sites can now be done literally within one or two seconds. The program is a *HUGE* time saver which frees up time for other aspects of your research.

I must admit that I have not tried all of the chart services available. I'm sure there are others that are good. I just know from talking with others and from my own experience that Worden's service is spectacular. Last time I checked, it was roughly $30 per month. In the spirit of free, I will let you in on a little secret. They also offer a free service: www.freestockcharts.com. It offers the same basic features but is supported by advertisements. The drawback is that the ads can cause the site to be slower than the paid version. Try it out.

## 4) FILING4.COM

This service will deliver a free list of all of the insider buys filed each and every day. I've tried most of the free services and this one seems to be the best. There are usually a hundred or so different stocks listed per day so it can take some time to weed through them all. If a company has insider buying and a good chart pattern, you can then move on to researching the fundamentals.

## 5) FINVIZ.COM

Most Superstocks will appear in the daily "biggest gainer" list on the day they break out from their base. It is your job to comb through the list of biggest gainers to see if any are moving higher due to spectacular earnings or outstanding fundamental developments. There are dozens of websites that offer such lists. For me, probably the easiest to navigate is www.finviz.com. It also offers a ton of different stock screeners to help find stocks that meet your technical and fundamental criteria. Again, rather than overload you with all of the other websites that show the same results, I will leave you with just one.

## 6) INVESTOPEDIA.COM

If you would like to learn more about basic technical analysis, look no further than Investopedia.com. The following is a link to a great free tutorial on basic technical patterns, moving averages, and indicators: http://www.investopedia.com/university/technical/default.asp#axzz2AjNaZMEM. It provides a wealth of information on the basics of technical analysis.

## 7) JESSESTINE.COM

Lastly, it would be irresponsible for me to omit my own website!

Well folks, that's really all you need to get started. You might crave more resources but that's all I'm going to give you. The only way to find the best stocks is to do the legwork yourself. I literally have 300 or so free and paid websites in my bookmarks that I could give you. There are also hundreds of people in the blogosphere and on Twitter that I could give you. There's no need for any of them. Once you master the fundamentals, none of the noise will matter.

# CHAPTER 14

# *Major Lessons from My Failures, Warts and All*

Now that we have learned all about how I achieved my past windfalls, I would now like to turn the tables and do something rather unique. I remember several "How I made my fortune" trading books being published in and around 2002. This was just after several of Wall Street's top traders were admitting that they had lost 50%, 70% or more during the .com collapse. When I flipped through these "How To" books, I noticed none of them contained information about losses, failures, or how they fared during the collapse. The books focused on the spectacular performance of the author's (mostly internet) stocks. Most books stressed that "you can replicate my performance" with "little or no experience necessary."

Several years ago, I listened to a Jim Rohn audio-book, and part of it stuck with me to this day. He spoke about how the success industry has a laser focus on only studying success. He said that very few people ever studied failure.

Rohn went into detail about how his terrible early life decisions led him to become completely broke in his late 20's. He went on to say that he would have given just about anything to have listened to a lecture by a homeless man so that he could have learned everything there was to know about what *not* to do in life. Rohn said that if he had learned from such a person, he may not have ended up making the same mistakes.

So in the spirit of Yin and Yang, right and wrong, good and bad, highs and lows, summer and winter—in addition to success principles and Super Laws, I give you the essential lessons I've learned the hard way. I relate lessons from the episodes that wasted thousands of hours of hard work, put me through indescribable agony, and cost millions of dollars in tuition.

I plead with you to learn from them, so that you never have to go through the drawdowns that I've gone through. Yes, I said that several of the top traders have learned immensely from gigantic portfolio losses but you don't have to experience such dramatic results in order to learn the lessons. Learn from my failures, and promise yourself that you won't repeat them.

## 1 – DON'T LISTEN TO "HOT TIPS" OR INVEST IN BIOTECH PENNY STOCKS YOU KNOW NOTHING ABOUT

As I entered my very first investment some 16 years ago, I didn't commit *one* cardinal sin. I didn't commit *two* cardinal sins. I didn't even commit *three* cardinal sins. Unbelievably, I managed to commit *four* cardinal sins! First, I listened to a hot stock tip. Second, because of the stock tip, I invested in a company that I knew absolutely nothing about. Third, it happened to be a penny stock. And lastly, it was the riskiest type of investment known to man: a dreaded early-stage biotech company. Uggh! If you'll recall, I lost 100% of my account equity during this first stab at investing.

## 2 – DON'T DRINK THE KOOL-AID

This is a fact: Everybody's significant other is their "soul mate," and there is simply nobody else out there that would ever compare. The same can be said of our children, our pets, our favorite sweater, our first car, and (gulp!) even the company that we work for. Everybody drinks the Kool-Aid in one form or another. It's ok, as long as we are grateful and happy with what we have, that's all that truly matters. But, although nobody would ever admit to it, the fact remains that given limitless options, there is always something better out there.

Think about this in terms of the stock of the company that we work for. The odds of it being the best investment out there are about, ummm... 1,000,000 to 1. But everybody keeps drinking the Kool-Aid and believing wholeheartedly that because *they* work at the company, it is *THE* best stock and the only one to own. Enron, Worldcom, Kodak, TimeWarner—at one point or another, they were all *THE* best stock in the world in the eyes of their employees. I drank the Kool-Aid the second time I invested in the stock market, and put everything I had into my company's stock. I lost every last penny. Enough said.

## 3 – DON'T TRADE THE NEWS OR CNBC "HOT STOCKS" YOU KNOW NOTHING ABOUT

On my third foray into the market in 1998, I started trading all of the volatile "hot stocks" that were on CNBC. I knew nothing about them except that the talking heads absolutely *adored* them. My thought process was, "Hey, these guys have extensive track records and appear to be making perfect sense on national television. They certainly know much more than I do. It would be stupid not to buy the stock if they say it is going to double." In addition to listening to the "experts," I bought and sold whatever was active on the scrolling ticker on CNBC. Well, this kind of trading lasted all of two or three months for me. This time, I didn't lose *everything*. I lost everything *AND* an additional $600!

## 4 – DON'T EVER DAYTRADE. EVER!

What is day trading? Day trading is picking up pennies in front of a steamroller. To me, day trading is trying to time a stock's price movement from minute to minute, hour to hour, or day to day. 99.9999% of long term day traders lose. Even If you do manage to make some money, day trading is perhaps the most stressful and least spiritually and emotionally fulfilling activities on the planet. Ever heard of Mark Barton? Atlanta? 1999? Trust me, I've day traded on numerous occasions over the past 15 years. Even when I was successful at it, I was a stressed-out emotional wreck while totally unsatisfied with what I was doing.

I have found that when I am in stocks that I have researched inside and out, and when I have a multi-week or multi-month time horizon, I sleep soundly at night and am much more fulfilled. Not to mention 1,000 times more successful. Every time I was fortunate enough to experience a 7-figure portfolio advance, it was entirely because I sat and did nothing.

## 5 – DON'T "PYRAMID" (ADD AS YOUR STOCK ADVANCES) OR USE EXCESSIVE LEVERAGE

I know I know...this is in direct contrast with what many of the "gurus" preach in their books. "Add to your winners" they say. Yes, adding to your winners can create miracles. But it can and often ends in complete devastation if you pyramid excessively. Personally, I know about this all too well. I added more and more shares to a few positions as the risk/reward ratio dramatically shifted out of my favor. I was almost entirely wiped out in a few cases. I made my first million over the course of several months and lost virtually all of it in a single day due to adding to my position near the top when risk greatly outweighed reward.

Today, I would consider using leverage if I had several positions near low risk buy entries. I would not consider adding risk as the positions moved higher. This is and has been a recipe for disaster. Very few people advocate adding to your position when risk is at a minimum. They recommend doing just the opposite. Never do what everybody else is doing.

## 6 – AVOID "FEATURE CREEP" AT ALL COSTS

Remember that "feature creep" occurs when your investing becomes more and more complicated over time. When you started, you found success just by reading *Investor's Business Daily*. All of a sudden, you find yourself spending hours per week scanning *Bloomberg, Zero Hedge, Barron's* and "Big Mike's Jersey Shore Boiler Room Stock Emporium." You started your successful career focusing exclusively on price, volume, and blockbuster fundamentals. All of a sudden you find yourself in a coma as you stare at "OBV," "Slo Stochastics," "Fibonacci Levels," "Bollinger Bands," "RSI," "MACD," "Keitner Channels," "Pivot Points," and God forbid "Ichimoku Clouds."

You find that you used to find all of your stocks on your own. One day you glance at your credit card bill and see that you are spending $2,000 per month on 30 different newsletter services! You used to find all of the market's biggest winners while you sat in a coffee shop with your ten inch laptop. All of a sudden, you look around and see an elaborate office with five computer screens all showing different data feeds.

Each of the above scenarios happened to me. They all served to cause massive over-thinking and overtrading. For crying out loud—I traded $2 *BILLION* (yes *BILLION*) dollars from 2006-2008! I can't tell you how complicated my trading became by the time I took a breather from the game in late 2008. Ridiculous is the only word I can come up with. Feature creep kills your returns and your spirit. Da Vinci said it best: "Simplicity is the ultimate sophistication." Keep your trading simple and streamlined, and you will prosper in the long run.

## 7 – WHATEVER YOU DO, DO NOT "TRADE THE MARKET"

As my trading became excessively complicated, I began to focus more and more on trading general market exchange traded fund (ETF) vehicles such as QQQ (NASDAQ 100), SPY (S&P 500) , IWM (Russell 2000 smallcaps), and EEM(Emerging Markets). In theory, when you enter a trade blindly, you have a 50/50 chance of success. Well, when I put money in ETF's such as these, I think I lost about 80% of the time. Do you know why? Because I had no edge and no conviction in the trades!

These are all "mainstream" investment vehicles that "everybody" invests in. "Everybody" is average and mediocre. By now, you know very well that "everybody," the "mainstream," and the "media" are our investing arch enemies.

If you have no research backing up your position, you have no price target and very little confidence that it will increase in value. As stocks fluctuate wildly around their mean, what do you think would happen almost every time one of these vehicles started trading for a loss? Without conviction, I would sell for a loss. Over and over again. I didn't learn my lesson. I urge you to only invest in prices whose underlying stocks you know inside and out and whose risk/reward is stacked heavily in your favor.

## 8 – DO NOT TRADE WITH UNSUCCESSFUL TRADERS

There have been times when I have traded with some of the best traders in the world. There is nothing like the confidence and inspiration that you get when you are bouncing ideas off of like-minded traders. The information exchange and discipline developed is truly rewarding.

Unfortunately, there have been other times over the past 16 years when I have found myself stuck in much less desirable situations. "Noisy" situations ruled by fear of success, where traders were overwhelmingly "news junkies" who felt safe being enveloped in a cloud of media-induced fear. Some of these investors were people who could not see the immense opportunity that lies just 3 feet beyond this cloud...a mere 36 inches outside of their comfort zone; traders who wanted to be right at any cost; traders foregoing potential fortune just to experience the instant gratification from five minutes of ecstasy—the ecstacy from being right in a group setting. The sad truth is that I just described a majority of the trading environments I've encountered over the years.

My trading has excelled in group settings where successful traders were able to see beyond the ridiculous nature of spoon-fed "stories" and "news." My trading has also excelled when I traded entirely in isolation. But I have never prospered when I traded in group settings where the majority of traders were led by their emotions and allowed their decisions to be influenced by others.

## 9 – DON'T TRADE ILLIQUID STOCKS AND DON'T BECOME STUBBORN

In 2007, I had the misfortune of becoming enamored by a Chinese stock by the name of Fuwei Films (FFHL). Like most other Chinese stocks, its earnings were exceptionally high and its PE was ridiculously low. I ended up taking a sizeable position in the company just after its earnings release. Within days, its volume completely dried up and I found myself unable to exit my position. Not wanting to sell little by little, I became stubborn, thinking that eventually I would exit at a higher price when the volume returned. Well, the volume finally returned— several months later when the company announced poor earnings. I was finally able to exit, but I took a *HUGE* loss to the tune of $675,824. Fortunately, the rest of my portfolio was faring much better at the time.

So, never enter a stock that you can't easily exit from in a timely manner. If you do find yourself in a similar situation, do not "buy and hope." Do not hope that things will change for the better. Start selling immediately, and sell for as long as it takes to exit your position. If it takes you ten trading days to exit while unloading 100 shares at a time, so be it. Just don't find yourself sitting on hundreds of thousands of dollars of losses from a single position.

## 10 – DO NOT LET ANTICIPATED MARKET DIRECTION DICTATE INDIVIDUAL TRADES

When listening to others or when focusing on broad market technical charts, on occasion I have let my *opinion* about the direction of the general market affect my investing decisions. I have let go of some of the market's biggest winners because I *feared* that the market was about to turn down. While lightly trading in the spring of 2009, I let go of several 500%-1,000% gainers because I allowed myself to listen to the prevailing opinions (groupthink) at the time. If there's one thing I've learned over the years, it is that the broad market usually does exactly the opposite of what we expect.

Outside of major market turning points (which I cover in the appendix), day-to-day opinions about the market rarely come to fruition. If you believe that the market is going to fall, chances are that it won't. And if it does, who cares? You have a stop loss in place, and you will buy the next low-risk entry when it presents itself.

## 11 – HOLD ON TO YOUR WINNERS

There have been times when I have found myself victim of the "right" vs. "rich" syndrome. When all of my experience dictated that a Superstock would surge several hundred percent, I would exit after a paltry gain due to letting my emotions get the best of me. Once you have entered your positions, don't give them any thought until they issue a major sell signal. Until then, focus on the garden of life.

## 12 – LEARN HOW TO SELL. LEARN HOW TO SELL. LEARN HOW TO SELL!!!

Early on, I knew just about all there was to know about uncovering the market's best fundamental stories as well as identifying their blockbuster patterns. What I had no clue about was the art of selling. I let millions and millions of dollars exit my account simply because I had absolutely no clue about when to sell. A parabolic pattern? "Cool" I thought, "It must mean that it's breaking out and going much higher." Ha! Little did I know that it was the kiss of death, and I was about to lose everything I had.

Like I've said throughout this book, knowing how to sell is more important than knowing what to buy and when to buy it. Very few investors study the art of selling. I'm sure by now that you can guess what I'm about to say, right? Since you *must not* do what everybody else does, you *must* do what nobody else does. You absolutely have to learn everything there is to know about selling. Selling high-risk situations makes a brilliant career.

## 13 – DO NOT!

DO NOT LOSE YOUR DISCIPLINE!
DO NOT OVERLEVERAGE!
DO NOT "GAMBLE"!
DO NOT TRY TO BE A HERO!
DO NOT TRADE "THE MARKET"!
DO NOT INVEST IN OPTIONS!
DO NOT INVEST IN ANY STRATEGY THAT IS NOT YOUR "BREAD AND BUTTER"!
AND NEVER, EVER "REVENGE TRADE"!

To make a long story short: I somehow managed to lose **discipline** and violate every single one of the above rules in a very short period of time during the "Great Crash of 2008." I won't recount the entire incident yet again, but suffice to say that I committed a series of tragic errors that resulted in a multi-million dollar hit to the tune of some 70% in a matter of days.

I lost a small portion of my account heading into the crash, so I backed off on risking capital. Once things totally unraveled, I figured that I would take **revenge** for my earlier small losses and emerge victorious with a mindboggling nine-figure fortune. I figured that such a reward required a massive **leveraged gamble;** a gamble that for one reason or another, I was ready and willing to take. A gamble that was encouraged by my army of computers, newsletters, and data services (groupthink).

Becoming an overconfident **hero,** I put all of my eggs into leveraged **broad market** ETF's and **options,** and divorced my time-tested successful **bread and butter strategy**. The rest is stock market lore. Do not let this happen to you.

## 14 – ALWAYS REMEMBER TO PUT EVERYTHING IN PERSPECTIVE

We need to remind ourselves just how insignificant our account fluctuations are in the grand scheme of things.

Look, one fateful night at the Atlanta Olympics in 1996, I sat on a bench speaking with a co-worker whose name you may remember—Richard Jewell. Four minutes after our conversation, a bag hidden under that very bench exploded, killing 2 and injuring 111 people.

While studying in Delhi, India in the spring of 1996, my tardiness caused me to board bus number "two" to the Taj Mahal. As fate would have it, bus number "one" careened off the road, killing 5 and injuring dozens of my fellow students.

 In 1999, I awoke one afternoon to find doctors telling me that after ingesting a lethal dose of GHB (unbelievably, it was legal and sold at GNC as a muscle builder!) it was a miracle that I was alive.

I could go on about my "Multiple Sclerosis" experience, my 15-day lung cancer scare in 2006, my night in a Mexican jail, or a dozen other near-death experiences taking place all over the world. The point is that we all can (and will) leave this great Earth in the blink of an eye. We need to always remind ourselves that, when put into perspective, our account balance has no meaning in the grand scheme of things.


**Update**—On the evening of December 11, 2012, I released the "advanced reviewer's edition" of this book to friends and family for the very first time. It was my announcement to the world that I had actually written a book. I was pretty ecstatic.

As you know by now, I talk quite a bit about "seasons" and "cycles" in this book.

36 hours after this long-awaited "soft-release" of this book, I went out for a long run in Sarasota, Florida. At the very tail end of the run, I slowed down to walk through the crosswalk of a major intersection.  I made it about 60 feet through the intersection before an accelerating car slammed me from behind.

The market has taught me that I can bounce back from anything life can throw my way. This time will be no different.

Put the market in perspective and never take one single day for granted.

# CHAPTER 15

# *Top Sixteen Things You Must Do Differently to Achieve Massive Success*

Now that we near the end of the book, I want to re-emphasize just how critical it is for you to do things differently from almost everybody else in the investment world. I want to drill the point home, so I will say it again for the umpteenth time. What everybody knows is not worth knowing. What everybody does is not worth doing. You must stand on your own and live life to the beat of your own drum. In so doing, you must invest entirely different than just about everybody else in order to put yourself in a position to radically outperform.

Here I will summarize a few of the key ways in which you can exploit different investing behaviors in order to succeed on a massive scale.

## 1 – RELENTLESSLY STUDY THE ART OF SELLING

You can buy any stock at any price. It does not matter what stock you buy or at what price you buy it. The only thing that ultimately matters to your success as an investor is the price at which you sell it. Most investors spend 99% of their time studying what to buy and when to buy it. They just figure that they will sell at some point in the future after their stock has advanced. As we have seen visually in this book's charts, stocks can violently collapse within hours or days after hitting a high risk sell point. If you don't become passionate about the art of selling, you might continually lose a majority of your gains as you sell with everybody else when fear becomes your sell signal. Fear is *NOT* a profitable sell signal.

## 2 – FOCUS ON WEEKLY AND MONTHLY CHARTS

An overwhelming majority of investors do not consider low risk timing when they purchase their stocks. "I like stock X...I buy stock X." A vast majority of investors, who actually *do* consider the proper point at which to buy, are focused almost exclusively on hourly and daily charts. Only a small number of investors ever consider making a majority of their investment decisions based on the gold standard of charts—the weekly chart. Smart money billion dollar hedge funds and institutions base their buy and sell decisions almost exclusively on longer-term weekly and monthly charts. They do so because weekly and monthly charts are much more reliable in terms of their predictive nature than shorter term charts. When I see an imminent breakout on a monthly chart, I hold on for dear life. Such long term breakouts can be colossal in scale.

## 3 – BUY WEEKLY BOREDOM

Most traders are taught to buy breakouts when excitement reaches a pinnacle. Many breakouts fail and these "chasers" exit their position at a loss. Very few investors would ever consider entering a position when boredom, volume, and volatility are at a minimum. Most investors need the instant gratification of buying a stock that has already moved higher. The most successful investors are quietly accumulating large positions while nobody is watching or discussing their stocks. Rather than buy excitement on the daily chart, focus your attention on high probability, low risk weekly entries when volatility (price range) has come to a standstill and volume is just a fraction of where it was just a few weeks earlier. It will seem like nobody is talking about your stock. You may have to practice patience and wait a few weeks, but the risk/reward is much more favorable in these situations. Remember to "buy light and tight" and "silent but deadly" chart patterns.

## 4 – BECOME "ONE" WITH THE "MAGIC LINE"

Outside of some institutions, very few investors know that most stocks have their very own "magic line." They don't realize that there is a very specific longer term moving average that a stock adheres to over time. The magic line is oftentimes the 10 week simple moving average, but it can be just about any other short or long term moving average. The 12 week moving average, 17 wma, 20 wma, 30 wma—you name it. The market's very best entries occur precisely when boredom (low volume) and low volatility (low price range) meet up with these magic lines. The results can be magical. And most investors have no clue.

## 5 – FOCUS EXCLUSIVELY ON SMALL CAPITALIZATION STOCKS

An overwhelming majority of investors buy into the "safety," popularity, and familiarity of behemoth large cap stocks. These are the stocks that are talked about all day every day on CNBC. If General Electric, Microsoft, AT&T, or Intel move 20% in twelve months, it is considered a "monster year." The very best stocks are the small caps that are moving 20% per *WEEK*. There is no information edge to be found investing in large caps or ETF's. Such an edge can be found in each and every corner of the small cap universe.

## 6 – WAIT UNTIL EVERYTHING LINES UP

Most investors invest immediately because they "like" a company or its product. Or they may invest if a technical indicator says to invest. They may even invest because a company is "growing" and has "rock solid fundamentals." Or they may invest often simply out of habit. They feel as though they have to do something in the market just to keep busy. These are qualities of your average investor whose returns mimic the major averages over time. There is only one way to put yourself in a position to hit a grand slam—*wait, wait, wait, and wait some more* until most of the technical Super Laws line up in your favor, most of the fundamental Super Laws line up in your favor, *and* the market conditions are favorable. By waiting until *EVERYTHING* lines up in your favor, your odds of massive success go through the roof. Only strike when the iron is hot!

## 7 – DON'T INVEST LIKE A MUTUAL FUND MANAGER

Mutual funds generally have a mandate to be "fully invested" in the market. They very rarely have more than 5% of their assets in cash. This is generally the case because being "fully invested" is outlined in their prospectus. Additionally, their investors generally frown upon large cash positions as the managers are paid to outperform "cash." Most average investors have a similar personal mandate. They feel that they must be in the market at all times. It simply feels strange to them to be in cash and to potentially "miss out" on a market advance. The very best investors spend a considerable time in cash. Cash is definitely a position. A very *POWERFUL* position at times. When the conditions warrant, being in cash allows you to have the emotional and financial firepower at your disposal for that rare fat pitch that is slowly lobbed in your direction. By being inactive a good deal of the time, you put yourself in a position to have massive portfolio bursts from time to time. Put yourself in the position to seize only the very best opportunities. The objective is to make as much money as possible. It is not to be "fully invested."

## 8 – INVEST ON AN ISLAND

Let's assume for a second that you were dropped off on an island in the middle of the Pacific Ocean. Let's also assume that on the island, you have no access to *CNBC, Bloomberg,* Twitter, Facebook, email, articles, friend's opinions, mass-media etc. etc.. *BUT,* let's assume that you had electricity, *ONE* laptop, access to a powerful chart pattern program (Worden for instance) and access to all SEC filings (Insider transactions, earnings releases, key developments etc.). Aside from the small problem that you have no food (!), there is not a single doubt in my mind that you would outperform your previous investment returns on a scale previously thought impossible. By eliminating all "noise," you open up the possibility of massive success. 99.99999% of investors would never physically be able to give up the "noise." It is powerfully addictive and powerfully detrimental to our investment success. Ignore the noise and make your own decisions. Grab some string, some wood, a paddle, and get rowing to that island!

## 9 – BECOME A "SWING TRADER"

A majority of investors are long-term "buy and holders." Their returns are generally dependent on the movement of the major market indexes. Over the very long-term, they generally succeed, but their returns are "slow and low." On the other extreme, you have day traders who buy and sell within minutes, hours, or days. These traders generally experience massive emotional swings and lose money over the long term. The sweet spot is right in the middle. The investors setting records are the "swing traders" who are timing their buys and sells over periods of weeks or months. They may even be in a stock as a "position trade" for a year or more if it proves to be a big winner.

## 10 – BUY THE $3 TO $15 "SWEET SPOT"

Most investors fall into one of three categories: those who buy "penny stocks," those who limit themselves to stocks above $15 or $20 (recommended by *IBD*), or those who invest at any price. Very few investors focus on high growth stocks within the $3 - $15 "sweet spot." This is the band within which a majority of my biggest gainers started their major advances. To go much above this threshold, the "law of large numbers" takes effect and severely limits your potential returns. Likewise, by the time a stock reaches the ever-popular *IBD 100*, a majority of its gains have already taken place.

## 11 – BUY INDIVIDUAL STOCKS, NOT MAINSTREAM ETF'S OR MUTUAL FUNDS

Exchange traded funds and mutual funds have exploded in popularity in recent years. They completely take thinking out of the investment equation. I can understand their appeal for those who don't have any time to make investment decisions. That's fine. But to beat the market, spending time on specific stocks is critical to your success. Information arbitrage exists in every corner of the market. The only way to exploit risk/reward imbalances is to invest in individual stocks.

## 12 – STOP INVESTING IN "WHAT YOU KNOW"

Enough of the Peter Lynch groupthink! Don't invest in your employer because you know it inside and out, do not invest in Coca-Cola because you drink it by the gallon, and don't invest in Facebook because you have no life outside of it. I hope you didn't invest in Groupon because you "love" their coupons. Invest in future themes that nobody yet knows about. If it is something new and you don't know anything about it, chances are good that others don't know about it either. In the future, when others "discover" this theme, their investment capital will flood into this new "must- have" trend.

## 13 – BECOME OBSESSED WITH CHARTS

Most investors pay no attention to charts. They invest in "solid" fundamentals for the long term. They end up sitting on losses for perhaps years at a time before the stock price catches up with the "fundamentals." To prevent this, you must have a diabolical focus on promising chart patterns. *ONLY AFTER* you have found a blockbuster chart pattern should you dig into a firm's fundamentals. *NEVER* reverse this sequence. Your only focus should be on making money from increasing *PRICES*. Unlike many others, your goal should never be to feel "all warm and fuzzy" about a fundamentally strong company that you have great love for.

## 14 – BECOME A SENTIMENT STUD

Most investors are led entirely by their emotions. They are listening to others and buying into the hype and euphoria. On the way down, they continue to follow the crowd as they sell into fear. You must learn to divorce your trading entirely from your emotions. As you master your emotions, you will find yourself buying boredom and fear and selling euphoria. Very few investors are able to do this. The investors making billions are the ones who are buying hand-over-fist during each and every global crisis. They were the ones buying the fear of "nationalization of all banks" in the spring of 2009. They were the ones selling every one of their holdings when one of the most euphoric news items in history was released—the killing of Osama Bin Laden—which marked *the exact* top before the "Fiscal Cliff"" crash of 2011. See Appendix A for my thoughts from this period.

## 15 – SELL AS YOUR STOCK RISES

Every book, every guru, every article is focused on the stop loss. *EVERYBODY* is programmed to sell at this magical price. With anything, what we continually focus on eventually enters our life. Because we are consumed by this stop loss, it inevitably gets triggered. Most investors enter a trade and have not thought for a second about where to sell on the way up. But I can almost guarantee that they have thought about when to sell *on the way down.* Even if a stock goes up 20%, most investors hold on long enough to sell at a loss at the old stop loss price. Most investors don't think even for a second about selling their stocks as they rise. When euphoric sentiment and technical extremes start kicking in, they think "this time is different." "This time" is *never* different. Be different. Everyone else is selling into a collapse. You need to be the one selling as your stock moves higher.

## 16 – DIVORCE YOURSELF FROM MASS MEDIA, AND CLAIM YOUR INDEPENDENCE TODAY!

We focused extensively on groupthink, news, and mass media. The only way to make a fortune is not to allow the opinions of others to influence your investment decisions. In fact, the media is not providing an opinion; the media is *actively* attempting to make you do the exact opposite of what you *should* be doing. Likewise, when "everybody" agrees with your opinion, or when you find yourself agreeing with "everybody else," it is time to run for the hills. Remember that when you consume anything pre-packaged from the mass-media, you slowly lose directed control over your mind. While you consume media (or anything else for that matter) on your television or while staring at your computer for hours on end, what have you created? What have you actually done? What do you have to show for your time? Has your life improved? An existence of constant media consumption sucks every last bit of life out of you. Next time you are about to sit on the couch, ask yourself how good you feel and how great life is *BEFORE* you sit down. Ask the very same question five hours later. Depression truly is a disease of the couch.

A few more important ways to be different:

- "Diversify, diversify, diversify." NO—Invest in only the very best stocks that give you a significant edge, know them inside and out, and always be ready to sell.

- "Pyramid your way to success." NO—Do not add as your stock advances. Risk/reward is shifting out of your favor.

- "Learn all of the indicators." NO—Keep your approach as simple as possible and become the best at reading price, volume, and the magic line.

- "Learn the efficient market hypothesis." NEVER—information arbitrage is everywhere. You *can* crush the market!

- "Study Finance." NO—Study psychology. The market is all about social mood and human behavior. Read Freud. Don't read manipulated economic reports.

- "Gather as much information as possible." NO—Simplify. Actively question the effectiveness of all of your information sources. Increased output = decreased input.

- "Watch your stock like a hawk." NO—Don't obsess. Do all of your homework, let go (have a stop-loss), and live your life. Watching like a hawk destroys vital energy.

- "Invest for long-term capital gains." NO—The cycles for the market's biggest winners are less than a year in most instances. By the time your long-term capital gain window opens up, your stock may be back where it began.

- "Read economic reports, government data, and "Macro News." NO—Just look for winning stocks. Any data provided by economists or the government is rigged for you to lose.

- "Learn every approach." NO—Have a laser focus. Master one method and do it better than anybody else.

- "Only buy breakouts!" NO—*EVERYBODY* is taught this. My biggest gains were low-risk buys *after* and well *below* the hyped "breakout." Buy when everyone else has already been "stopped-out" for a loss.

- "Invest through thick and thin." NO—If something changes at the company or if your stock isn't acting right or...*whatever,* always be able to change your mind on a dime. Be able to sell at a moment's notice. This is hard to do. John Kenneth Galbraith said it best: "Faced with the choice between changing one's mind and proving there is no need to do so, almost everyone gets busy on the proof."

# CHAPTER 16

# *The Road Less Traveled*

*"The question isn't who is going to let me; it's who is going to stop me."*
Ayn Rand

Well, we now find ourselves at the end of this "Road Less Traveled." Give yourself a well-deserved round of applause. You have officially endured my personal story, all of the exhaustive charts, as well as my long rants against the media. Making it this far, you must really be passionate about investing! I truly believe that you are now equipped to step out of the shadow of the backward-focused mainstream market historians. You are now ready to become a future-focused market visionary.

Writing this book provided me with immense personal fulfillment from start to finish. I enjoyed every second of writing it. It has been a journey of deep personal introspection. I remembered investment rules and stories that I had long forgotten. As a result of the process, I am more energized than ever before to pursue the most exciting opportunities in the market. I hope that, as a result of our journey together, you are now more motivated to take control of your financial destiny and to pursue immense future financial independence.

Now that you have the knowledge, it is up to you to turn that knowledge into wisdom through vigorous practice and application. Remember that you can't achieve anything important in life until you get into motion and the magic of momentum takes hold.

I challenge you to keep learning as much as you possibly can—study psychology, learn through trial and error, and study the market's biggest winners (stocks and investors). Once you do experience a level of success—don't stop. Trust me...*NEVER* stop! Keep stretching, keep moving, keep refining your thinking, and keep making mistakes—make it a continuous lifelong pursuit. Make investing your passion.

Don't study others exclusively; take the time to study your own successes and failures. I should have taken the time to study my own history several years earlier than I did. I can't put into words how much I learned from this experience.

In learning from your past investment successes and failures, do not rely on your memory. Keep a folder of "market notes" and keep adding to it. This book would not be possible without the personal notes I collected over the years. I would urge you to develop your own laser-focused "bread and butter" strategy, and get better and better and better at it as you gain experience.

Make a powerful decision today to master the market. Get moving, and remind yourself that there is no finish line in the market marathon. Remember that everything worthwhile is just a few feet outside of your comfort zone. Remember what Muhammad Ali said: "I hated every minute of training, but I said, 'Don't quit. Suffer now and live the rest of your life as a champion.'"

Why not go for it? Why not this very moment?

I wish you all the best in your pursuit of greatness.

*Jesse Stine*

PS- Feel free to keep in touch. Send me an email at jesse@jessestine.com with any questions, comments or collaborative ideas. Visit www.jessestine.com to receive my "friends and family" emails. I hope our paths cross in the future.

*"I'd dare to make more mistakes next time.*
*I'd relax. I'd limber up. I'd be sillier than*
*I've been this trip. I would take fewer things*
*Seriously. I would take more trips, I would*
*Climb more mountains and swim more rivers.*
*I would eat more ice cream and less beans.*
*I would, perhaps, have more actual troubles but*
*Fewer imaginary ones. You see, I'm one of those*
*People who was sensible and sane, hour after hour,*
*Day after day.*
*Oh, I've had my moments. If I had it to do over again,*
*I'd have more of them. In fact, I'd try to have nothing else.*
*Just moments, one after another, instead of living*
*So many years ahead of each day. I've been one of those*
*Persons who never goes anywhere without a thermometer,*
*A hot water bottle, a raincoat, and a parachute. If I could*
*Do it all over again, I would travel lighter than I have.*
*If I had my life to live over, I would start barefoot earlier*
*In the spring and stay that way later in the fall. I would go*
*To more dances, I would ride more merry-go-rounds, I*
*Would pick more daisies."*

85 year old Nadine Stair

# APPENDIX A

# *How to Spot Major Global Inflection Points*

*AND my SECRET indicator—the DEADLY canary in a coalmine.

I have said that the market has a habit of doing exactly the opposite of what we expect it to do. However, after a long market move, it becomes quite a bit easier to pinpoint inflection points. It is often much easier to call a bottom or top in price than it is to call one in time. Thus, even if you know a top or bottom is in place, it can take several weeks to several months for the market to reverse course. When the market makes a big reversal, its objective is to have as few people onboard as possible able to profit from the move. In light of this, even if we know that the bottom or top is in, the market will ultimately time the move to take place when we are no longer watching....when we least expect it.

## *1 – "THE CANARY IN A COALMINE"*

Over the years, I have noticed that my individual portfolio tends to perform horribly in the days leading up to a large market decline. Just prior to a "crash," I have noticed that even if the market continues to slowly advance, I get stopped out of position after position for a loss. It took me several years to finally realize it, but virtually *ALL* of the best performing momentum/ Superstocks start their decline *in advance* of a market decline. Since my entire portfolio can consist of such stocks, I have seen my account take a substantial beating 1-6 sessions *BEFORE* an all-out market route. The reason for this is simple. It is because the best performing stocks are held by the most experienced investors. These are the "smartest guys in the room" who are heading for the exits just hours or days before the masses. This is my "Canary in a coalmine" indicator.

As a general rule, there are typically a dozen or so momentum stocks at any point in time that are considered "in play." These of course, are the stocks that have had the largest advances and are known throughout the trading community. When you start seeing these stocks take significant hits out of the blue, it is best to begin getting defensive. There's a good chance that the rest of the market will follow suit sometime within the next 1-6 market sessions.

On the other hand, when trying to identify market bottoms, we want to see the former leading stocks setting up in solid low level bases before the general market bottoms. As the general market is in free-fall, the very best stocks often are setting up powerful reversal patterns (after already falling substantially) as they prepare to outperform when the market reverses course.

## 2 – 1,000 POINTS SIGNALING A MAJOR CRASH

Perhaps the most reliable way to "predict" an imminent all-out market crash is to simply look at where the Dow is in relation to its 34 week moving average. *EVERY SINGLE* time it gets stretched 750-1,200 points *ABOVE* its 34 week moving average, a major crash comes out of nowhere to surprise everyone. In recent years, the media blamed each and every one of these crashes on a "Crisis" somewhere in the world. I now laugh out loud whenever the media comes up with a major "reason" for each and every mean reversion. If only the media would take a minute to learn about the dynamics of chart patterns, standard deviation, and mean reversion. If major averages get stretched from long term moving averages (34 wma in this case), they get pulled back to these averages no matter what. Stretch, reversion, stretch, reversion...rinse and repeat. Just remember that every global media crisis happens within days of the indexes reaching unsustainably overbought conditions.

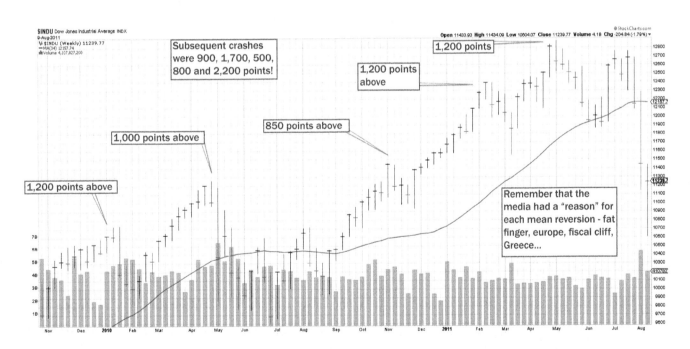

Courtesy of Stockcharts.com

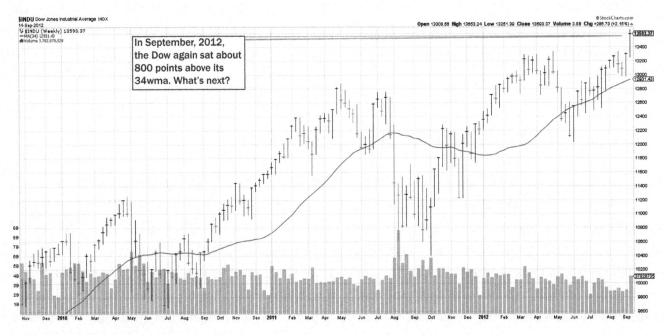

In September, 2012, the Dow again sat about 800 points above its 34wma. What's next?

Courtesy of Stockcharts.com

## 3 – SOX SIGNAL

Throughout my trading career, I have noticed that the semiconductor index leads the overall market. On mornings when the market is down yet the semiconductor index (SOX) is up, chances are very good that the overall market will turn around and follow the SOX. Likewise, when the SOX is down while the market is up, there's a good chance that the overall market will follow suit and turn lower.

The same principal applies over the longer term. When looking at chart patterns, I have noticed that a stretched semiconductor index signals a market reversal even if the general market is not showing any discernable reversal patterns. So, when looking for a top (or a bottom), I go straight to the semiconductor index.

## 4 – WORLD MARKETS

Everybody" tends to analyze the S+P 500, the Dow, or the NASDAQ when trying to position for market tops and bottoms. In recent years, I have noticed that global markets such as China, India, or Brazil will signal a global market turning point even if there are no clear signs in the United States. Whenever I'm looking for a turning point, I put much more weight on an alignment in global markets than I do on U.S. markets. Since the average investor is focused almost exclusively on the Dow, S+P, and NASDAQ, I want to make sure that my attention is focused elsewhere.

## 5 – THE OTHER INDICATORS TO WATCH

In addition to the above factors, for tops and bottoms, I keep my eyes on the VIX, the Credit Suisse "fear indicator," the "NYMO," 90%+ volume into advancing and declining stocks, low 20 and 100 day put/call ratios, "ROBO" (Retail Only, Buy to Open) dumb money option indicator, large speculator positions, and the spread between "smart money" and "dumb money" confidence. Out of the hundreds of indicators, I have found these to be the most effective at predicting market turning points. I generally like to see them all hit extremes within a relatively short time frame. After hitting extremes, a market decline generally will begin sometime within the next few weeks. There are literally dozens of other such indicators that I don't feel are nearly as important as these. These indicators are beyond the scope of this book. There are many websites and books devoted entirely to such indicators. The best website by far devoted to pinpointing sentiment extremes and possible turning points is Sentimentrader.com.

## MY ORIGINAL ALERTS DISCUSSING IMPENDING INFLECTION POINTS

The following "friends and family" alerts discuss exactly what conditions I monitored prior to major market turning points. Outside of my discussion of the Global 2009 historic low, I limit the alerts to 2011 and 2012 as they are more current in the reader's memory. In my "friends and family" alerts, I generally focus on the overall market and specific sectors to the exclusion of individual stocks. On occasion, if a market is gearing up for a run, I might suggest individual stocks. I do not send out alerts at regular intervals. I have gone months without sending out an alert. At other times, when conditions dictate, I can send out several within a matter of days.

These are all unedited original emails sent to friends and family or postings in public forums. Even if my views are entirely dependent on technical indicators, I generally try to keep the discussion of them to a minimum in the spirit of simplicity for readers.

I would also add that most of my alerts were rarely proofread and were written rather quickly in a free-flowing, stream of consciousness style. By no means were these part of a formal newsletter. Again, I apologize for any mistakes in spelling, grammar, or any informalities from these original notes.

# 1 – CALLING FOR THE BIGGEST BOTTOM IN HISTORY

This is what I saw heading into the spring of 2009. I saw an immense opportunity. At the time, I called for a 40-45% upward market reversion. I certainly could not foresee the extent of the ultimate advance.

3/01/09

"MAJOR MARKET/ BANK BOTTOM/ PREDICTING THE BIGGEST BOTTOM IN HISTORY (Email Subject)

Bank Stocks

Here's my investment thesis. Due to multiple indicators pointed out below, my belief is a major low will be reached by March 15th at the latest. Odds favor bottom closer to day 1 than day 15 per *Sentimentrader.* My guess is that 3-5 month return on major averages COULD be 40-45%. This of course is still within the bear market. Banks are in a very defined bullish falling wedge with positive divergence. They have led us down, so my guess is they lead us up. If this plays out, there should be several banks returning 2,3,4,500% by sometime this summer. I also continue to be married to oil. I LOVE steel as well. I sent out an email about FAS earlier which is how I will play the banks until I find some individual bank plays. I'm starting to look into RF. SFI has an interesting chart as well. Lastly, I like DDM which is the ultra Dow ETF. The Dow is the most oversold and there appear to be many individual Dow stocks setting up.

This is an interesting article written by a tax attorney on how bank profits may surge....

http://seekingalpha.com/article/123194-the-end-of-the-credit-crisis?source=article_sb_popular "

The email below shows the kinds of indicators I look at when predicting major market inflection points. This is one of the few where I go into great detail regarding individual technical indicators. I shared them in this instance because although most were hitting historical extremes, it appeared there was a little work left to do on the downside. The included links most likely no longer work. Ultimately, the indexes had a few more days of selling and the indicators hit extremes in unison.

3/5/09 -

"Bottom Indicators (Subject)

10 day moving avg. put call ratio WAY too low. Should be at 1.25, now at .94 - middle of page http://stockcharts.com/def/servlet/Favorites.CServlet ?obj=ID369857&cmd=show[s137347942]&disp=O

Dollar charts appear to be topped out

NDX vs. S&P outperformance is totally off the charts. S&P needs to outperform or NDX needs to crash. Very bottom of page http://stockcharts.

com/def/servlet/Favorites.CServlet?obj=ID369857&cmd=show[s14750168 6]&disp=O

XLE backtested prior low- bouncing off former bottom to the downside

NYSE new lows should be over 1,000 for bottom (770ish today)

Gap in the monthly chart from February to March- Needs to fill? I can't find any other unfilled gaps on monthly charts.

Daily put/call is under 1- should be 1.20 or above.

Would like to see indexes break below their bolinger bands.

Dow MACD breaking previous positive divergence

Where is the VIX spike?

BKX at bottom of channel

XBD retested previous channel and bouncing lower off the channel

Would like to see double bottom in XBD on year chart

Would like double bottom in SOXX

Would like double bottom in NDX

RUT retested old low, bouncing lower

SPX retested prior low, bouncing lower

NAAD MACD should hit -3,000 to -4,0000 (at -2500 now)- last chart...http:// stockcharts.com/def/servlet/Favorites.CServlet?obj=ID369857&cmd=sho w[s157306645]&disp=O

Nasi summation MACD -200 (-100 now) 2/3rd down http://stockcharts. com/def/servlet/Favorites.CServlet?obj=ID369857&cmd=show[s12994756 0]&disp=O"

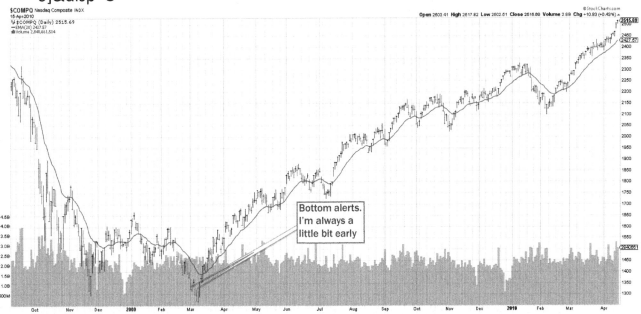

Courtesy of Stockcharts.com

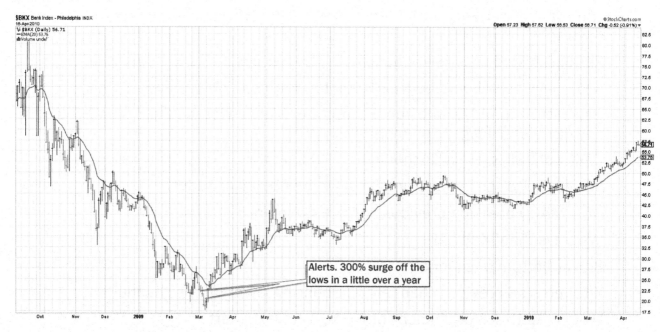

Courtesy of Stockcharts.com

5 days later, within a day or two of the 2009 low, I sent this email out to point out what stocks would go ballistic during a market rally. Many/most of them ultimately offered life-changing returns within a very short period of time.

### 3/10/09

"These are my favorites should a rally unfold. (Subject)

*C($1)- new book value $4. Could be best capitalized out of big banks now. Many banks priced at 1.5 times book now.*

*CENX- highly levered to aluminum. If aluminum returns to where it was 8 weeks ago, this is a 10 bagger.*

*FAS- triple financials*

*MTL- miner- play on the Russian market which is soaring through its 50 day moving average for first time since crash.*

*LCC- Transports have more than likely put in a bottom. Highly levered to transport index.*

*AMR- same as above*

*KWK*

*RF*

*MBI- lowest price to book in entire stock market. Something like .07. If mark to market adjusted....*

*TCK- I just like the chart*

No tech on this list. Tech to under-perform in my opinion whether the market goes up or down."

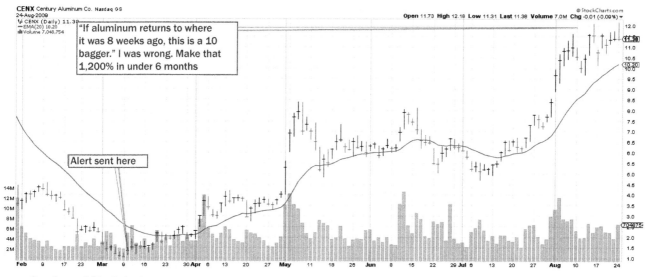

"If aluminum returns to where it was 8 weeks ago, this is a 10 bagger." I was wrong. Make that 1,200% in under 6 months

Alert sent here

Courtesy of Stockcharts.com

160%

Alert

Courtesy of Stockcharts.com

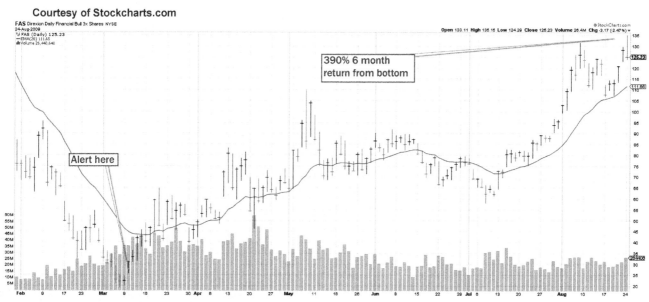

390% 6 month return from bottom

Alert here

Courtesy of Stockcharts.com

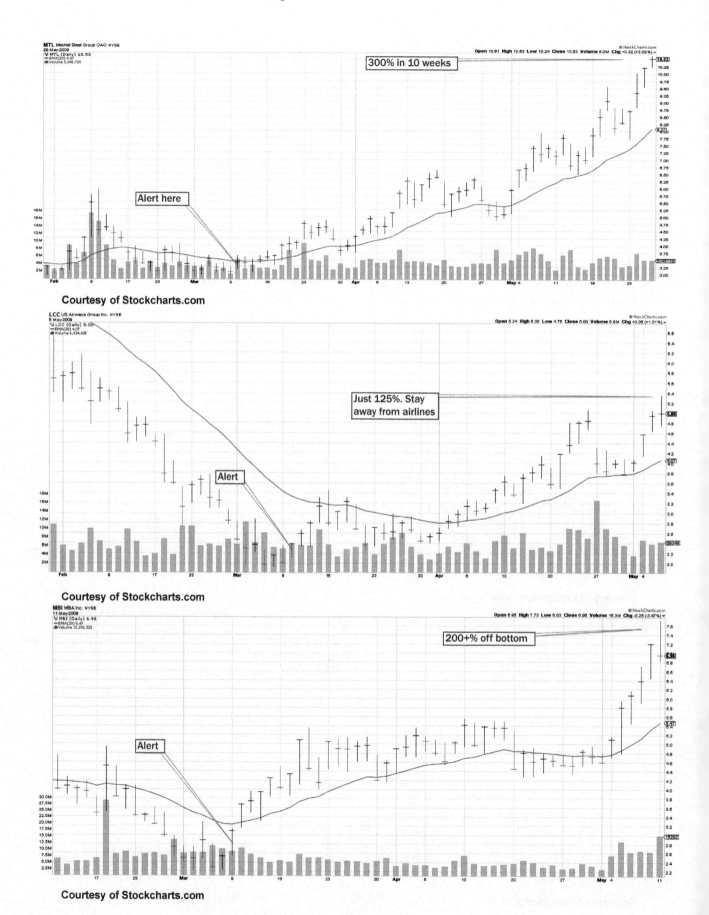

Courtesy of Stockcharts.com

Courtesy of Stockcharts.com

Courtesy of Stockcharts.com

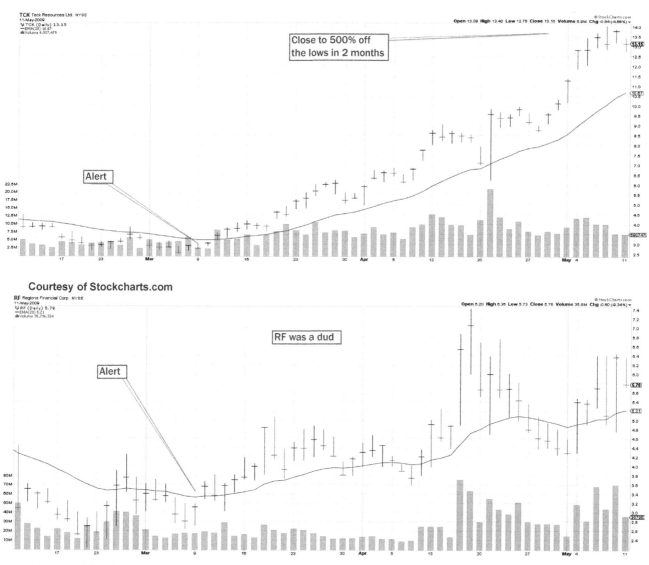

Courtesy of Stockcharts.com

Courtesy of Stockcharts.com

## CALLING THE BIG BLT: "BIN LADEN TOP"

As the technical indicators were getting wildly stretched in the late spring of 2011, I began putting on my bearish cap. When the news of Bin Laden's death was released, I was VERY confident that reward was exhausted and market risk had shot through the roof.

### 4/29/2011

"Guys—

I have been looking at the bull market since the '09 low. The Dow has hugged the 34 week moving average most of the way up. The index reached "extremes" above the 34 week moving average on 3 occasions. Here are the deviations from the moving average and the reaction over the next few weeks.

01/2010: 1,000 points above the 34 week moving average. 800 point reversal within a couple of weeks.

04/2010 850 points above 34 wma. 1,300 point reversal w/in 2 weeks.

02/11 1150 points above 43 wma. 900 point reversal w/in 3 weeks.

Today: 1,070 points above 34 wma."

In the alert below, note how I discuss the "canary in a coalmine"—momentum stocks starting to fall across the board while general market was holding up. The Bin Laden news on this day proved to mark the *EXACT* top in the market for months to come. It was the last hurrah before a 2,300 point crash.

## 5/2/2011- BIN LADEN TOP

"BIN LADEN TOP! (Subject)

Pretty much all of the big boy momentum plays down on the day- REDF -13.5%, TZOO -5%, MOBI -21%, PLAB -5%, APKT -5.5%, SFLY -2.3%, LULU -3.8%, ARUN -4%, OPEN, NFLX, MITK barely survived.

In my experience, this type of action usually results in a pretty big pullback w/in 3-4 sessions as professional traders exit the market while big funds still have funds to put to work, thus propping up the majors.

At major lows, you want to see terrible news being bought. At tops, you want to see unbelievable news being sold. I can't think of any other news that would have the entire country rejoicing."

Coinciding with the Bin Laden Top was a massive reversal setup for the U.S. dollar. If you can recall, there was tremendous "death of the U.S. dollar" groupthink around this time. Everybody suddenly became an expert on what foreign currency was about to take over as the global "reserve currency." In the midst of this dollar groupthink, the dollar was signaling a powerful advance was around the corner. Remember that the dollar is inversely correlated with stock markets. This fit in precisely with my Bin Laden Top premise.

## 5/2/2011

"4/26/11- U.S. dollar public opinion- 18.8%. That's the lowest as far as the chart goes back. This level is outside of lower Bollinger Band which has marked dollar turning points in the past.

IMO, this presents a major inflection point for the Dollar and for the markets."

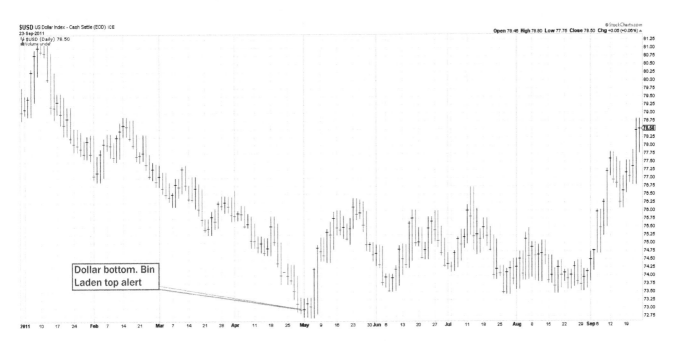

Courtesy of Stockcharts.com

Courtesy of Stockcharts.com

# WHAT I SAW IN THE HOURS LEADING UP TO THE 1,900 POINT "FISCAL CLIFF" OF 2011

The following is what I saw heading into the big crash of 2011 aka "The Fiscal Cliff of 2011." Notice the canary in a coalmine indicator. I got pretty passionate in a couple of these. I pleaded to stay in cash. These alerts were written the day before a 10-day 1,900 point crash.

## 7/26/2011

"I have been busy w/ a couple new business ventures, thus I haven't been involved in the market too much of late. However, I have seen 4 separate headlines in the past 2 days commenting on how the debt ceiling debate has absolutely no bearing on the stock market. Why the stock market will continue to be strong in the face of this gridlock...Saying how "strong" the market is in the face of the chaos. I think this is a set-up.

I have seen leading indicators- TZOO, NFLX, CVV, REDF, SIFY, MITK, X, STLD (all of the leading indicator commodity stocks with the exception of rare elements- MCP, REE etc...all start to fall. Usually these leading indicator "momo" stocks fall 2-6 sessions before the market drops substantially. I think it all started about 4 sessions ago.

There are a couple of stocks that I really like here. However, all of the above is the type of crap that results in a 3 hour market drop of 1,000 points or more (aka the "flash crash"). I am heading to Laos and am hoping the Nasdaq can break out to the upside so we can have a 1,000 point breakout over the next 6 months.

In the meantime, I would be VERY hesitant to recommend "buy and hold" for those looking for +20% annual returns."

## 7/26/2011

"Yes, everybody is saying that stocks are "safe" in light of the chaos.

From a long term perspective, there is still a HUGE;... let me reiterate... MASSIVE weekly and monthly head and shoulders pattern on all of the indices- IWM, RUT, SPX, DJIA etc. etc...IF, IF, iF this starts breaking down, we see a MASSIVE drop.On the bullish side, we are at the cusp of a multi-year cup and handle, which would lead to a HUGE breakout to the upside.W/ the leading indicators selling off.....HARD.... These momo stocks are not just selling off a little bit, but selling off SUBSTANTIALLY, I am not willing to bet on the long side just yet.There is *ABSOLUTELY ZERO, ZILCH, NADA, NONE, NO* reason to be long or short here.If you get long, the market will crash. If you get short, the market will skyrocket.I think the best course of action is to wait on the sidelines, be entertained by *CNBC, CNN, Barron's* etc. and invest your hard earned money in a month or two- whether its at 1000 SPX or 1500 SPX..."

7/26/2011

"And don't forget about the "BLT" top that I have been talking about since the first trading day of May. It still stands."

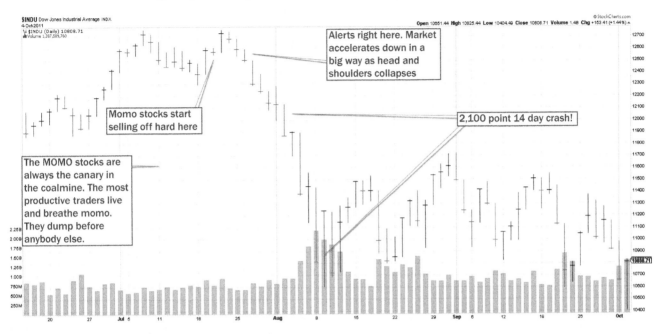

Courtesy of Stockcharts.com

## ANOTHER "CANARY" TRIGGER THE DAY BEFORE THE 750 POINT SELLOFF

This alert was written the day before a 750 point 3 day drop. Although not expressed in words, the implication was watch out, I hear the birds in the coalmine.

"From my "momo watch list" today:

JVA -14%

CVV -10%

VHC -6%

OPEN -4%

TZOO -2%

IDCC -2.5%

MCP -1.5%

LULU -1%

NFLX -1%"

*This was particularly troubling as it was on an up day in the market.

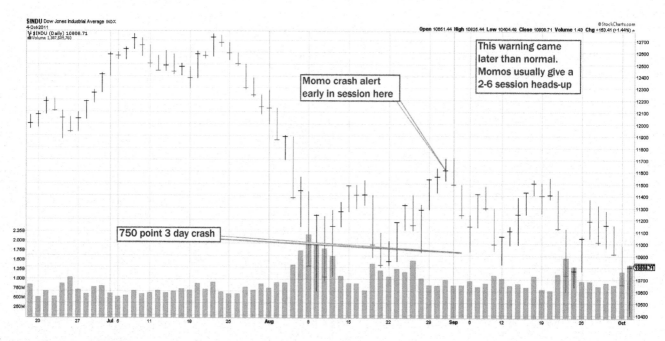

Courtesy of Stockcharts.com

## MULTIPLE CANARY IN A COALMINE ALERTS BACK TO BACK BEFORE 1,100 CRASH

These 4 alerts were in the few days leading up to a 1,100 point 10 day crash.

### 9/16/2011

"My super-oversold watchlist always surges leading out of a market collapse. Here's my watchlist:

PCX -10%

FRO -4.5%

TEX -4%

MTL -3%

BAS -3.5%

TZOO same old same old

Then I could go on about the horrendous performance of the momo's: CVV, MITK, NFLX, OPEN etc"

### 9/19/2011

"I commented about my watchlist being down big on Friday. More of the same today.

MTL -6%

FRO -6%

PCX -4%

TBSI -10%

TEX -4%

BAS -5%"

**9/20/2011**

"MAJOR WARNING GUYS.

We haven't seen anything like this since July 17th (ish). This is actually much worse than the day when I said "market collapse w/in 2-4 sessions." (There was a) **Total collapse in all things momo today on a fairly flat day in the markets.** I'm not putting money into puts, but be high alert over the next 6 trading sessions.

MCP -22%

REDF -11%

JVA -10%

NFLX -9%

TZOO -13%

DTLK -9%

VHC -8%

IDCC -6%

LNKD -6%

STMP -5%

OPEN -4%

LULU -3%

PANL -5%

MITK -3%

RESOURCES

PCX -9%

MTL -5%

FCX -4%

X -3%

AKS -3%

……too many to list"

**9/20/2011**

> "If history is any guide, after a total collapse of "trading vehicles," we should see a flat/up day tomorrow and possibly Thursday. If history repeats (as it continually has in my trading career), we could see some sort of meltdown starting Thursday, Friday, or Monday."

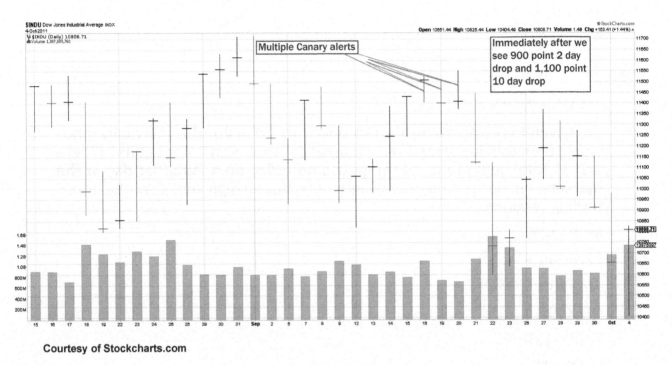

Courtesy of Stockcharts.com

## CANARY AND HEAD AND SHOULDERS PATTERNS EMERGING BEFORE MAY EUROPEAN CRISIS

These were my alerts just prior to yet another European crisis in May of 2012. Remember that the SOX tends to make its move before the overall market.

**5/03/2012**

> "I haven't been watching the market, so not sure if this is making the rounds or not. Be aware of pretty clear Head and Shoulders patterns starting to break down in key indices such as RUT (small caps) and SOX (semiconductors). I have to keep reminding myself that the Fed always gets what they want. And I keep hearing QE3 being discussed in Fed minutes. There's only one way their/Obama's wishes can come to fruition (market collapse to get public on board for QE). Back to work for me..."

**5/5/2012**

> "We had SOX and RUT setting up in H+S (Head and Shoulders) pattern. Now

S+P will most likely open below its 13 wma on Monday which has been the bull staircase since the crossover in November. The market is toast. Not sure how dramatic the decline will be, but I would take long walks in the park and perhaps pull out old Nintendo NES from the attic over the next 1-2 weeks as H+S patterns happen so quickly, they are usually only evident in hindsight.

The early signal has been several key stocks getting whacked 30%,40%,50% over the past few sessions. (Canary in Coalmine) As always, will it (crash) happen? The heck if I know. But in the rare event when the indicators line up, its best to shift focus *IMMEDIATELY* to those things that truly matter in life and take a market vacation."

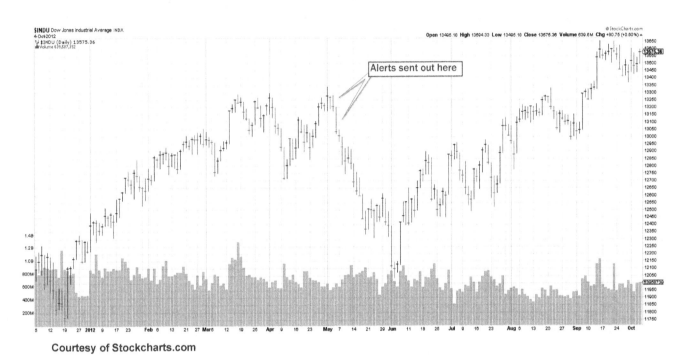

Courtesy of Stockcharts.com

## THE LIGHT THAT I SAW WHILE "CHAOS" ENSUED IN EUROPE

PREPARING FOR A MAJOR BOTTOM WHILE WALL STREET PANICS

As the mass-media speculated that the EU "catastrophe" was about to take down the rest of the world, as CNBC had its first-ever Sunday evening emergency broadcast ("Markets in Turmoil"), and as a Goldman Sachs alumnus circulated his Armageddon article, I was preparing for an imminent birth of the next mini-bull market.

**5/21/2012**

"WPRT looks like it might have a V shaped bottom w/ an 80% move in the next 1-2 months. IBD stocks that get sold off hard tend to have enormous rallies after a market bottom.

Always buy the stocks that have severely sold off in a well-defined channel coming out of a bottom. Stocks that have held up well vastly *under-perform* going forward (contrary to conventional Wall Street teachings)."

## 5/30/2012

"The more I look at the dollar, treasuries, and Euro charts, the more convinced I become that they could trigger a "Black Swan" rally event simply from funds pouring out of the safe havens of the dollar and treasuries. (General market) stock charts don't signal such an event, but given the dynamics of treasuries and the dollar, money flow would simply overwhelm the stock market."

## 5/31/2012

"Humans can only panic for so long. There is a definite point at which worrying starts to slowly demoralize us and kill us and at that point we say "I don't give a FU*K anymore." We then go on living our lives and ignore all the BS being thrown at us by the media.

I think we may have reached that point yesterday and today."

## 5/31/2012

"CRB (commodity index) waterfall pattern looks to be at completion. Anything commodity related could see a serious snapback. (Commodities roared going forward)

The S+P weekly SLO STO's (Slow stochastics) have been this oversold 8 times in the past 12 years.

03/2001- 20% 3 week rally

09/2001- 22% 6 week rally

05/2002- 5% 1 week rally

03/2003- Start of major bull market

06/2007- 18% 6 week rally

01/2008- 10% 2 week rally

05/2008- 9% 2 week rally

03/2009- 25% 4 week rally"

## 6/04/2012

As nobody believed my thesis that a major buying opportunity was at hand, I got a little emotional:

"For years to come, they'll be talking about the Sunday night CNBC special, "Markets in Turmoil" marking the exact low at Dow 11,985.

They will say that it was so obvious; that the dollar was about to collapse due to China and Japan (transitioning from the dollar as trading currency).

They will say that the Treasury bubble was so obvious as it was extended outside of its multi-decade channel.

They will say it was so obvious as QE3 -or at least trader's anticipation of it- was only 3 weeks away.

They will say it was so obvious after world markets had *ALREADY* traded down 13 weeks in a row.

They will say it was so obvious as world commodities were in the final stages of an impulsive waterfall decline.

They will say it was so obvious because an ECB/EU announcement regarding Greece and Spain was imminent.

They will look at P/C ratios, weekly stochastics, media obsession w/ a crash, smart/dumb $ ratio, % of stocks under 50 dma (87%), Naz summation index....and say a mega rally was so obvious.

They will say "Man 2008 really fu%ked with my perspective.

They will say it was so obvious because the Prez, Ben, and Tim needed to jack the market up prior to their re-election party."

## 6/05/2012

To really drive the point home about just how pessimistic EVERYBODY was, I re-posted this simple 5 liner. Some of these guys have been in the business for decades and it still blows my mind that they still become swayed by groupthink in light of high probability reversal patterns and technical indicator extremes.

1. "Richard Russell: "the bear market goes on. I'm afraid it has a long way to go."

2. Gary Shilling: "S&P 800"

3. Muhammad El-Erian: "Investors should be concerned with the return of their money and not just the return on their money."

4. FT(Financial Times): "Europe needs its "Lehman Moment."

5. Der Spiegel: Big Investors Don't Know Where to Put Their Cash."

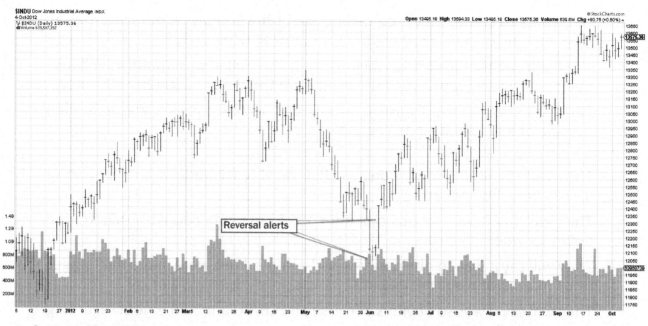

Courtesy of Stockcharts.com

## MY 2012 GLOBAL FACE-RIP PART DEUX

Just after the major June bottom in the markets, I sent out this email which was part 2 of my 2012 annual forecast ("Global Face-Ripping Stock Smorgasborg")

### 6/13/2012

This was the follow-up to my 2012 forecast for a "Global Face-Ripping Rally." For my 2012 forecast, please see annual forecasts in Appendix B.

> "GLOBAL FACE-RIP PART DEUX (Email Subject)
>
> Hi guys-
>
> This evening I was asked about my thoughts on my bearish email(s) sent 3 weeks ago. Well, it appears quite a few things have changed since then. In the interim, many longer-term oscillators have gotten REALLY oversold. To be brief, here are the biggest factors for a possible huge global rally starting sometime in the near future.
>
> 1,2,3,4,and 5) Parabolic move in treasuries. The first chart below (not pictured) shows the entire treasury bull market since 1980. Bull markets end with a parabolic move ABOVE the upper channel on panic buying. This is exactly what we witnessed 2 weeks ago. Because of the vertical parabolic nature of the move outside of the 30+ year channel, it is my belief that this is the EXACT END to the 30 year bull market in bonds. This has immense ramifications. Outside of rising mortgage rates etc., there should be a FLOOD of money out of treasuries into stocks.

6) Several world markets bottoming in unison similar to late December (actually Jan. 2) when I sent out my first "Global Face-Rip" email. Spain, Greece, Brazil have most likely bottomed. India is forming a multi-year very bullish double bottom.

7) Outside of '08, crude oil is more oversold (several indicators) than it has been in many years. It should surge out of oversold readings soon resulting in a huge surge in the most highly levered oil markets such as Russia and Brazil.

8) Commodities (CRB-Chart #2) have been this rsi oversold twice in the past decade. Each time lead to a massive multi-year bull market.

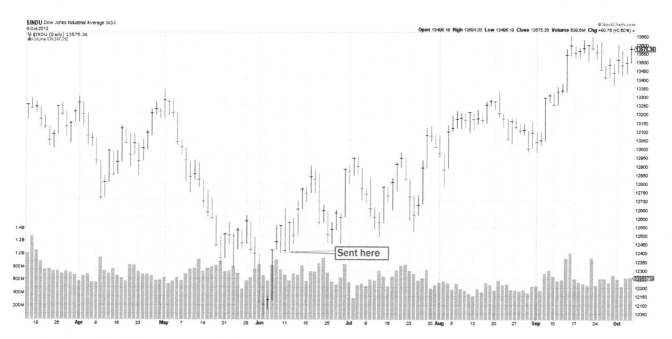

Courtesy of Stockcharts.com

9) We are seeing extremes in sentiment. The Bespoke financial panic news headline indicator triggered 2 weeks ago w/ the number of financial panic news headlines hitting an extreme seen only before prior major market bottoms. Additionally, for the first time I can remember, the average newsletter recommendation is 40% short (unfortunately I don't have the link). This is *VERY* rare. As I intentionally do not read any financial headlines (I actually try to near inflection points), I have no idea what is going on in Europe, but it seems like there is blood in the streets. Cap it all off with the CNBC special "Market in Turmoil" spectacular on the 3rd when Dow Futures reached 11,980 and you have an extreme sentiment trifecta.

10) As for NG, it looks good down here for a long term investor. Dumb money rebound players are mostly out.

This may not be the start of a massive bull market, but I see a snapback at a minimum.

Don't forget that a) Obama needs to be re-elected and b) bearish dollar groupthink should ensue soon w/ China/Japan dumping it for trade, and c) QE3 wildcard."

## *WHAT GLOBAL MARKET COULD SURGE 500% POST BOND BUBBLE?*

I sent out this alert as a long-term call on the rebound of Greece. Within nine weeks, Greece rallied 50% higher. That's nice, but my call is a long-term multi-year mean reversion play. I discuss the largest hidden global stimulus in history. I mention First Solar (FSLR) and the solar sector as well. At the end, I reiterate my stance that I don't know why the U.S. will bother holding an election in 2012.

8/15/2012

"What market could surge 500% post bond bubble? (Email subject)

A quick update:

-As you probably know the 32 year global bond bubble popped this past week in dramatic fashion.

-30-year Treasuries touched the upper trendline 6 times over the past 32 years. Afterwards, the average Dow Jones 12 mo. return was 50%.

-FSLR did in fact break out on its monthly chart- it is up 50% w/in 2 weeks. The solar sector theme I spoke of has officially begun.

-Resource-based emerging markets began their run.

-Steel has begun its run (but I'm not nearly as bullish anymore).

-The gold mining stocks have followed plan and significantly outperformed gold.

-Coals have been pretty lethargic. The smaller guys should rally big time over the next year once the downtrend line is broken.

-Greece should significantly outperform all global markets over the next 1-2 years based on the chart alone. It has 2 mammoth monthly reversal hammer candles in May and June w/ the 2nd candle undercutting the 1st and reversing dramatically. These graphically illustrate massive capitulation. The monthly chart has strong monthly positive divergence and has completed 5 waves down as well. From today's close at 621, Greece should hit 1451 w/ relative ease w/in 12 months on mean reversion alone. There's also a likelihood it hits 2938 w/in 1-2 years- a return of some 500%.

-And if you're one of those media followers who need a "fundamental reason" to invest. Well,Greece is now trading at 1989 levels. Greek GDP in 1989 was $73 Billion. Today's GDP- $300 Billion. Price makes news. As Greece's market rises, the media will focus on improving GDP figures. Their yoy GDP hit -8% 3 quarters ago and has been trending higher. When GDP growth hits 0% over the next year or so, the market could be double or triple its current price.

-The shipping sector is highly correlated w/Greece. The Baltic Dry Index/ S+P 500 ratio is at an all-time low. It has nowhere to go but up.

-The popping of the 32 year interest rate bear market is the largest hidden global stimulus in history. Trillions will flow out of bonds looking for a new home.

-I'm actually not bullish at all in the short term here. This is a BIG macro theme that should play out over the next 1-3 years.

-In the meantime, tell me how bad unemployment is, how bad housing is, how Europe is finished, tell me about the U.S. fiscal cliff. All of these media themes are essential to keeping main street (dumb money) out of the market. Most of the biggest market advances in history have climbed the proverbial "wall of worry".

-And as I've been saying since December, I don't even know why they are going to bother having the election. No, I'm not a Dem."

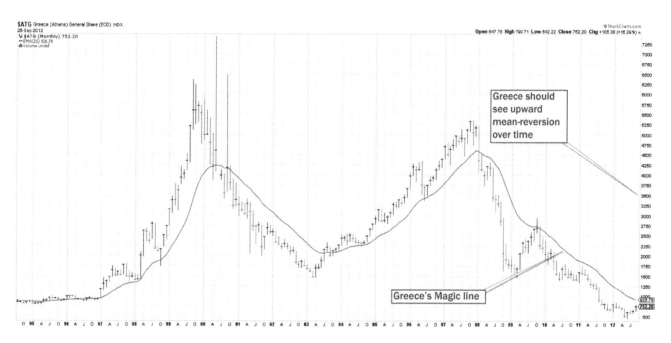

Courtesy of Stockcharts.com

## *AND TO SHOW THAT CHARTS ARE NOT JUST FOR STOCKS... THE 2012 ELECTION*

I include this alert to show that all markets are based on human emotion. Whether we are dealing with charts of stocks, bonds, or elections, it makes no difference. I sent this out on October 10 as the general public believed that Mitt Romney was taking the lead leading up to the election. My chart said otherwise. Unfortunately, I can no longer locate a chart displaying public opinion leading up to the 2012 election.

### 10/07/2012

"The Election Chart (Subject)

I know I said no more market updates, but this is pure entertainment. Fun stuff. I just saw some headlines about Romney taking the lead. So I thought I'd look at the charts. This is pretty cool. A chart is a 100% reflection of human emotion, human nature, human behavior etc....Since the beginning of time, human emotion has repeated in 100% predictable patterns. The election is 100% emotion.

The chart of the election is a textbook "breakout" chart (for Obama) on exponential volume as it broke out of its 2 year base. Look at the 2 year base between 50% and 60% (Obama's odds of winning). Look at the volume when the chart breaks out above the 60% threshold.

We are now seeing a textbook re-test of the breakout pivot point which just so happens to coincide with the lower Bollinger Band. If true to form, the chart should see a very high volume reversal to the upside within a couple/ few days. If it traded much below 60%, I would sell my momentum stock (Obama) and put on my Romney cap. Until then, it's a very bullish pattern. Unfortunately, (Obama) shareholders have to sell at 100."

# HOW TO SPOT MAJOR COMMODITY TOPS AND BOTTOMS

## *INDICATORS SHOWING MAJOR TOP IN SILVER IN 2011*

While the world was piling into silver due to massive "devaluation" groupthink regarding the U.S. dollar, I saw a *GIANT* bubble that was about to burst at any moment. I saw that big money was going to be made by those betting *against* Silver. Below were my thoughts about what I saw technically, and ultimately how big the debacle would be.

### 4/21/2011

"BTW-

Silver closed 51% above its 200 dma in April of 2004. It went from $8.50 to $5.45 in the next month.

Silver closed 68% above its 200 dma in May of 2006. It went from $15.21 to $9.48 in one month.

Silver closed 47% above its 200 dma in late March of 2008. It went from $21.44 to $16.06 in one month and to $8.40 in six months...

Today's close? 68% above its 200 dma. Tomorrow's open? Close to 70%.

When the dollar has its inevitable, yet seemingly impossible 10% (upside) retrace, we will truly see "shock and awe" when it comes to silver as well as other commodities. I even saw that Cramer yelled buy, buy, buy SLV 2 nights ago while it sat 65% above its 200 day.

Now, we just have to wait for Goldman to put Silver on its "conviction buy" list when it hits $50.... 4 weeks after their "recommendation"? $30.

### 4/21/2011

"I just hung out at SLV message board. Two words- utter pandemonium.

SLV closed today (around $46) at a record 72% above its 200 day moving average at $27.

Going back to 2002, all prior instances above 50% touched the 200 day moving average within one month."

**4/28/2011**

"More silver stats:Silver- closed 75% above its 200 dma. (It) hit 82.4% earlier this week. (Previous parabolic moves popped in a big way at 47,51, and 72%)Here's one I find really interesting. SLV avg. weekly volume is 120 million. Previous record weekly volume was 350 million. W/ one session left, this week is on pace for 850-875 million. But here's the kicker- W/ that MASSIVE volume, SLV is only up 3.79% (for the week). I suspect SLV will close the week just about at $47."

Courtesy of Stockcharts.com

## GENERATIONAL BOTTOM CALL FOR OIL

In February of 2009, there was literally a "sea" of excess oil on the market. There were tankers literally parked all over the world with millions and millions of barrels of oil that nobody wanted. Analysts were calling for a return to $15-$20 a barrel oil. I saw a large opportunity. Here is exactly what I saw then. Unfortunately, the links no longer apply.

**2/22/09**

"Subject: UCO/Oil bottom?Clues to a possible major oil bottom last week.

-Blowoff top for DTO (oil inverse) on weekly chart.

-Contango bubble may have popped?

-Bullish hammer on USO weekly chart http://www.fxwords.com/b/bullish-hammer-candlestick.html

-Oil monthly chart down 8 months in a row. My guess is if USO breaksFebruary's monthly high in March, USO projects to 35 to 40.

-If oil rallies, a world stock rally would probably ensue. RSX would most likely be most highly levered market (doesn't make much sense since economies are imploding.... but charts are charts)

-Oil charts - see page 10 http://stockcharts.com/def/servlet/Favorites. CServlet?obj=ID369857&cmd=s how[s122127438]&disp=O

-Possible double top for dollar which moves inversely w/ oil -USO weekly volume would have been an all-time record if not for the shortened trading week. Here is a very interesting post from the UCO board... "There is virtually no contango between the just expired March contract and the April contract. The March contract expired yesterday at 39.48 and the April contract ended at 40.03, roughly a 1.4% contango spread. Last month this was very different. The February contract which expired on Jan 20th ended at 38.74 while the March contract ended at 40.84, roughly a 5.4% contango spread. Additionally, through the month of February, there was a steady 6-8 dollar differential between the front month (March contract) and the April contract...which was roughly 15-20% contango spread.

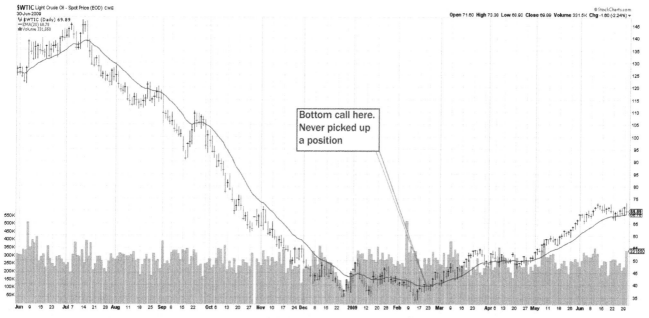

Courtesy of Stockcharts.com

As UCO now holds the May contract, should contango come back into play and the front month contract (April contract) hold its ground at 39-40 per barrel, we could see a 15-20% rise in the May contract to be more in line with the sperad between front month and next month out during February. This would mean a 30-40% rise in UCO price, without the front month contract moving anywhere.

Summary: There are ways to benefit from Contango. One of those ways is to own UCO just after contract expiration on the hopes that the Contango effect broadens without the front month moving. I believe UCO will be at 8.00-8.10 by end of week, a 25% increase this week. I don't believe the front month will rise much over $40 during the period"

## NATURAL GAS LIFETIME BOTTOM—THE IMPENDING NATGAS SUPERCYCLE

*I had to cut some sections of these emails out due to excessive length.

### 4/05/2012

"Biggest bull thrust we'll ever witness starts w/in days (Email Subject)
Buenos Aires 4/05/12

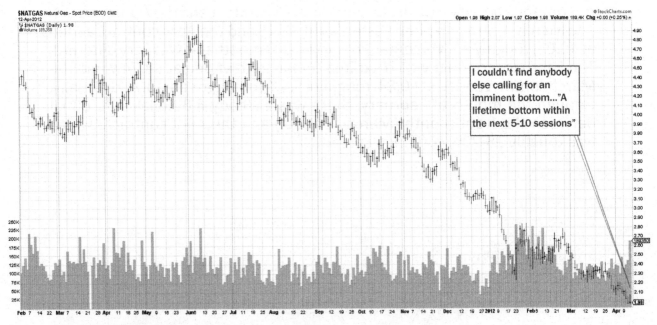

> I couldn't find anybody else calling for an imminent bottom..."A lifetime bottom within the next 5-10 sessions"

Courtesy of Stockcharts.com

I now take a brief hiatus from what has literally been a non-stop journey entailing hundreds of hours of bus travel throughout S. America. Over the past 2-3 years, if memory serves me correctly, I think I've recommended a natural gas trade on 2-3 occasions. Well, I'm now recommending a natural gas *INVESTMENT*.

-The charts are telling me that we will witness a simply breathtaking natural gas rally commencing ***w/in the next 5-10 trading sessions*** which will be unlike any typical general market or commodity rally we've seen in recent memory.

-The current natural gas pattern is what we might call a bullish descending longer-term wedge on declining volume. I have witnessed and traded many similar patterns in the past. The upside explosion can be historic.

-As far as my charts go back (12 years),natural gas has traded above its monthly bollinger band 5 times. After each upward bollinger band piercing, there has been a very powerful reversal back w/in the bands. We have now violated the lower monthly bollinger bands for the VERY FIRST time AND have stayed below the band for 5 MONTHS IN A ROW! The band is now at 2.12. On a long-term basis,natural gas is more oversold by any measure (rsi, slow sto, roc (just about there)) than it has ever been in its history. Once re-entered (The Bollinger Band) on a monthly basis, after 5 month stretch outside, the longer term reversal will be the most violent we've ever witnessed. Btw- the bands are simply a measure of standard deviation-most things in life eventually revert to the mean over time.

-The Natural gas continuous contract is in the process of completing its Elliott Wave fifth wave down from last summer. Once completed, 5th wave reversals are very powerful short term moves in the opposite direction.

-Rig count/supply was 1650 when natural gas was probing $14 in '08. As of this afternoon, rig closures have taken that number down to 647. Going forward, there will be an HISTORIC demand/supply dislocation that will cause prices to literally skyrocket virtually overnight. Simply put, demand has increased over 10% since '08 while potential supply is down what 60+%.

-Producer's marginal cost is in the $6 per bcf range just to BREAK EVEN. The CASH COST for a very small percentage of the lowest cost producers in the industry is around $1.85. Assuming natural gas is TOTALLY FREE to them, it costs them $1.85 per bcf to pay employees, pay shipping costs to customers, variable overhead etc. Well, in the past week, Henry Hub spot prices have probed the $1.85 level on 2 occasions.....

-If you monitor the natural gas forums and sites, the dominant theme is that ABSOLUTELY nobody will come w/in 10 feet of a natural gas etf. If they are bullish on natural gas (not many), they are piling into natural gas or coal producing stocks. For many, many reasons, during extreme price spikes, the producers tend to follow the underlying commodity to a much, much, much lesser extent. Natural gas has more or less a market negative beta. Thus if it falls, the stock market tends to rise. If gas rises, the market tends to fall....and thus the producers tend to fall, stay flat, or at best increase slightly (much of this has to do w/ very long-term forward contracts which limit downside and upside dramatically).

-In 2002, many investors anticipated a natural gas rebound. They piled into mega producers such as CHK. While the stock market languished, the producers went nowhere. Let's just say that natural gas budged slightly..... Ever so slightly....up 600% w/in a few months.

-DO NOT read any article relating to natural gas oversupply. There is TREMENDOUS oversupply at the moment. Did you guys closely follow the oil market in 2009 when there was SO MUCH supply vs. ZERO demand.... so much so that every hedge fund was storing oil on their rented tanker off the coast of Singapore? In the midst of this, I sent an email to (name confidential) in March of 2009 telling him to forward my oil charts to his readers. The charts indicated a HUGE rally during perhaps the biggest oil oversupply in history....you simply couldn't give oil away at $40. In the next 6 weeks, oil traded from roughly $40 a barrel to the mid $70's while there was NO DEMAND AND literally a sea of supply. And yes, he sent that email out.

-Such a potential rally REQUIRES an historically oversold market. Natty closed at $2.09 today. Thus, the further natty trades down...... **($2, $1.90, or even $1.80)**, the tighter the rubber band becomes, and the larger the rebound rally becomes.

-Its coming in a BIG, BIG way. Next Monday, Tuesday, Wednesday, Thursday, Friday or the following Monday, Tuesday, Wednesday, **Thursday (this was the day),** or Friday. It will catch the world entirely off guard. It will be so fierce that the millions of people waiting to enter on the sidelines will have no opportunity to re-enter until its too late. Traders will not buy a stock or etf that is up 20-25% in a single day (this didn't happen - just a relentless, steady climb). They will simply miss 90% of the move like everyone else. There are a handful of producers, end users, hedge funds, I-banks, and institutions that own 95% of the forward contracts at the moment. They will not sell until the 4's,5's, and 6's or higher. The S/D dynamics of such a situation could take the spot market to those levels w/in weeks or a couple months.

-And over the next 1-2 years, the forward curve WILL reach and exceed old highs. You can do the math. The market's main job is to ensure that everybody remains on the sidelines (w/ the exception of a dozen billionaires who slowly accumulate during the panic) during massive runs. It is my opinion that the market is sending a very clear signal that next few weeks will not be an exception.

-One more tidbit... and going back over the course of history, the oil to natural gas ratio is 6-10. It closed at an ALL-TIME high today of 49.45. I bet my life that it will trade again w/in its long-term historic bands. Do the math. And what if oil spikes???

-Lastly, don't forget that the U.S. will soon begin massively exporting natural gas worldwide into markets (most of the world) that pay $14-$16 per bcf in the free market.

-A massive sea change will soon be underway. And 99.999999999% of the world has no idea.

Cheers,

Jesse"

**4/6/12**

"Just received from a friend who is a natural gas executive at a large regional player in the SE:

"Our natural gas traders believe we are going lower. All the means

Of storage are 100% full. Warm spring means no demand.

I'm hoping for a natural gas play later in the summer. Hope for a hurricane and a European winter!"

I've heard very similar comments over the past month from others in the know w/in the industry.

Against all odds, I stand by my email."

**4/09/12-**

"My last gas email – this is a doozy (subject)

-There is more natural gas in storage than any other time in history. Record setting oversupply.

-The only way to get rid of this oversupply is to see substantially lower prices going forward.

-There is now 900 BILLION more cubic feet in storage than last year!!!

-There has only been ONE other time in HISTORY w/ such a demand-supply imbalance.

-ONE other time when gas in storage deviated this much from the 5 year average.

-What happens when there is such an imbalance? Producers do whatever they can to fix the situation by whatever means necessary. What happens otherwise? Their shareholders simply fire them and replace them w/ a team that can simply cut production by a meager 10% to raise prices 100% to give shareholders (aka "the boss") a fat return.

-When was the ONLY other time when demand and supply were this imbalanced? History runs in cycles and repeats itself over and over again. The only other time there was such a scare regarding oversupply and capacity limits?

-Well.....How about this? *EXACTLY* 10 years ago. *EXACTLY* 1 decade ago.

-What happened to the natural gas price during the following 3 months? 125% upward mean reversion.

-What happened to the natural gas price during the following year? You won't believe this. Nothing short of a 561% return. Yes.

-The smart money (institutions/hedge funds) do their buying based on the monthly chart. Well, going back to 1999, the lowest monthly close was at 2.13 in 2002. The price bottomed while supplies continued to increase for a couple months.

-Do you know what the monthly close was last month? You guessed it! Ever heard of a *MASSIVE* multi-year, decade-long double bottom? Here is the potential outcome- contrary to "expert financial analyst forecasts" the world over, we could see a MASSIVE multi, multi year rally exceeding old highs by an enormous percentage. Think about the implications.....especially from $2 natural gas.

-Can you find anyone else in the *ENTIRE* world who is predicting a rally from current levels?

-The guy below is the biggest bull in the natural gas arena....and he is predicting a 25% DECLINE from current levels before we turn around! Even Gartman threw in the towel today. All of the bulls are calling for a re-test of $1.80 for crying out loud. Usually you have all of the bulls or all of the bears on the same side of the boat, but not the bulls and bears sitting side by side!

-For many, many reasons, the crude oil to natural gas ratio has always traded between 6-10 for as long as the 2 commodities have traded publicly. The current pattern has gone parabolic and/or has entered a waterfall decline depending on your perspective. The one thing I can promise in this email is that over time, there will be a mean reversion back into the historic range (I could write a separate email on this). So....if oil eventually trades to $200, $250,$500, $1,000 (peak oil?) and the ratio reverts to the historical range.... well, you can do the math. Mind boggling.

But then again, everybody who makes 7 or 8 figures along w/ every single person who has the charisma to appear on financial television every few weeks is predicting further declines into the lowest inflation-adjusted levels in the history of the commodity. Maybe you'll see Jesse on tv in 5 years at $100 natural gas calling for $200. If that's the case, sell all you can.....and then some:)"

## 4/16/12

A reply to the alert above:

"Being the only natgas bull in the universe, I looked far and wide today for somebody....anybody to comfort me in my loneliness. Anybody who can see from my vantage point. I couldn't find a single bullish article... Anywhere. I think we have all been around long enough to remember the significant articles we read in the past at major market tops and bottoms.

(Media called for) "QCOM to 1,000. AAPL to 1,000. Oil back to $10. Silver to $100. Dow 30,000, Dow 1,000" etc....

Here is what I found:

1)-4/13/12 -Natural gas bottom nowhere in sight....."there's going to be a price shock -- where these caverns fill up so quickly that there's nowhere else to store this gas, so you're dumping it on the cash market. You could see the market collapse down to all time lows...$1" - Senior Analyst RJO futures.

http://www.bnn.ca/News/2012/4/13/Natural-gas-bottom-nowhere-in-sight.aspx

2) 4/12/12 "SIMPLE ECONOMICS SAY THE PRICE SHOULD BE CLOSE TO $0"

http://seekingalpha.com/article/493521-natural-gas-why-prices-are-headed-lower-and-how-to-profit?source=yahoo

3) 4/12/12- GOLDMAN SACHS downgrades natural gas....no rebound till 2013.

http://blogs.wsj.com/marketbeat/2012/04/12/goldman-sachs-natural-gas-prices-wont-rebound-until-2013/

4) 4/13/12 - Morgan Stanley downgrades natural gas (no link)

"Morgan Stanley this week revised down its 2012 price forecast for natgas to $2.40/mmBtu from $2.70/mmBtu...stemming largely from continued warmer-than-normal weather. Through the summer, Apr-Oct, we see gas prices averaging $2.20/mmBtu"

4) 4/16/12- UNG going to $10

http://seekingalpha.com/article/501231-sub-10-ung-is-coming-to-a-market-near-you?source=yahoo

5) 4/12/12 "Face-Ripping trade of century" author throws in towel

http://allstarcharts.com/the-natural-gas-crash-revisited/

6) I posted a link last week about the most bullish guy I could find calling for a massive ng rally. YET, he's bearish. Calling for $12 UNG in the short term. I can't find the link at the moment.

7) I posted another link 2 weeks ago about a guy calling for a rally, but saying we need a 15-30% single day crash in order to do so.

The stage is set."

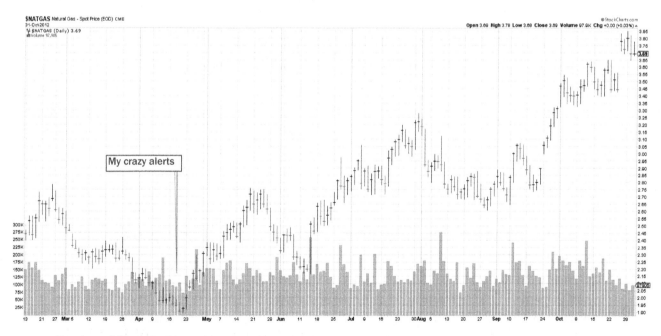

Courtesy of Stockcharts.com

# APPENDIX B

# *My Annual Global Market Forecasts 2010-2013*

A glimpse into my thought processes heading into new calendar years. My annual calls are meant to be for entertainment purposes only. They are my best guess for what may play out in worldwide markets. As you might expect, it is quite difficult, if not impossible to generate a reliable forecast for the following 12 months. But for laughs, I try anyway...

"* To view my 2013 forecast of "200%-500% Sector-Specific Anomalies," please visit www. jessestine.com.

## MY 2012 GLOBAL MARKET FORECAST: "EXPLOSIVE FACE-RIPPING WORLDWIDE STOCK SMORGASBORD" (GOLDMAN CALLS FOR UP TO 25% S+P DECLINE)

*Note—includes summary of 2011 forecast (for 2011, Goldman called for 25% S+P advance led by bank stocks).

I posted the wildly bullish forecast below as Wall Street strategists predicted the lowest return in seven years: http://www.bloomberg.com/news/2012-01-03/smallest-s-p-500-gain-since-05-seen-by-strategists-after-u-s-beats-world.html

I was wrong about a few of the points, but all in all, things have turned out pretty well to date.

01/02/2012

"My2012 market prediction- an explosive, face-ripping, worldwide market smorgasbord (Email subject)

I also posted this (without charts) at http://explosiveface-rippingstocksmorgasbord.blogspot.com/

As many of you know, I have been moderately market bearish over the past 2 years. Quite frankly, the environment for traders and investors has been crap for quite some time now. One year ago, I sent out my "market forecast" for 2011 based almost entirely on The Royal Bank of Scotland's own forecast. I have learned to take their forecasts very seriously ever since June 6/18/2008 when the research team from Royal Bank of Scotland (RBS) warned investors to "get ready for a full fledged crash in global stocks and credit markets over the next three months." Global markets immediately

238

crashed w/ the S&P going from 1350 to 850 in the next 4 months.

Anyway, I sent this out (one year ago-my 2011 forecast): "…..as of this morning, The Royal Bank of Scotland has advised clients to take out protection against the risk of a sovereign default by China as one of its top trades for 2011." *Having been on the ground in China for close to 3 months now, my belief continues to be that China is priced for perfection for many years to come. Any missteps will be reflected in the market(s) in an exaggerated fashion.* China is forecasted to grow at 10% per annum for years to come. As the article states, any hiccup (such as 5% growth) will take markets down by 25%."The result of such a hard landing (+5% growth) would be a 20pc fall in global commodity prices, a 100 basis point widening of spreads on emerging market debt, a 25pc fall in Asian bourses, a fall in the growth in emerging Asia by 2.6 percentage points, with a risk that toxic politics could make matters much worse....Albert Edwards from Societe General said the OECDs leading indicators are signalling a "downturn" for Asias big five (Japan, Korea, China, India, and Indonesia). The China indicator composed by Beijing's National Bureau of Statistics has fallen almost as far as it did at the onset of the 2008 crash."

(Back to 2012)- The day I sent that 2011 note out, the Shanghai index closed at 2857.18. As fate would have it, 2 sessions ago, the index hit 2134.32....a fall of 25.3%! It is my contention that the low of 3 sessions ago in China will be the low going forward (the index just recently tested this low in September of 2012) and perhaps its low for the rest of our lifetimes! I have now spent much of the past 2 years in China, and the real estate situation is simply dire. Imagine walking around ANY CITY in China at night and literally seeing *MILLIONS* of empty condos with no lights on. I don't know what will happen to Chinese real estate but the charts are telling me that the Shanghai Index has *BOTTOMED* and may never look back. (I was very close in price but a little off in the timing of the low).

(For 2012) I see a possible giant transition taking place right this second throughout worldwide markets. As you will see in the charts below, I see:

1. An imminent end to the 30 year bull market in 30 year U.S. treasuries resulting in a flood of capital into worldwide equity markets.

2. An imminent bottom in worldwide equity markets- especially China, India, Vietnam etc. out of severely oversold levels.

3. The Dow Jones 13 week exponential moving average (ema) just crossed above the 43 week ema (a rare occurrence) signaling a bull run. Prior instances have resulted in *short-term thrusts upwards of 30%+.*

4. According to Oppenheimer (see below), 2011 was THE MOST VOLATILE year on record going back to 1950. There were huge drops in March, June, September, October, and November...not to mention a "once in a lifetime" mega-drop in August. The individual investor has simply given up in frustration. After periods of extreme volatility, markets go up...a lot.

5. The "Ted Spread" (measure of credit risk in the economy) has topped

out. Its rsi (14) of over 81 is higher than at any other time during the crisis of the past 4 years. This extremely overbought rsi indicates an imminent fall in the "Ted Spread" resulting in money flowing out of the safety of bonds and into more risky assets- stocks.

6. The American market flat performance in 2011 masks an *ALL-OUT* worldwide market crash in 2011. Much of Europe is down 50% from its highs, Cyprus is down 72%, Vietnam is down 50% (VNM), China is down 33% from its highs this year, India is down 45%, Russia is down 30%, Brazil is down 28%, Copper is down 28%, Japan down 25%, biotech index down 33% from its highs, networking index down 28%...... and basically every sector in the U.S. market is down big time. If you look at every sector in the States, it is literally impossible to figure out how the S&P, Dow, Nasdaq etc. finished the year flat. Put simply, 2011 was an *ALL-OUT MAJOR MARKET DEBACLE WORLDWIDE.* A once in a lifetime worldwide market decline. My friends, we are due for a worldwide market reversion higher!

7. Goldman Sachs. I will never understand how Goldman Sachs will forever be allowed legally to purposely mislead investors. It is what it is. At the end of 2010, the indexes surged over 20% resulting in an end of year weekly rsi (14) in extremely overbought territory above 70...a level consistently leading to significant market declines or crashes. SO.... I've seen it over and over and over w/ Goldman (as with many other houses), as they upgrade at unsustainably overbought levels and downgrade at unsustainably oversold levels. Anyway, their forecast for 2011 was for a 25% S&P surge LEAD BY........ BANKING STOCKS!!!!! Just take a second to look at some banking stocks over the past year! This brings us to 2012. What is Goldman's forecast??? Any guesses???

8 "Our 3-month, 6-month, and 12-month forecasts are 1150, 1200, and 1250"!! And how about this: ***"We estimate the S&P 500 could fall by 25% to 900 in an adverse scenario in which the Euro collapses." Wow!*** By the way, the average portfolio manager predicted a 17% S&P return heading into 2011. A USA today poll of individual investors was right at about 17% as I recall. Euphoria at very overbought levels is a recipe for disaster. Things got so out of control that I bought index puts for the first time in my career in February.

9 The U.S. market has survived! It has survived *EVERYTHING* in 2011. The most volatile year in history. The entirety of Europe collapsed in spectacular fashion (already priced in), S&P downgraded U.S. debt, dismal GDP figures, depression-level consumer confidence numbers, lackluster earnings, riots in the UK, Tunisia, Greece, Syria, Israel, Egypt, Libya, the occupy Wall Street movement in the U.S., possible warfare with Iran, bursting of the world's biggest property bubble in China, municipal debt crisis in China, the collapse of MF Global, the uproar against quant trading, the runaway debt crisis in the U.S., ...the worldwide debt bubble etc. etc. etc.... Guess what? The U.S. markets survived everything. What happens if we get any good news? Anything. We get a *HUGE* market surge.

240

10. There have been 97 negative earnings pre-announcements issued by S&P 500 corporations for the fourth quarter, compared to 26 positive pre-announcements, resulting in a negative-to-positive ratio of 3.7. That's the highest in 10 years, according to Thomson Reuters data. The earnings bar is now set much lower. These pre-announcements came in early, meaning estimates have been coming down across the board in every industry. This now sets the stage for some significant "beats" for those firms who meet or exceed their initial guidance set at the start of the quarter.

11. The U.S. market is a complete and total wasteland. The leading sectors like banks, solar (down 80%!), shipping(down 50%), and coal (down 50%) have simply been devastated. They have priced in a total collapse of the worldwide economy. The good news is that from a sector-down approach, I see dozens and dozens of setups within these sectors suggesting a massive rally in many of the individual stocks. I see many "cash cows" trading at absurd Buffet-esque discounts. Take coal company ACI for example. 3% dividend, $38 enterprise value, $2.90 EPS run-rate in Q1 2012, profitability booked well into the future through forward contracts....all for $14.50 per share. I haven't done enough work on solar yet, but the charts suggest a big turn for several of these firms in the coming year. For example, lottery ticket solar firm HSOL w/ $3.50 in cash, backed by a multi-billion dollar Korean company is trading at $0.98. $33 FSLR, is projected to earn $6 in 2013, RDN w/ a book value of $8.50, highly leveraged to a housing rebound (yes, it is coming) trading at $2.34. I have dozens of companies like these on my radar. I see many potential 100-600% "rebound plays" this year (my coal, solar, shipping thesis turned out to be wrong).

12. Industry reports are suggesting a surge in some leading indicator consumer and industrial activity. Sales of new cars have been surging very late in the year. TSM (Taiwan Semiconductor) is the big boy in the semiconductor space (the leading of all leading indicators in my opinion). I just received this note from CSFB the other day: "Taiwan foundries opening up order spigot. We analyzed the equipment orders made by Taiwan chip makers in Taiwan public filings. Orders from TSMC & UMC in 4Q11 have increased to $2.63bb (up 421% q/q from just $504mm in3Q11). The order levels are higher than the $1.62bb average levels in 1H11. With sales of ultra-laptops surging in the second half of 2012 combined with the intro of revolutionary TOUCH SCREEN Windows 8, we could see a huge computer upgrade cycle setting up a second half technology bonanza.

13. Presidential Cycle. The average 3rd year return for the presidential cycle is 17% while year 4 is around 10%. Its my guess that the market over the next 12 months will combine year 3 and year 4. I have spent 80% of my time outside of the U.S. over the past 3 years and 2 themes consistently emerge whenever I meet somebody. 1) Obama, Obama, Obama! (Similar to Tebow mania) and 2) "The U.S. is no good anymore....it has collapsed, right?" There is/will be a worldwide push for Obama to remain president of the United States. Unlike any other president in my lifetime, he is almost universally loved outside of the U.S. As always, big money the world over

will want to preserve the status quo by making conditions conducive for his re-election, jobs will be created, markets will surge, everyone will be happy, and Obama will win in a landslide (and no, I am not a democrat nor an Obama supporter). By the way, Intrade and other markets are forecasting only a 52.5% chance of his re-election. I don't think that figure will stay there for very long. The other point is that the world has totally given up on the U.S.. Everyone I meet abroad thinks that the United States is in a terminal state of decline. It is precisely when you see this kind of universal dour sentiment that the U.S. (or any company/country etc.) comes back swinging and surprises everyone in a *BIG* way.

14. The U.S. real estate collapse is over. *Period*. Nationwide U.S. real estate futures are slowly starting to reflect this-http://www.recharts.com/cme.html. Banking stocks and indexes will surge when the data show that prices are no longer falling. If prices start climbing (at all), we could see an all-out market moon-shot.

15. Professional traders are totally out of the market. During my career, there have always been at least 30-40 stocks at any point in time that are "in play." There are virtually none at the moment. Well, there are a small handful, but they are nothing like what we are used to "playing" in good markets. The "momo stocks" of 2011 have all been completely decimated. TZOO, GMCR, OPEN, REDF, MITK, MCP, NFLX, VHC, JVA, SFLY etc. have been absolutely crushed reflecting a depression scenario. Should we enter a less volatile, uptrending market in 2012, professional traders will return en masse pushing the next generation of "momo stocks" through the roof similar to the 2003-2006 momentum heyday.

16. Lastly, I can't find any other commentators or traders looking for a huge market surge this year. Being an ultra-contrarian investor, this single fact alone makes me even more confident that 2012could be the "Big One."

Bottom line, I see a possible once in a generation market move this year with scores of individual stocks making "multi-bagger" moves over the course of the year. Everybody has an outlook for the stock market. For the reasons stated, I just feel particularly bullish this year. Unfortunately, market outlooks are wrong more often than not. According to Steven Kiel at Arquitos Capital, "If you want to keep yourself in check, head on over to this BusinessWeek article from December 20, 2007. Some very talented analysts, some of whom I really respect, put out their end of the year 2008 stock market predictions. William Greiner, Tobias Levkovich, Jason Trennert, Bernie Schaeffer, Leo Grohowski, Thomas MacManus, and David Bianco all are included. Their S&P 500 predictions ranged from 1520 to 1700." Do you all remember S&P 666?:)

The charts below show the mega bullish crossover for the Dow (happening in other indices as well), a mega-bullish 4 year cup and handle formation for the Nasdaq, the bottoming formation in the Indian market, descending bullish channel for coal stocks, descending bullish channel for networking stocks (NWX), the same pattern for the Nikkei, a chart showing natural gas closing on Friday at its cheapest level (relative to oil) in its history. This will prove to be its lowest monthly close (I was off by 3 months) in our lifetimes w/ future 1-3 year returns of 100-800%, a bullish emerging markets formation, a chart of 2011 being the most volatile year ever, a chart of 30 year treasuries hitting their long term 30 year upper channel (I was a little early here on the bottom), a chart of the TED spread, charts of the Shanghai index, a chart of the solar index (TAN), Oil services index (OIH) and its bullish descending channel, a chart of the agricultural index (GKX) suggesting a possible 100%+ move over the next year or so, and a long term commodity chart."

## 01/03/2012

"There are literally hundreds and hundreds of former "high flyers" in every sector coming off of low bases.

FSLR, IGPG, DRYS, EXM, CREE, BTU, DANG, PEIX, BAC, AUMN, WFR, GMXR, SSRI, OSG, HSOL, SOL, SMSI, AA, MTL, RDN, CENX, anything oil related....

I've never seen so many longer-term, multi-bagger setups in all my years trading.

Bill O'Neil's pants are wet. There are classic IBD setups all over the place.

This is the year we've been unpatiently waiting for since 2006. Astute traders are going to make a *BOATLOAD* of money this year. There will be no pullback."

## 01/03/2012

And just to show that I am not always making friends. In response to the comment above:

"'There will be no pullback.'" WTF? Are we traders or psychics? There is *NO WAY* to know what the markets will do. No one knows, *NO ONE*."

Courtesy of Stockcharts.com

## MY MARKET CALL FOR 2010 – "DO ABSOLUTELY NOTHING"

*My 2011 market call was summarized in 2012 forecast.

This was my forecast heading into 2010. Just days before a 900 point drop and a few months before the now infamous 1,800 point "Fat-Finger Flash Crash" of 2010.

### 1/3/2010

"My 2010 investment forecast – comments on the U.S. dollar (email subject)

Again, I find myself on Bangkok time on a Sunday morning:) One last thought regarding the status of the U.S. dollar as an "investment" in 2010. Everywhere I look, I see articles and commentary on the imminent collapse of the U.S. dollar due to quantitative easing/massive fiat currency expansion and our parabolic debt explosion. While abroad, I saw Time and Newsweek covers (sometimes the covers are different in foreign nations) about the "demise of the U.S. dollar." That was precisely when I started to become bullish on the U.S. dollar. I follow about 15 excellent technicians on stockcharts.com And one- Matt Frailey has been spot on over the long run regarding the U.S. dollar (and the general market as well). Like many successful investors, his timing isn't always exact, but he gets the major movements most of the time. Rather than listen to the talking head group-think and financial journalists, I choose to follow chartists who have proven themselves to me over time...........If I was pressed to recommend any investments for 2010, I would recommend doing absolutely nothing......So, from my vantage point, as we enter a new decade, my recommendation is to invest in yourself, enjoy life a little bit more, perhaps expose yourself a bit more to foreign travel to gain perspective, perhaps quit your job and pursue your passions, appreciate those around you a little bit more, and make a conscious effort to enjoy each and every moment.

Here's to a great 2010!"

*Remember that the U.S. Dollar is highly inversely correlated with the stock market.

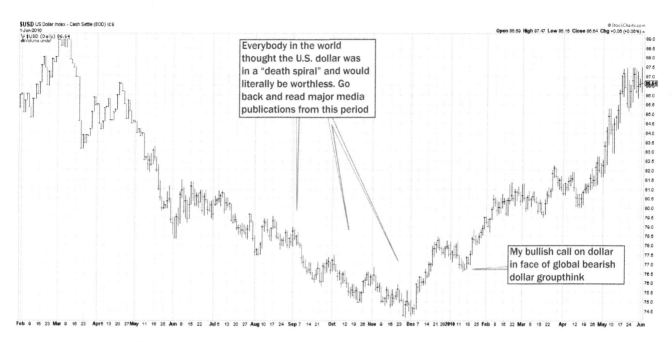

Courtesy of Stockcharts.com

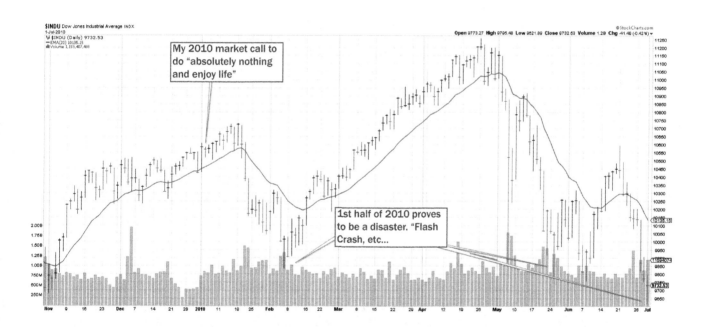

Courtesy of Stockcharts.com

# APPENDIX C

# *And Finally, Some Things Never Change*

Last but not least, I stumbled upon these old message board gems during the editing process of this book. What struck me in particular was just how much my investment philosophy has *NOT* changed over the years.

### 3/26/04 – "INVESTMENT PHILOSOPHY"

"Essentially, this adventure will lead us to future IBD 100 stocks. The secret is to find them before they do. I think all of us knew from the get-go that TRM was destined to be an IBD powerhouse. Not only do I want to find great long term holds, but I would also like to uncover (with your help) some great swing trades. No day trades please!

Since I don't have too much time this evening to go into specifics about what I would like to look for, I will leave you with an earlier post from the TRMM board about my trading style. Since I don't have enough space to post it here, please read the first board post. Happy investing!"

### 3/26/04 – INVESTING THEORY; EFFICIENT MARKET THEORY / "IT FACTOR"

"Here is a little bit about my Investment philosophy:

First, let's go over the efficient market hypothesis. The theory basically holds that stocks are always fairly valued and it is impossible for an investor to consistently beat the market. Of course, I will do my best to disprove this theory. Since the stock market is efficient, stock prices rapidly reflect all available information. There are 3 forms of market efficiency: weak-form, semi-strong form, and strong-form. Weak form states that all info. contained in past stock prices is fully reflected in the current price. Therefore, recent stock "trends" are of no use in selecting stocks. For instance, if a stock goes up 3 days in a row, this tells us absolutely nothing about what the stock will do tomorrow or anytime in the future. So, this theory postulates that technical analysts are wasting their time. Semi-strong-form states that the current price reflects all PUBLICLY available info. It is of no benefit to the investor to read a 10k or any other past release because market prices have already adjusted to all of the information contained in those reports. When information is released, the stock price will change only if that information is different than what the market expects. The last implication of this theory is a very important one. Insiders, who have information that is not publicly available consistently earn substantially higher returns. Strong-form efficiency states that current prices reflect all information whether public or private. Nobody can achieve market beating returns. Except for a portion of semi-strong-form, I think that the academics who came up with these theories were actually commissioned by Fidelity and some of the other large Wall Street players to promote their index funds!

In short, if you have an ability to predict what the herd will do in the future, the market is a joke and can be trounced on a consistent basis. Yes, you do need to have an idea about how the company will do fundamentally, but you need to have an ability to predict how investors will feel about the developments. Its very hard to explain. Its a talent that takes time to develop. Before I even think about how investors will react, there are several keys to finding future winners. They are listed in order of importance.

1.  Small-cap, small-cap, small-cap. Small caps, especially micro-caps beat the general market by an average of 2% annually. I read somewhere that micro-caps average somewhere in the area of 20% per year, but I find that very hard to believe.

a)  Co. must be undiscovered or relatively undiscovered at buy point.

2.  Insider buying. The insiders know what will happen before the market. Insiders are the only group of investors to consistently beat the market.

3.  Company must be profitable.

4.  Earnings must be growing sequentially quarter over quarter and year over year. TRMM- (.54), .05,.11,.15,.20. I think I got the first 2 wrong, but you get the point. The market loves to see this type of progression.

5.   Stock must have a great chart. If the stock meets the above criteria, but chart is flat, I will not buy until I see an uptrend. I could go into great detail concerning what constitutes an acceptable chart, but that would take hours.

6.  Great mangagement team who don't have a history of secondary offerings, mega stock options etc. NO DILUTION! With TRMM, from day one the new team made a big difference. Employees were crying because their highly paid co-workers were shown the door. YES!

7.  Low float/low # of outstanding shares. When I see a small cap with over 100 million shares, I run for the borders. Why is management issuing more and more shares?

8. "It factor"- There must be a certain mystery factor that will keep investors guessing. OK, this co. is undervalued, its receiving more attention, good mgnt team, insider buying, good future, etc. but what could really turn this puppy loose? The "IT" factor. With TRMM, we know that the co. is adding ATMs and the co. is focused on profitable growth, but the "IT" factor or the unknown is the agreement with Triton as well as other service agreements that may or may not be in the pipeline.

9. IBD factor. Co. must have a legitimate chance of being featured in IBD and having good numbers. If so, stock will skyrocket when #'s come together.

Well, I think that is most of it. The number one element is research, research, research, and more research. Read every 10k, 10q or any other 8 or 10 that is released. Read every post on the message board. Yes, takes a long time! Talk to people in the industry, people at the company. DO NOT talk to stockbrokers or listen to analysts. When a stock is universally loved and everybody is recommending it and every wall st. house has upgraded it, who else is left to buy? 5 days before I purchased TRM, not 1 share was traded. Undiscovered, yes.

After researching hundreds of stocks on a weekly basis, there are only a few that meet my stringent criteria. TRMM, Parl(I don't like the chart right now at all, but the fundys look good), and Wire. Eln is another one of my biggest holdings, but it doesn't meet these criteria. I held it because of other knowledge the public didn't know about.

Anyway the "It Factor" at Parl is its future product launch with Guess. With Wire, it is a few factors such as the launch of a new production facility, skyrocketing copper prices, and general industry buzz concerning the future of their business. I have held all of these companies prior to their breakouts. I am not recommending anybody buy any of them. These are just my rules of investing. It takes a lot of trial and error, but the market can be consistently beaten by a rather large margin if you are motivated to learn."

## 7/16/05 - MY METHOD

"These are the most powerful charts you can find. FORD, CMT, SMTI, BOOM, NGPS, ANTP, CKCM, RURL were all considered earnings breakouts.

This is probably dealt w/ in O'Neil's book. The ideal situation takes place when a stock has traded in a tight range for a LONG period of time (preferably years) The stock is forgotten. No volume.

Suddenly, the company releases earnings that blow the market away.

Something materially has changed at the company. Oftentimes, a company

248

will sell or drop a money losing division which will rapidly increase its earnings per share. These stocks will spike on earnings day taking out all previous resistance (all older highs) and keep on heading north for the long term. I probably find 4 of these per year and put a large percentage of my portfolio into them. I found FORD at $4, SMTI at $7, BOOM at $9, NGPS at $8, ANTP at $8, and CKCM at $9.

When I find one of these rarities, I literally can't sleep at night. I analyze every aspect of the business and the stock and play them over and over in my mind thinking about the possibilities. I felt the same way about VPHM when I bought it at 3.94. I'll be sure to let you know the next time one of these is uncovered. Earnings season starts next week, so we might uncover one or two. I'm finally done!"

CPSIA information can be obtained
at www.ICGtesting.com
Printed in the USA
BVOW07*2331110118

504966BV00002BA/3/P